Welcome Home Me

Sue Skilton Orrell

Welcome Home Me
The Story of A 54-Year Journey
All Rights Reserved.
Copyright © 2023 Sue Skilton Orrell
v3.0

The opinions expressed in this manuscript are solely the opinions of the author and do not represent the opinions or thoughts of the publisher. The author has represented and warranted full ownership and/or legal right to publish all the materials in this book.

This book may not be reproduced, transmitted, or stored in whole or in part by any means, including graphic, electronic, or mechanical without the express written consent of the publisher except in the case of brief quotations embodied in critical articles and reviews.

Marsutonell Press

ISBN: 979-8-218-96007-0

Library of Congress Control Number: 2023913524

Cover Photo © 2023 Valerie Maggitti. All rights reserved - used with permission.

The Neil A. Kjos Music Company graciously granted permission to use page 5 of *Celtic Benediction* by Sue Orrell (2007) as the background for the front cover of this book.

PRINTED IN THE UNITED STATES OF AMERICA

KEY TO FRONT COVER LOCATIONS

1.	DeLand, FL	1968
2.	Boston, MA	1968
3.	Gaffney, SC	1968
4.	Rock Hill, SC	1970
5.	Indianola, IA	1974
6.	Kansas City, MO	1975
7.	Indianola, IA	1976
8.	Ann Arbor, MI	1977
9.	Indianola, IA	1978
10.	Houston, TX	1980
11.	Frostburg, MD	1991
12.	Houston, TX	1993
13.	DeLand, FL	2023

TABLE OF CONTENTS

PART ONE: DEPARTURE
TRAVELING, TEACHING, DATING

Introduction iii
1. A Weekend in Charleston 1
2. From South Carolina to Salzburg 12
3. Das Team in Vienna 22
4. Das Team in Salzburg 36
5. From Salzburg to Italy and Zermatt 43
6. From Zermatt to Paris for Bastille Day 51
7. Kindred Soles on Interstate 10 59
8. From Foothills to Corn Fields 67
9. Mile-High Surprise 86
10. From Manchester to Edinburgh 98
11. My Brother's Hands 103
12. Dreamscape on Writing 108
13. A Mighty Good Time and a Stop Sign 112
14. Children's Voices 120
15. Butter Pecan Delight 156
16. A Mailbox Post, a Few Small Screws and a Mountain
    of Mulch 161
17. Sixty-Eight and Ready to Date 173
18. Click It or Ticket 180

PART TWO: RETURN
WEATHER, REAL ESTATE, AND RELEASE

Introduction 189
19. Gramma Skilton's Teacup and Saucer 192
20. Snowmageddon 196
21. Two Gallon Limit 206
22. Mead in The Elusive Grape 211
23. Coincidental Incidences That Led Me Home 215

24. Discovery of Childhood Home 233
25. Instructions if I Were a House.. 239
26. Car Registration and Florida Tag: Application 245
27. Florida Tag: Receipt and Installation 253
28. Release to Peace.. 260
Acknowledgments.. 271

DEDICATION

This book is dedicated to the children whose lives touched mine in schools, churches, choirs, and in my piano studio. Teaching and nurturing them enriched my life. Their enthusiasm energized me. The emotional and musical ties grounded me. The painful experiences they told me about kept my heart soft and tightened my sense of purpose. The joy of observing their progress not only as young musicians, but also as individuals with multiple gifts to share within their world, will stay with me as long as I live.

Additionally, I dedicate this collection of stories and essays to thousands of parents who supported my work and their children's progress over the course of nearly 60 years. Because of you, my life is filled with contentment while my mind focuses on writing.

With deep gratitude, I also dedicate this book to my fellow travelers—particularly Chris, Cathy, Virginia, and Camie; to colleagues who are dear friends, especially Valerie, Michele, Tina, and Jennifer; and to the multitude of strangers, friends, and relatives who smoothed the way as my journey home grew from dream to plan and from plan to action, especially Georgia and Betsey. I am indebted to each of you, including many unnamed herein, for the strength and courage you shared.

PART ONE: DEPARTURE
TRAVELING, TEACHING, DATING

Only that traveling is good which reveals to me
The value of home and teaches me to enjoy it better.
Henry David Thoreau
(1817-1862)

But the great Master said, "I see no
best in kind, but in degree;
I gave a various gift to each,
To charm, to strengthen, and to teach."
Henry Wadsworth Longfellow
(1807-1970)

Thirty-five is a very attractive age.
London is full of women of the very highest
birth who have, of their own free choice,
Remained thirty-five for years.
Oscar Wilde
(1854-1900)

INTRODUCTION

During massive upheavals of cultural and political unrest in 1968, I sought solace on the campus of Stetson University in my hometown, DeLand, Florida. The peace of the canopied grounds where acorns popped on sidewalks and palm fronds rustled above competed with the challenge to plot my future. The respite I found in walks through the Forest of Arden (now planted with Presser Hall, which houses the School of Music) strengthened my resolve to embrace peace where I could find it and to follow the call to goals that seemed unreachable.

Much of the time, I felt as though my own life was in as much turmoil as the entire nation. I believed that my own world would implode if I told my truth. The person who had abused me was so effective in his indoctrination, which reflected the code of secrecy of the time, that my sense of self was as much at risk as the lives of national leaders who dared to speak their own truth.

Stetson Students certainly were informed of national and world events but limited in their political expression. Instead of overt protests, energy more commonly was spent on community involvement in the mostly segregated part of town.

Not all news was negative. The first successful heart transplant took place in January of that year. In September, a group of about 150 women protested the Miss America pageant in Atlantic City. That awakened my awareness and changed my own attitude from an uninformed teenage preoccupation with trying to make my physical measurements and proportions match those of the beauty queens to a realization that the parading of superficial beauty objectified by sexualization was simply wrong. Although I later attended two small pageants in South Carolina, I was uncomfortable at those events.

Amid the protests over the war in Vietnam and the struggle for civil rights and women's rights, it seemed like a monumental leap of progress when President Lyndon Baines Johnson signed the Civil Rights Act in April.

After my first divorce occurred about the same time as the signing of the Civil Rights Act, I prepared to leave town in time to begin graduate school in the summer school sessions at Boston University. On the surface, the divorce and the drive to Boston gave me a sense of freedom and opened possibilities while also providing relief to be away from the need to dodge the abuser. I had a mistaken underlying assumption that geographic distance could squash the memories that festered in a simmering brew of reminders that they could exceed my strength and coping mechanisms. Because of the code of silence, I was alone in my world of dark turmoil.

The excitement of getting into graduate school and out of town was temporary. The sense of deep unrest, even danger, became personal in Boston. When I saw African American students in the registration line at Boston University give a Black Panther salute when they greeted each other, it stunned me. They stood behind me, and when they overheard me talk with the registrar, they started good-naturedly teasing me about my accent. To be clear, they did not threaten me in any way. It was simply my own inexperience that caused my discomfort. I had not witnessed the few sit-ins at DeLand's Woolworth's. Segregation was real to me, but direct social protest was foreign. Until then.

I chatted with the fellow registrants briefly before they laughed and one of them chanted, "You're from the South. We know you. You don't drink, cuss, smoke, or chew, and you don't run with boys who do." The only time I had felt uncomfortably *different* was in elementary school when I was teased for being a redhead. But the taunt in Boston went far beyond anything so superficial as hair color. The registrar corralled my attention and welcomed me to the campus.

Hours later, after I found my dorm room, unpacked my car, and put it into a storage garage, I figured out that what I felt was a degree of white guilt. I thought perhaps the young men were attempting to make me feel as different as my race had made their race feel.

A week or so later, for the first time in my life, I heard gunshots fired when I visited a new friend. We were in his apartment when shots rang out within the block where we were. I was scared to walk to the bus stop. My mind churned with the realization that I was fearing a social ill that had plagued people of African descent for centuries. I feared that a stray bullet might hit me or my friend. When I expressed reticence to walk to the bus stop, my friend assured me that the issue had nothing to do with us and that we would be okay. He had heard that it was only gang rivalry.

The nation still hurt and reeled from the assassinations of Dr. Martin Luther King, Jr. and Robert F. Kennedy before there had been time to heal from John F. Kennedy's assassination. Those monumental events became even more immediate for me as I sensed the crackle of unrest in the very air I breathed.

Apollo 8 orbited the moon that year, foreshadowing the landing on the moon the following summer. But it was almost impossible to focus on that achievement or Boeing's new 747 jets that launched a new era in the airlines industry. The routes the 747 planes used and the exploration of space gave a brief alternative to the pervasive angst. But like my own excitement, it was short-lived. On the seas, a Navy intelligence ship, the USS Pueblo, was lost to North Korea with a claim that it had been in North Korea's sovereign waters.

As the list of national and world-wide jolts grew longer, my own list grew in number and scope while I tried to maintain the façade of a young woman off on an academic and cultural adventure with grit and adequate preparation. I hoped that the successes and triumphs would outdistance the failures and tragedies—not an unusual desire—but because of my personal history, I held a tilted view of my future. My grit was admirable, but I was woefully unprepared for much of what I would experience.

In my first book, *Cries of the Panther on Mockingbird Hill* (2020), I told much of my family's background story and focused on my history of sexual abuse perpetrated by a brother-in-law. But I did not go into depth regarding other significant aspects of the broader story. In this book, I have chosen not to go into detail regarding the loss of my children at birth, although I do reference those tragedies to inform the reader and to place those events in my chronology.

In Part One of this book, I flesh out the background of my leaving and tell some of the stories I lived during the 54 years I was away from my hometown. While away, much of my life was centered on traveling, teaching, and dating.

It is impossible to relate and reflect upon every situation that I enjoyed and learned from. My intent is to emphasize the incidents of fun and adventure. If I am successful, those who read this book will gain insight into my pilgrimage and find pleasure as they read. Many will relate to these stories through their own personal histories.

No matter how much artistic license I use, I cannot describe my journey as a circle. Even though I left my hometown in 1968 and returned in 2022, the trail of coincidental connections that led me home formed an angular maze that eventually became a chain. Various sizes and shapes of links gave flexibility to follow topographical angles. Even the smallest link was soldered with as much strength as the largest. When I placed dots on a United States map to show places I lived during the 54 years away, the connected dots resembled routes of a small airline. Yet, in some sense, I have come *full circle.*

The angularity of my journey's route was a labyrinth of *tos* and *froms* too far flung to be linear, and too convoluted to be circular. Circumstantial tangents were a mixture of necessity, misfortune, and opportunity. One of my primary challenges was to winnow out opportunities while withstanding the consequences of choosing to leave and to stay away for so long.

There were times when I felt like a *prodigal daughter* of my town, but my story does not conform to that notion. It lacks the characteristics of notorious riotous living and squandering of birthright generally found in the understanding of the Biblical parable of the prodigal son. But I often wondered if I would be welcomed, shunned, or even remembered if I ever did return.

The motivation that fueled my 54-year journey was a combination of conscious and subconscious forces—some that pulled me to explore a world larger than what I already knew—and some that pushed me away from the trauma I had known in DeLand. The pull and the push were equally strong, and both were vital for my emotional survival and future growth.

Both sets of grandparents came to Florida in the early 1900s. After marrying in 1926, my parents moved frequently, including a trip to the state of Washington right before World War II ended. We returned just a few months later soon after my fourth birthday.

As an older child and adolescent in DeLand, I saw the seasonal influx of visitors soaking up winter's sun or cooling off in summer's beach breezes. Going places, whether on short trips or moving elsewhere, seemed to me to be the norm, even though my family did not take a vacation until the summer I graduated high school. At school or church, I often heard tales of trips to the Carolina mountains or fall leaf-viewing trips to New England. My own wander lust latched onto vicarious travel that matured into my determination to travel.

After years of therapy and untold hours of reflection, a pull toward DeLand and a push out of Houston reversed the process of 1968 and brought me back to reclaim the peace of place and to write this second book of personal episodes that marked the journey.

Regardless of my marital or employment status, I consistently sought ways and means to travel. Stories of my travel range from the Tricentennial celebration in Charleston, South Carolina to Paris on Bastille Day and a visit to the Playboy Club of Denver. Rather than dulling my urge to travel, each trip confirmed my desire and gave me stories to remember, to tell, and to write. In each locale and with each person I met, I learned a little more about myself and a lot more about humanity.

I avoided majoring in Education because I wanted to have a career different from my mother's. But once I tried it, I knew it was the best choice for me. Teaching in different states and in various types of communities gave me a wealth of experience that fed my thirst for personal growth and my commitment to make an honest effort to impact young lives.

Teaching led to associations with some of the most talented and gracious mentors I could have imagined. Most importantly, though, teaching gave me the opportunity to nurture children through Music while those young minds and voices unknowingly mended tears in my heart. Teaching in a school district with at least 36 different cultures and languages present among the school's enrollment enriched my life and taught me a little about cultures beyond those I visited personally.

In addition to wanting to travel and teach, after I left DeLand, I wanted to date. When I left in 1968, I was still grieving the first divorce and loss of identical twin daughters who lived only a few hours. I knew that I still loved my first boyfriend, Jack, and that he was happily married. He was four years older and had enlisted in the Army soon after his high school graduation. His discharge occurred in time for us to be in the same class at Stetson until I dropped out for about two years after the sophomore year.

I could count on one hand the number of dates I had in high school beyond his fairly frequent visits, not because he demanded it, but because I had no interest in anyone else. It was all I could do to keep my emotional head out of quicksand while sexual abuse was relentless at home, academic pressures built, and I waited for the boyfriend I adored to find a white horse and rescue me. He was a dear friend until he died—one I will never forget, and one I could never adequately thank for supporting me through the writing of my first book.

I also had bought into the Hollywood myth that there was only one person on earth meant for me. When the relationship with Jack did not lead to marriage, at age 19, I chose to marry someone else. Shortly before the seventh anniversary, the divorce became final. Despite the reality of living in an emotional desert, that marriage served its unadmitted purpose: it got me out of an unsafe environment and out of town for about two years while the person I married completed his military commitment. After he was discharged, we returned to DeLand so that I could complete the Bachelor of Music degree at Stetson and he, a Stetson alum, could take additional courses in the School of Business.

During those years, the abuser and his wife (my sister) and their children moved back and forth between Missouri and Florida. They were back in DeLand during my last years at Stetson and were still there when I left. By then, I was strong enough to challenge him verbally when he tried to manipulate me, but it was exhausting and emotionally debilitating to still have to wonder when and where I might run into him. At the same time, I attempted to maintain my connection with my sister and their children—a juggling act with no possibility of success. I had to get away to heal, to grow into much of my potential, and to be able eventually to be at peace in DeLand.

While I waited for the divorce (the first of three) to become final during the 1967-68 academic year, I took additional courses at Stetson so that I could support myself by teaching. An undergraduate degree in Church Music/Organ was almost useless for a female seeking employment in those days. I also continued to study organ with Paul Jenkins in case I was accepted into graduate school.

I left DeLand by myself in late spring, 1968, and went to Boston where I enrolled in the School of Music at Boston University and began a full load of courses in summer school. That long trip included first driving from DeLand to Missouri to pick up my mother and then taking her to Connecticut to visit her relatives before I went on to Boston. It set into motion what would become my 54-year journey.

Outwardly, I appeared to be an incredibly confident and independent young woman who had found her footing after the divorce and loss of the twins. People congratulated me on being accepted into the three graduate schools to which I applied. I even was offered a provisional scholarship to one of them, and the chairman of the organ department at Boston University notified me that he would be my teacher.

Numerous times, I heard statements such as, *Sue, you are so strong* or *You've weathered the storm.* But no matter how well-intentioned those statements were or how much truth they contained, the messages that wielded the most power were those that I told myself: *You are in way over your head, a fake at getting through life, just like your brother-in-life predicted.* True self-confidence was far beyond the horizon I saw. This is not an unusual experience for many people as they pursue education and establish careers. But for me, it was exaggerated because of the long-term effects of the abuse I had internalized.

Behind the façade of victory, in the heart of who and what I was, I was awash in a cocktail of pent-up brokenness from the sense of self I lost at age 13, grief, the stigma of divorce, and the reality of diving into graduate school. My insides quivered as much as my hands wanted to tremble the first time I drove in Boston traffic. It seemed like a chronic condition inflamed by self-blame—a place of shame with no exit.

That pursuit of graduate work ended with my withdrawal after marrying the second time following a two-week courtship. That is how I ended up in South Carolina and began my teaching career. That marriage lasted for two years—perhaps a credit to both of us under the circumstances.

As the marriage disintegrated, I refocused on graduate work and moved from Gaffney, South Carolina to Rock Hill to earn the Master of Music degree at Winthrop University (then Winthrop College). At that point, my delayed adolescence set in, and I learned a lot about dating.

After the second divorce, each time I was single between marriages, I had long-term relationships, but did not date around or play the field. Two years after my last husband's death, at age 68, I decided it was time to see what it was like to just date. Not only was it a different century since the last time I had been single; it was a different world. Enter the phenomenon of internet dating.

These three aspects of my search for home and peace (travel, teaching, and dating) coalesced to provide adventure, fulfillment, and entertainment as I followed the lanterned path, determined to keep going despite the self-doubt that took so long to work its way out of my system, and never knowing until 2022 that it would lead me back to DeLand. I am grateful for the expertise and care of my therapist, Dr. Sonia Simone, and for all those who believed in me when I questioned the validity of their belief.

CHAPTER I
A WEEKEND IN CHARLESTON

When you come to a fork in the road—take it.
Yogi Berra
(1925-2015)

About three weeks after arriving, I left Boston University to marry an organist I had met in one of the practice rooms. Our courtship lasted two weeks; we married in a historic church and enjoyed an exciting honeymoon in Northeastern Canada. Two years later, the marriage ended.

Following my second divorce, I reclaimed my dream of doing graduate work that eventually would lead to completing a doctorate. Because my second husband and I had spent ten weeks in Europe the previous summer (1969), I also hoped to claim travel, both foreign and domestic, as part of my life, regardless of my marital status.

For the first and only time, I had a female roommate while I completed the Master of Music degree in Rock Hill, located about three hours from Charleston. By birthdays, the roommate was about eight years younger than I, but in experience, she was a toddler, and I was in the throes of a long overdue adolescence.

I'll call her Jane. She had grown up in Rock Hill, where the university is located, just as I had grown up in the town where my undergraduate school, Stetson University, gave the town much of its identity. I sympathized with her regret that she had not been able to live in a dorm. That similarity in our backgrounds marked the line where similarities left off and significant differences irked both of us.

My three siblings and I were more like two families—sisters eight and eleven years older and our brother three years younger than I. Jane had no siblings and still was compliant with childhood family rules and Sunday School lessons that, in my opinion, represented superficial commands of an angry god who perceived us to be ignorant—one I did not aspire to imitate or emulate. But at the same time, there was an attractive young woman inside my roommate struggling to unweave scratchy threads of a strait-laced corset and find a way to fly away with chaffed, weak wings that fluttered toward fledgling independence.

The security and fun of her small family unit had ruptured after she enrolled at Winthrop and her parents' marriage ended in divorce. I met her mother only once. I came home from campus one afternoon soon after Jane moved in and found her in a cleaning frenzy. Even the crinkled red linoleum around the hot water heater in the kitchen did not escape her manic scrubbing. She caught the look of surprise on my face. "My mom's going to stop by tomorrow to take a look at my first home away from her."

"Everything looks nice. I'm sure she'll approve. I'll just be here long enough to get a snack and change clothes. I need to get back to campus and practice some more before the choir concert. You'll probably be in bed by the time I get home. I'll try to get here tomorrow in time to meet your mom."

That night when I got home after practicing, singing in the concert, and grading papers, I wanted to relax with a glass of wine before I crashed. There was no wine to be found. I looked in each of the few kitchen cupboards; I looked in the refrigerator; and I checked the countertop. I knew she was a teetotaler, so assumed she had not suddenly changed her habits. Baffled, I gave up and went to bed.

The next morning, as I was grabbing a cup of coffee, she came in, dressed and ready to go to her job interview. "Do you know where the wine is? I looked for it last night, and it seems to have disappeared."

"You don't think I could let my mother come and see it right out in the open, do you? It's behind the hot water heater."

"I decided long ago that I would never hide wine from my own mother. I'm going to take the two bottles out from hiding and put them back where they belong. You can tell your mother whatever you want regarding my use of wine, but I won't agree to hide it. You are an adult, out on your own now, and probably will discover that differences between you and either of your parents must be acknowledged and talked through so that you don't lose your chance for independence."

The next day, Jane answered the door and invited Connie in. I stayed in my room while they *toured* the living room and kitchen. I met them in the short hall, and Jane introduced us. I said, "I'm really happy that Jane can share this duplex with me and hope that she gets her dream job soon. It's an exciting time for both of us."

After a brief look into both bedrooms and the bathroom, we went back to the living room. Jane and her mom sat on the red couch, Connie's posture as stiff as the scratchy upholstery and her mouth set in a strained half-smile. She clutched her purse on her lap and frequently smoothed her hair while her eyes darted as though in search of assurance that her only child had made a good decision. I sat across the room on the bench of the picnic table that served as a dining table. Connie began to relax a little and moved her purse off her lap and onto the couch. I offered iced tea, but they both declined when I told them it was not sweet.

Connie said, "I hope Jane will enjoy living away from home. It's a big move for her." I thought, *It's even a bigger move for you—probably the most difficult since you enrolled her in Kindergarten.*

After a few more minutes, I excused myself to return to campus and felt somewhat confident that Connie would find Jane's choice of housing acceptable. I guess the place and I passed the test, despite the bottles of wine, because she did not demand that Jane move home.

I remember more clearly spending time with Jane and her father, Roy, out in his boat on Lake Wylie, a large lake that had sprung from a reservoir in 1960. The lake was still an object of wonder in the early '70s. Roy not only had a rustic lake cottage but a boat that could pull skiers and make the wind turn long red hair upside down and short hair into a precursor of the spiked '*dos* waiting to be discovered.

Soon after moving in, Jane invited me to go with her when she visited her father at the lake house. She marveled at my lack of hesitation when her dad offered to let me steer the boat. I had been in boats in Florida but had never taken the wheel before. She soon learned that I had no fear of the water, the boat, or the speed. "Slow down," she shouted from the back seat as she tugged on her hat.

Her father turned to face her and said, "It's okay. Sue's been driving a car a lot longer than you have. She knows what she's doing."

When we angled toward shore as the sun was setting, Jane asked, "Dad, did you bring stuff to make ice cream?"

"Sure did. It wouldn't be a trip to the lake without homemade ice cream."

I recalled Uncle Bob and Aunt Ruth's ice cream churn. Electric churns were popular at the time, but Jane's dad was a purist. When she asked him about getting an electric churn he said, "None of those electric churns for me. Stuff tastes better when you work for it."

We went to the cabin and brought the supplies back down to the dock. He set to work on the first round of churning. We each took our turns on two batches—one peach and one coconut. After overeating the dessert of our labors, we lay down on the long dock and dozed to the sound of white caps hitting dock posts until the lull became a buzz of mosquitos and the too-cool breeze sent us shivering to the cabin.

Back at the duplex, it wasn't long before Jane asked what I was going to fix for dinner. "I don't expect to cook for both of us. You're welcome to put whatever you want in the fridge. Why don't you use the top shelf, and I'll use the second one?"

On another evening, she made a more specific request. "Could you cook some sauerkraut?"

"All you need to do is heat it."

"I know, but I'm afraid to light the gas stove."

"Okay. I'll get it started, and you can watch it. I'll show you how to turn off the burner when you're sure it is heated."

Sauerkraut was not a favorite of my family, but I had learned to appreciate it while I was in Germany the summer before I moved to Rock Hill. It was apparently one of Jane's favorite dishes—so much so, in fact, that she used one of my silverplate forks to eat a second helping right out of the bowl after I had already gone to bed. Not only did she use the fork to eat out of the bowl, but she left it in the bowl.

The set of silverplate flatware was a wedding gift from my parents for my first marriage, which had ended in divorce a little over two years before I met Jane. Since I ate most of my meals, such as they were, on campus, I did not discover the intrusion of the fork into the bowl of leftover sauerkraut until the tines were so black that I thought the polish might expose the base metal before I could make the silverplate shine again. We had a chat about the use of utensils and quick clean-up of the silverware to guard against corrosion.

A month or so later, I found a serving spoon left in potato salad in the refrigerator. Like the fork in the sauerkraut, it was black. I showed it to Jane and told her I was going to buy a couple of place settings of stainless steel and a few serving pieces so that we wouldn't have to worry about tarnished silverware again. For over a year, the chest full of eight place settings of silverplate flatware and serving pieces that my parents had bought through a layaway plan collected dust under my bed until once again, I lived alone.

Jane graduated within a week of moving in with me and was ecstatic when she found out she had a job offer with the city school district. I was happy for her. At about the same time, I heard of a house that was available because a professor was taking a sabbatical. I jumped at the chance to have more space for just a little additional rent, and we agreed to remain housemates for the rest of school year, figuring that by the end of that year I would have completed my degree and she would have saved enough money for her own place.

Jane offered to get her dad to help with the move. He and one of his friends moved the apartment contents and set up the beds for us at the house. Having a little more space eased some of the tension between us. I completed the degree that August and was hired to teach in a brand-new school. The principal supported the arts and encouraged me to order equipment to furnish the music room as I thought it should be equipped.

One of Jane's graduation gifts was cash from an aunt with a stipulation that she take a short cruise. I suggested that she contact a travel agent to make plans for the cruise. Her dad gave her extra money so that she could purchase several new outfits. She told me it was the happiest thing she had ever thought about. She had ordered her passport in time to get it before she graduated in anticipation of her first trip by herself and her first trip out of the country. She modeled each of her new outfits and asked for suggestions about accessories. I loaned her a necklace and a scarf that could be worn in several different ways.

Those few days on the cruise to the Caribbean changed Jane. Her inquisitiveness regarding my comings and goings toned down as she became more accustomed to being alone some of the time. And she no longer tried to hide my stash of wine when her mother came to visit.

At her suggestion, we started planning a weekend trip to Charleston while the tricentennial celebration was still going on, even though it was a few months beyond the actual tricentennial date. I drove because I had been to Charleston a few times and always seem to be the driver whenever I am involved in even a short road trip. She had never been to Charleston and wanted to get acquainted with it because she was to start seeing a dermatologist there for treatment of severe acne soon after our weekend trip.

We had been settled at the new location less than two months when we decided to take the weekend trip. I had heard from someone that the place to stay in Charleston was at a circular-shaped Holiday Inn near one of the bridges. It was easy to spot as we approached the city. I stepped up to the registration desk and asked for a room with two beds. We were in luck. At the height of the tricentennial celebration, there would not have been a chance of getting a room without a long-standing reservation, but with the turn of the season from summer to fall, our walk-in request was honored.

After getting settled into the room, we spent the afternoon doing various touristy things, including a harbor tour with a sighting of Fort Sumpter. We strolled the old streets and wandered through one of the historic cemeteries. A highlight for me was seeing Catfish Row, the setting for *Porgy and Bess*. I recalled seeing the movie in 1959, my senior year in high school. It was the first time I had seen African American talent displayed in a serious way. That sparked one of the first conversations I had with my parents regarding the inevitability of integration.

Charleston was still abuzz with the celebration of its tricentennial. One of the most entertaining sights unique to the timing was the abundance of fire hydrants that were transformed into statues of many designs. Many of them provided the scaffolding for creative transformation into caricatures of historical figures.

We enjoyed a seafood dinner near the hotel. In my home state, Floridians are convinced that their seafood is the best in the world. Charlestonians believed the same about their seafood. And, many years later, when I lived in Maryland and then in Texas, both of those states made the same claim.

I cast my vote in favor of wherever you first learned to relish seafood and the associations it brings. For me, it conjures up Aunt Ruth's fried shrimp (Florida); Daddy's fried speckled perch or bass (Florida); steamed shrimp from the Gulf of Mexico; and Maryland crab cakes such as friends served when I lived there. If there is any discernable taste difference in seafood in different parts of the country or world, I have not tasted it. The differences are in the seasonings and cooking methods with the deciding distinctions being in the associations and memories.

After changing clothes, Jane and I went to the hotel bar to enjoy live music, hoping to dance. Soon after our drinks were served, two attractive men came to our table and asked us to dance. They were dressed in navy blue slacks and light blue dress shirts, making us assume they were businessmen in casual Friday attire. Jane showed off the moves she had learned on the cruise. With her rum and Coke, she was losing her inhibitions and obviously having a good time. The men were good dancers and offered to buy the second round of drinks.

The one I danced with and I really hit it off. He told me that he sometimes had business in Rock Hill and asked if he could call me when he was in town. I hesitated because the person I had been dating had just begun to ask me out again after he had pulled out of the relationship for at least a month. But there was no commitment, and I felt certain there never would be. With some reluctance, I gave the dance partner my unlisted number and thought, *Yeah, right. I won't hold my breath for that phone call.*

To my surprise, about 10 days later, when the phone rang, Jane answered it, placed her palm over the mouthpiece, and whispered, "Remember that man you danced with in Charleston? He says he's here and wants to speak to you."

I grabbed the phone from Jane. He said, "Remember me? We danced together in Charleston a week or two ago."

"Of course, I remember you. I didn't realize you'd be in town so soon."

"I'm here and was just wondering if I could see you tonight."

"Yes, but not for long. Tomorrow's a school day, you know." I gave him the address, hung up, and started to set an instant preparation into motion—cat put on the back porch, table cleared, and a few swipes with a dust cloth before brushing my hair and teeth and refreshing my lipstick.

He wasted no time getting to the house. When I let him in, the attraction was just as strong as it had been in Charleston. Jane politely went to her room, and the man and I sat on the couch, curtains drawn, lamp turned low. Sandalwood incense swirled in the dim light, and the taste of red wine lingered on my tongue. His physical advances escalated, then stopped abruptly. He put his elbows on his knees, and his face sank into his hands. For an instant, I wondered if he felt ill. He wiped his face as though he had been in the hot sun all day, then looked at me and said, "I'm sorry. I've got to stop and talk to you."

I thought, *Here it comes. He's probably got a girlfriend and is going to 'fess up.* What came out of his mouth went so far beyond surprise that I was stunned.

"I know where you teach because you teach my son, Bobby. I live right here in Rock Hill. When I watched you conduct the fifth graders at school last month for the opening ceremony of the new school, I thought, *Hot damn! They didn't make teachers like that when I was in school.* My son adores you. His mom and I don't get along very well, and he knows I'm unhappy. When I saw you in Charleston, I couldn't believe it."

I realized why he seemed vaguely familiar when we first met. His son looked exactly like him. I moved to the end of the sofa. "Why didn't you tell me this right away?"

"Because when I felt so attracted to you, I was afraid you wouldn't even dance with me if you knew the truth. Will you ever see me again?

What if we run into each other at school? Bobby's really into sports, but as long as you're the music teacher, he'll be in the choir. He also likes to play the xylophones and drums. He says you teach folk dances and really know how to dance. He's right."

My mind spun with disbelief and disgust. I wanted to verbally attack him, but knew I had to be able to keep a level head if I ran into him at school and that I did not want to escalate the situation into such a mess that I would need to request a transfer. I loved my school and the program I was building there. But I also knew that I would not allow him to manipulate me into conniving against his wife or into paying the price of social and moral compromise in order to keep him quiet. He had mentioned being a member of a fraternal order where the person I had been dating also was a member. The possibility of locker room exaggeration ripped through my mind.

The barrage of thoughts finally quieted enough for me to speak. "Your son is a very good student and seems happy every time I see him. I will not be able to look at him now without thinking of how dishonest his father has been. This is his last year in elementary school, so the chances of our running into each other at school are slim."

I squelched a momentary urge to thank him for leveling with me but calculated that the weight of deceit was far greater than his guilt-based change in behavior. I continued, "If I ever do see you at school, I will make certain that others are nearby. I will not be alone with you again, and if you ever approach me in person or by phone, you will regret it. Furthermore, if I ever hear that you have spread rumors about me or tall tales about meeting me in Charleston, I will make sure that your wife is aware of your behavior. Meanwhile, I will have to figure out if I can ever trust a stranger again. Right now, I need a way to get rid of this throat full of bile before I spew it all over you."

He grabbed his cap and left with the weight of dejection gouging his shoulders and the sting of shame singeing his face. He apparently had a conscience but had no trouble ignoring it while out of town. I felt sorry for his wife and wondered if she was yet aware of his talent for deception. I also wondered whether she might have been equally devious with him and if perhaps he felt her behavior justified his behavior.

But I had no desire to spend enough time with him to root out the answers to satisfy my wonderings.

Jane heard the front door open and close and came out of her room. "What was that all about? Sure was a short visit."

"It's too tangled to even try to explain now. I won't be seeing him again, so please don't give him the time of day if he calls. I don't think he will, though. I've got to get some sleep. The choir's first rehearsal for the Christmas concert is tomorrow before school starts. I'll be out of here earlier than usual."

On the way to school the next morning, my mind kept flip-flopping between the logistics for the rehearsal and the wishing that I had been able to speak up for myself when I was much younger. Now, decades later, I understand that my experiences in Charleston and Rock Hill were fundamentally different than the ongoing abuse I had suffered within my family. Randomly acute situations tend to be somewhat easier to face, process, and recover from than the ongoing trap of familial abuse. But that comparison comes close to saying it is less painful to drown in water than to boil in oil.

My strength of voice was silent only regarding the sexual abuse. I don't mean to say or imply that the dance partner in Charleston physically abused me; he did not. But he certainly misled me and betrayed his wife.

During rehearsal that morning, I tried to avoid eye contact with Bobby. His bright eyes and energetic smile seemed to say, "Don't you remember me?" I hoped he did not feel discounted or invisible as I tried not to interact with any other student more than I did with him. The internal excuse of getting the semester of rehearsals started with no time for individual chit-chat about their summers or sports teams or whatever else may have been on their minds both set the tone for rehearsal expectations and gave me a little reassurance that I was not singling him out with my unusually cool demeanor. Full focus on the seating chart, vocal range checks, and the introduction of one or two songs filled the time and placed a layer of insulation between my heart and the student who excelled at Music and Little League.

As I drove home that afternoon, I again reflected on my ability to confront the student's dad once I learned the truth and wished I had been able to find my voice when first attacked by my next-older sister's husband almost twenty years before the handsome young man asked me to dance in Charleston.

If Bobby's dad showed up for the choir concerts that year, I did not see him. But I had to assume that he would attend the fifth-grade graduation ceremony. When I made the choir award presentations, I announced that for the sake of efficiency, photo ops would be for students only, meaning that I would not pose with students. I could not run the risk of having a picture taken of me standing beside Bobby.

Since other teachers stood with their students, I felt cheated to miss out on having visual memories of the students I spent the most time with because a dad had been so devious. I doubt if it mattered a lot to the students but it mattered to me.

When the graduation ceremony was over, I busied myself with moving instruments and sound equipment while parents left. I was almost finished when the principal came up and said, "Don't you think you've spent enough time here today? I'll take care of the rest of the equipment. You run on home and get some good rest. The parents really liked the music. I think the newspaper photographer got some good pictures, too. Thanks for helping me get this school opened and off to a good start."

On the short drive home, I thought about how unfair it seemed that dancing with a stranger out of town would require me to watch my steps at school for almost an entire academic year. Avoiding any other encounters with the man was relatively easy, but every time I saw his son, I couldn't help but recall that bit of history and hope that the student was happy at home.

CHAPTER 2
FROM SOUTH CAROLINA TO SALZBURG

Our memories are independent of our wills. It is not easy to forget.
Richard B. Sheridan
(1751-1816)

In the spring of 1973, my student teacher, Virginia, competed in the Miss Rock Hill beauty pageant. I met up with her mother, Brenda, for the competition at the civic auditorium. Since Virginia had recently given her senior recital at Winthrop University, I was primed to enjoy her part in the talent segment of the contest. If she placed in the top three, she would win money to go toward some of her expenses on the trip to Europe I was planning for that summer. Chris, one of my friends who was a junior high school band director in Rock Hill, and her sister, Cathy, who lived in Hawaii, also were going on the trip.

When I had spent the previous Thanksgiving with Chris and Cathy and their family in North Carolina, their mother told me, "I raised my four kids to have roots and wings. I just didn't expect the wings to stretch so far—two sons in Germany, one daughter in Hawaii, and the other daughter a state away."

When we first talked about the possibility of making the trip, I asked Chris, "Will Cathy be content to be on her own while the three of us are in class?"

"Oh, yes. She's very independent and is used to taking solo trips."

"Great! I'll feel better knowing she'll enjoy the trip when she's on her own."

Chris, Virginia, and I registered for the two-week Orff-Schulwerk summer course at the Mozarteum in Salzburg. After completing the Master of Music degree in 1971, I attended a three-week summer workshop to study with Grace Nash at Ithaca College in New York in 1972. I was instrumental in getting her to teach a similar course at Winthrop that summer (1973), which led to her being invited to teach there the next two summers. In 1974 and 1975, I was her assistant in those courses.

At that time, there was a professional tug of war among music educators between followers of Carl Orff's and Zoltan Kodaly's respective teachings. Orff lived and worked in Germany, and Kodaly in Hungary. Both of their philosophies honored cultural heritage as represented in the folk music traditions of their countries. In the United States and elsewhere, leading music educators tended to align with one or the other and became loyal followers and proponents of their views as well as consumers of their materials.

Grace Nash, who became my most important mentor, disagreed with what she viewed as the *bandwagon* mentality of many in the field of music education. Rather than subscribing to a commonly held view in the late 1960s and early 1970s that distilled Orff's work into an emphasis upon creativity and Kodaly's work as an emphasis on music literacy, she became one of the few who studied with both Orff and Kodaly in person. In addition, she went to England to study with Vera Gray, a protégé of Rudolf Laban, most widely known for his system of notation for ballet, *Labanotation*.

After absorbing the philosophical and practical strengths of each of these pedagogues, Grace synthesized the complementary strengths of Orff, Kodaly, and Laban. She understood that none of the three drew lines of distinction between creativity and music literacy in their original writings and that the best of Music Education would include the values of all three, as well as others. To support the spread of her work, she also wrote an abundance of materials for use with American students and trained thousands of music educators, both domestically and internationally, in her unique approach to music education.

Even though I chose to study with Nash every chance I could and felt extremely honored when she insisted that I be put on salary as her assistant for two of the three courses she taught at Winthrop, I also knew that the most outstanding place to study *pure* Orff was at the Mozarteum in Salzburg. It was the international headquarters for Orff's work related to Music Education and attracted students and faculty from all over the world. Enrolling in the summer course at the Morzateum seemed like the perfect combination of furthering my professional credentials and embarking on international travel.

I organized the trip. At the time, travel expenses related to a profession could be used for itemized deductions on IRS statements. So, I reasoned that about half of the expenses would count toward tax deductions for the three of us who taught music.

My immediately former husband at the time and I had travelled in Europe for ten weeks during the summer of 1969, and I felt a strong need to prove to myself that I could come up with a way to make such travel a part of my life apart from a marriage or anyone else's planning. I also knew that Virginia and Chris would enjoy the course and that it would be beneficial in their work.

Three things controlled the overall planning for the month in Europe. We couldn't leave until the course at Winthrop ended; we had to be in Salzburg on the dates of the course; and we were determined to be in Paris on Bastille Day.

Grace, the dean, and two Music Education professors all agreed that we should set the date for the course at Winthrop as soon as possible after school districts in the state began the summer break. Once the dates for that course were firm, I began to finalize our plans. Chris and Cathy planned to fly a few days before Virginia and I so that they could have a short visit with their two brothers who were members of the military and stationed in Germany. They also planned to extend their time in Germany after Virginia and I left.

I planned the trip so that we would travel by train at night as much as possible to minimize lodging costs. But that did not mean we had a sleeping berth. The seats on the European trains were designed so that they faced each other. On the window side, there was a small drop-leaf table that came in handy for snacks and beverages. A small lever released the seats so that they slid forward and abutted to form a single bed that could accommodate the two passengers who normally faced each other.

The converted seats were reasonably comfortable for one night at a time. The only tricky things were to lie on your side and keep your feet out of each other's face. If one was a calm sleeper and the other one restless, that added to the number of tricks to master—sleep by collaboration. Raincoats doubled as blankets, and purses pillowed our heads. We found it workable, but in retrospect, I believe the thing that made the narrow *bed* work for two was the youth of those using it and the spirit of adventure that fueled us.

I took care of all reservations and informed the others of each step in the planning. I instructed them about using the lodging addresses for parents to send air letters, and I cautioned all to pack lightly. I ended up with the heaviest load of all because I chose to take an extra recorder—a wooden soprano and a plastic alto—so that I would not have to sit out any playing time while waiting for the wooden recorder to dry out. I also took more printed resources for the course. Once we arrived in Salzburg, I sent a small suitcase full of extra clothing to our final reservation's address in Amsterdam so that I would not have to lug the excess on the last week of the trip.

Once the skeleton for the schedule was outlined, Chris and Virginia collaborated in planning the sightseeing portions of the trip. It worked out so that we would travel for a week, attend the course for two weeks, then travel for one more week before Chris and Cathy headed to Germany and Virginia and I headed home from the Schiphol Airport in Amsterdam. Plans were set, but Virginia needed to place in the top three of the Miss Rock Hill contest to have money for her expenses. She did not want her mom to take out a loan.

I had attended one other small town beauty pageant in a smaller town the previous year and had promised myself I would never again attend such an event because I had lost the teenage awe of objectified contests. But when Virginia told me she needed to place in the contest to pay her trip expenses, I felt compelled to support her.

At the previous event, one of the contestants was at least 20 pounds overweight, but confident enough to make it through even the bathing suit portion of the pageant. The emcee asked the first question, "What is your favorite food?"

Without hesitation, she answered, "Macaroni and cheese."

When some of the audience members failed to contain their laughter, which was mostly stifled by seatmates' elbows, the teenager looked bewildered. Her yes darted back and forth between the emcee and the audience. Question marks filled her eyes as her mantle of confidence melted. It appeared that she needed some subtle clue to know whether to laugh or cry.

When it was her turn for the final question—the serious one—the emcee put on the mask of studious consideration and said, "What is the most important attribute for a young Southern lady to have?"

"Uhmm—could you please say that again?"

"What is the most important quality for a Southern lady to have?"

"Oh! I get it! To be sin-cere." (first syllable emphasis)

The other four finalists apparently appreciated her answer because they all gave the same response with identical inflection. The emcee was experienced enough to treat each of the repetitious opinions as profound insights. The winner (not the one who liked macaroni and cheese) basked in the low-wattage limelight as she cradled her roses against the glittered sash across her chest and donned the rhinestone tiara atop her high beehived hair.

At the Miss Rock Hill pageant, Brenda and I shared a sense of pride in her daughter's accomplishment and potential. Virginia had managed to avoid the plasticity of superficial beauty and exuded the genuine charm of a young Southern woman with confidence and without pretense. Our pride melded into a stream of support, lightening normal performance jitters as the almost-graduated student made the piano sing Brahms' long phrases with passion and nuanced musical authority. When the judges were ready to huddle for calculating the vote tallies, the emcee's circus-toned voice boomed, "Ladies and Gentlemen, a 15-minute break, please."

Brenda went to the restroom while I mingled in the lobby. A short man with an aggressive walk approached me and thrust out his hand, trapping mine between both of his. "Hi. I'm (garbled). Who you?"

"Excuse me. I didn't catch your name."

"I said, I'm Strom Thurmond. I'll 'preciate yore vote." In sales-speak, he knew how to *assume the sale*.

With barely hidden disgust, I gave in to social custom, "Pleased to me you."

The tone of my obligatory response meant, "Move on, Buddy," but I doubt if he possessed the gift of interpretation.

On the way back to our seats, Brenda and I locked steps. She was as giddy as a rural schoolgirl on her first trip to a state fair. "I saw what just happened. I can't believe you got to meet Senator Strom Thurmond and shake his hand."

"I didn't have much of a choice. He just assumed I wanted to meet him. I didn't even know who he was, but he seemed to expect me to recognize him. It sounded like he had a mouth full of snuff, so I didn't understand his name. When he repeated it, he sounded miffed."

"Yeah—he does like to be recognized, and he loves to hang out at beauty pageants. I guess you know his wife was a beauty queen."

I shook my head, indicating more incredulity than response. "No. I'm from Florida. I don't know anything about him except that he filibustered in favor of segregation. He can assume my vote all he wants, but he'll never get it."

Her giddiness calmed down and settled into confusion. I could almost see the mental wheels turning in her head. She liked and respected me but could not fathom why I was not thrilled that a glad-handing vote-beggar had sought me out. Brenda apparently had never heard anything less than high praise for the Dixiecrat politician.

We sat down to wait for the results. The announcer revealed the name of the second runner-up. Polite applause and demure acknowledgement followed. That meant that Virginia was either Miss Rock Hill or the runner-up, or she had not placed in the top three.

The announcer revealed the name of the second runner-up. Polite applause and demure acknowledgement followed. That meant that Virginia was either Miss Rock Hill or the runner-up, or she had not placed in the top three.

"And the runner-up is Miss Virginia Jones." We clapped and

cheered. Brenda jumped to her feet, too caught up in the moment to settle down and listen for the winner's name to be called. I touched her elbow and motioned to the seat.

The emcee called out, "If audience members will please be seated, we'll get on with the grand finale of announcements."

Brenda sat down and whispered, "Now I know for sure that Virginia will be able to go with you to Salzburg, take that course, and have a little spendin' money. I thought I might have to take out a loan, but since she's the runner-up, she'll have enough money for the trip. That's all she talks about besides how much she enjoys bein' your student teacher."

"She's really good with the kids and prepares excellent lesson plans."

"She's got several friends over there and hopes to look 'em up. Some boys from around here are in the Army, stationed in Germany. If you're able to meet up with 'em, they'll treat you to a real good time. They've known Virginia since she was a toddler." The emcee asked again for quiet. We hushed.

"And the winner of Miss Rock Hill, 1973, is Miss Jennifer White."

Everyone stood as though giving a standing ovation after a symphony orchestra concert. I cupped my hand over my mouth and spoke into Brenda's ear, "The two sisters who are going with us have two brothers stationed in Germany. Wouldn't it be something if Virginia's friends and Chris and Cathy's brothers know each other?"

She said, "Not impossible, but prob'ly not likely. That family's from North Carolina, right?"

"Yes—High Point."

When the roar quieted, I whispered, "Thanks for encouraging Virginia to go."

So—the first Southern beauty pageant I attended was not necessarily the most memorable, though I have not forgotten it. What distinguished the second, and last, beauty pageant I ever attended was that it helped launch the trip that took me, two other music teachers, and one of their sisters on a month-long trip to Europe. For my companions and me, such a trip was neither a rite of passage nor anything less than a dream come true.

I used Frommer's *Europe on $5.00 A Day* for travel tips and data for reservations. I also bought a copy of the current *Eurail Guide*, which gave a table of all European train routes and schedules. With those two tools, I could secure reservations and make the puzzle pieces of the plans fit the picture we wanted to live in for a month.

A few days later, Virginia asked me about the plans. I assured her that I had the tickets for our charter flight with a short layover in Philadelphia. We were to land in Frankfurt and spend one night in Heidelberg before leaving by train for Vienna. The Eurail passes, which had to be purchased in the United States, would arrive soon, and almost all the reservations were confirmed.

She said, "I wonder if any of my friends in the Army will be near Heidelberg."

I told her that I didn't know where the US military bases were located, but that distances within Europe were much less than we were used to. I also mentioned that I was trying to get us into Hungary to visit the Franz Liszt Academy but was not sure that it would work out.

Virginia seemed to tense up a little before she said, "Now you know I have to be careful about my weight. If anything happens to the new Miss Rock Hill, I'll have to take over her duties. I've heard they weigh themselves in kilowatts over there. I don't know how I'll even know how much I weigh."

"I think you mean kilograms. We'll get it figured out when we get there. People are usually friendly and enjoy helping Americans. I think there are scales in the train stations."

Behind the scenes, Brenda made sure that Virginia's friends' moms knew about our plans. She even gave them the name of the Gasthof where we would be staying in Salzburg.

One of the budget items was a splurge on a nice dinner once a week. On our first night in Salzburg, a Sunday, a couple of the young men Brenda had mentioned showed up at dinner time. We were already seated in the restaurant of the Gasthof and were just about to order when Virginia jumped up, thrust out her arms, and said, "Hey, Bill! Hey Bob! What are ya'll doin' here?"

Bob said, "Nothin' much 'cept tryin' to chase you down. Your mamma told our moms where you're stayin' at. Our base is not too far from here. How come you're out here in the country? We thought you were gonna' be at some fancy school in town."

"Well, I must say, it is a bit confusin'. The Mozarteum is in the city of Salzburg. But the summer course we're attending is held at Schloss Frohnburg. You know that yellow buildin' in *The Sound of Music*? That's Scholoss Frohnburg. It's cheaper to stay here than close to that buildin'. By the time we registered, all the cheap rooms near there were taken. The manager here says it's about a 45-minute walk to the Schloss. He told us about a shortcut that goes through a cow pasture, though. Hope we don't walk into class with stinky cow poop up to our ankles."

"Now, don't you be worryin' 'bout that. I'm sure you'll find a good path."

As Brenda had predicted, the US soldiers who had known Virginia all her life insisted on paying for the entire group and encouraged us to order with eyes on the menu items, not the prices.

Bill ordered what he thought would be chicken. With rumors of horse meat being disguised as beef, a fellow couldn't be too careful. When the waiter brought it, complete with red cabbage and pommes frittes, Bill looked at the plate, then at the waiter and said, "Chicken, right?"

"No, hare."

Trying to use my smattering of German vocabulary words, I turned toward Bill and said, "That's a term of respect, sort of like 'Sir.'"

The waiter's English was excellent. He said, "Nein, Fraulein, I meant rabbit. The meat is not chicken. It is rabbit."

The hometown boy old enough to do a man's job in the Army, but who was not used to eating rabbit, covered his mouth and mumbled, "Toilet?" The waiter pointed, and Bill raced, still covering his mouth.

Virginia batted her Southern blue eyes at the waiter and said, "Could you please take that away and bring some real chicken for my friend?"

The waiter obliged. Soon, with gray-white pallor, Bill returned to the table. Virginia said, "Ready for a beer?"

"Nah. Just water, please. Gotta' take it easy, ya' know."

Cathy and Chris and I reminisced about the family Thanksgiving weekend while Virginia and Bob and Bill talked about their childhood in Fort Mill. Bill and Bob also talked of their hopes to use GI benefits to go to college after being discharged. They must have been about two years older than Virginia. The affection shared among them was almost stronger than family—the bond of tight friendship encouraged by their mothers and nurtured by their shared Fort Mill and Rock Hill roots.

After dinner, the soldiers gave each of us a warm hug and headed back to the base that served as home while they served their country.

We went upstairs, finished unpacking, and laid out things we would need the next morning. We also set up a schedule for the hall bathroom that served everyone on our floor. We learned that we had to let the proprietor know ahead of time if we wanted hot water for a shower because there was an additional charge for that; otherwise, cold water was the mean alternative.

We had no complaints, though—just a time of adjustment to the dorm-like life for the two weeks and enthusiasm for what we were about to venture into—a course in the outskirts of Salzburg with people from over three dozen different countries taught in English by a woman from England; a course founded by a world class composer who also was an educator, located near his birthplace in southern Germany where he developed his pedagogy before World War II; folk dance classes taught by a very pregnant dancer from Greece whose due date was a few days after the course ended; incredibly talented classmates who helped us stretch our individuality and creativity while making music together and getting acquainted despite whatever language challenges we encountered. And Cathy mapped out her routes for exploring the city and outlying areas for sightseeing and photography.

CHAPTER 3
DAS TEAM IN VIENNA

Danger and delight grow on one stalk.
Scottish Proverb

Not long after the Miss Rock Hill Pageant, Virginia and Chris came to my apartment for a light supper and to discuss our plans for the trip. I gave Virgina and Chris the details of our flight schedules and the reservation confirmation for the room in Heidelberg. Virginia wanted a copy to show her mom, and Chris needed a copy in case we missed each other in the Frankfurt airport.

Virginia and I flew out of Charlotte with a layover in Philadelphia on Monday, June 20, 1973. It was a charter flight through one of the major airlines of the time. My husband and I had used the same flight arrangements in 1969 and discovered at the airport that we would be on a KLM flight. I hoped that the flight in 1973 would be just as pleasant—and it was—although I do not recall which airline serviced the flight. My understanding was that large companies chartered flights and sold any leftover seats at a deep discount.

After we boarded, stowed our take-on luggage overhead, and settled into our seats, Virginia said, "Why are we just sittin' here? Looks like everybody's ready to go." I was too inexperienced with flights to have become a Nervous Nellie flyer yet, but I did wonder if there might be a mechanical problem.

"I don't know, but I'm sure they'll tell us soon, or we'll take off."

Finally, one of the attendants announced, "Sorry, folks, but we cannot take off until at least two of you agree to accept a $10.00 reimbursement in lieu of dinner. Regulations state that we must have enough meals on board to serve everyone. We're fine for snacks and breakfast but are two short for dinner." Half the passengers raised their hands, eager to give up an in-flight dinner in exchange for a take-off. The attendant was standing near our seats and waved the vouchers at us. I was seated in the aisle seat and stretched my arm to accept the vouchers while fellow passengers cheered as the jet engines revved.

Like me four years earlier, Virginia was taking her first flight. I hoped the hook of travel would sink as deeply into her as it had in me. Her mom had made cookies and put fruit and nuts in individual care packages for both of us. We would be happy with the snacks along with airline-supplied drinks until we had crossed enough of the Atlantic to be ready for breakfast.

As planned, Chris and Cathy were in the lobby of the airport in Frankfurt and spotted us. I had picked up enough German vocabulary on my previous trip to understand some conversations if the speakers spoke slowly, especially if I knew they were discussing music. But I had no delusion that I knew the language. When we got into a cab, I showed the driver the air letter confirmation for the hotel, which was just across the river and within walking distance of the Heidelberg castle.

We rested a little and then ventured out for our first German meal about mid-afternoon. Excited with the prospects of adventure, we set the tone for the entire trip—input from all of us regarding when and where to eat, a general plan for the next day, and activities prioritized. After a walk long enough to work out the kinks from the flight and a heavy German meal washed down with a stein or two of local beer, we set out to return to the room. A car pulled up beside us, and a young man in the passenger seat said, "Need a ride, ladies?"

His accent was American, and he seemed to be above-board, but I said, "No, thanks. We don't have far to go."

"You sure? I'm not sure you should be walking in this part of town after dark."

Cathy spoke up. "We've already said 'No.' You need to move along and stop blocking traffic."

I felt no threat because the street was well-travelled, the man had no hint of threat in his verbiage or tone, and we were armed with Mace. I did realize, though, that four of us would not fit into the car and knew we should not split up. I thought about Brenda's telling me about Virginia having friends in Germany and Chris and Cathy's brothers being there also and assumed that these American young men were simply trying to be helpful to a small group of young women who were walking on a sidewalk after dark. It seemed to set our mindset of being open to forming new friendships while also being cautious.

The man said, "Alright. Me and my buddy are just tryin' to make sure you're okay. Some of these people over here really don't like Americans. Good to hear your accents." They drove on and we walked the last few blocks to our room, feeling secure in the surroundings and a bit smug in our freedom and independence.

The next morning, we walked around the Old Town portion of the city before hiking up the Burgweg through Kornmarkt Square up to the castle. By the time we reached the top, we wondered why we had not taken the funicular train. But with our budget of $5.00 per day, spending funds for a train when we were all perfectly healthy seemed like a waste.

Once we made our way to the main entrance, we paid for a guided tour. It was worth it though because of the outstanding guide who made the fascinating history of the castle that was built in the 1300s come alive. We especially marveled at the library on one of the upper floors and the 34,000-gallon wine barrel in the basement.

With plans to board a train for Vienna that afternoon, we did not linger at the castle. It was a long ride—over 14 hours—with the advantage of avoiding paying for a night's lodging outweighing the disadvantage of missing much of the scenery. But proverbial *starving students* could not cut corners on the budget without also cutting out some of the sights that better-budgeted passengers enjoyed.

Despite my effort to double-check every detail to assure our trip would be smooth, especially regarding reservations, I failed to account for the night train ride pushing our arrival into the next day and made the reservation for the day we left rather than the following day. If we had arrived on the same day, we would not have saved the cost of a night's lodging. What a difference arriving past midnight makes! I was completely mistaken and confused about the mistake I had made. I had alerted the proprietor of the pensione that we would be getting in very late, and he had assured me that we could check in at any time. Both of us had been diligent in our attempt at accuracy, but I had overlooked a critical detail.

We had no trouble finding a cab at the train station and getting to the pensione not far off the Ring Strasse a few hours before the kitchen began breakfast preparations. We managed to climb the four flights of narrow steps without having to take a rest break. But when we rang the bell for the desk attendant, I had to do some quick talking to get us into the room.

The desk clerk said, "Yah, Fraulein, we are expecting you, but not this day. We expected you yesterday. But you may check in after 15:00 (3:00 PM) for the remainder of your reserved time with us." Crestfallen, I showed him the confirmation letter.

"See? Here is the date."

"Yah, I see."

"And I called to let you know we would get in very late."

"Yah, I recall the conversation."

"Then may we please have the keys and go on to our room?"

About then, a man and woman with American accents and two children approached the desk. The man presented a note with a confirmation number on it, expecting to be checked into their room immediately. The proprietor explained to all of us that there was only one large room available and told me again that we should have checked in the previous day. I would later understand that when it appeared we were a *no-show*, he allowed the man with the family to reserve the four-sleeper room for that night.

"But, Herr Braun, my friends and I have been on the train for over 14 hours and were counting on this room. We have no other place to stay between now and when the room will be available."

The strength of my earnest conviction seemed enough to convince him that he had made a mistake and that I was in the right. While I do not claim that I would never have tried to bend circumstances to my advantage, that time, my plea was simply a mistake. I was speaking out of sincere belief in the facts as I (mis)understood them.

The proprietor said to the man with the family, "I am very sorry, Sir, but it appears that I have made a mistake. May I offer you a room in our sister property just around the corner?"

"Are you sure my family cannot have the big room now?"

"Yah. These ladies made a reservation for three nights."

"And will you pay for the taxi?"

"Of course, Sir. Shall I call for one now?"

"Yes, please."

Herr Braun gave each of us a key. When we got to the room, Chris said, "Guess this means we won't be goin' to Hungary, right?"

"Yes. I am so sorry that I didn't account for the long train ride from Heidelberg. It's a shame to get this close to Budapest and not visit the Liszt Academy."

"It might have made the trip a bit too hurried to try to do that this time. We'll just have to come back some time."

Chris' sweet spirit and understanding went a long way to make me feel better about the mistake in timing.

We set the travel alarm clock and crashed for the few hours before breakfast. When we sat down for breakfast, the proprietor came over to our table. He seemed a bit peeved and addressed his remarks to me. "You have made a mistake. Your arrival time should have been for this day, not yesterday. I was so tired when I talked to you that my mind got fuzzy. I hope our other guests were not offended."

"You mean that our reservation was for an afternoon check in yesterday but should have been for today?"

"Precisely! I am sorry I got confused when you arrived."

"I understand. I am so sorry that I caused the confusion. I see that it was my mistake because I had not accounted for the train time from Heidelberg when I made the reservation. If you talk to the man who had to leave, please pass along my apology to him. We are so happy to be here and appreciate your kindness." To myself, I wondered if it was even legal for him to release the room to someone else once an expected guest appeared to be a *no show*.

I filed my wondering away and then asked him about visiting Grinzing that evening. I told him that I had visited that area when I was there in 1969 and still remembered how much fun it was. I asked, "Is it still like it was then?"

"Yah, yah. Been like that since the 1800s. Won't be changing any time soon." He cautioned us about the bus schedule. The last bus returning to the city was at 23:00 (11:00 PM). The city center bus station was just a few blocks from the pensione. He explained that at that time of night it would be difficult to find a taxi and that if we managed to find one, it would be very expensive. I thanked him for the information and assured him that we would be sure to catch the last bus back to the city.

We spent the day seeing typical tourist attractions in the city and splurged on a cab ride to the cemetery where a section includes gravesites for many of Europe's greatest artists, including Beethoven and Brahms. We placed flowers on those two graves and at Mozart's memorial, feeling overwhelmed with admiration and gratitude for the talent buried and memorialized there.

Back in the city, we climbed to the roof of St. Stephen's Dom. Leaning over the parapet around the iconic tiled roof, we noticed heavy equipment repaving a section of the road. A pedestrian tried to dash between two cement trucks and was trapped between them when one backed up. We heard the screams and saw his twitching body as moments later a siren blared while the truck lurched forward to free the struggling man. His limp body fell to the pavement.

Our realization of what had happened threatened to cast a pall over our time in Vienna. But one tragic incident could not blot out the wealth of history we witnessed and our reaction to it. The juxtaposition of walking among the graves of some of our musical idols, seeing the incomparable tile roof of the cathedral up close, and hearing the heartbeat of the city in the clip-clop of the horses' hooves as their owners took tourists on carriage rides was almost too much to process.

The lives represented by the headstones in the cemetery had become real in ways that a textbook or recording could never convey. The work of craftsmen ages ago that still symbolized Vienna from the roof of St. Stephen's Dom set in our consciousness both the practical and aesthetic importance of every detail of a work of art. And the casual ease and rhythm of the hooves bounced us back to much earlier times when composers often walked the Vienna woods for relaxed inspiration or rode horse-drawn carriages to concert halls or patron balls.

Virginia said, "I don't know if I can walk past that place on the sidewalk where a man just got killed."

Cathy said, "I feel sorry for the cement truck driver. He couldn't have seen the man."

Chris said, "Why would he have been in such a hurry that he tried to walk between two cement trucks that were obviously trying to get a job done?"

I said, "There are no answers. We just need to refocus on thinking about something else right now."

We climbed the stairs down to street level and scurried around the corner to put the scene of the accident behind us, then stopped in a park to eat a gelato before going back to the room. After a nap, we freshened up and headed to the bus stop to go out to Grinzing for roasted chicken and green wine—the first wine from the current harvest.

We walked several blocks perusing many rustic wine houses, smelling the chicken on rotisseries, and catching the jovial cadence of animated conversations. It seemed that everyone's determined purpose was simply to enjoy life.

Musicians formed small bands to play what may be described as music appropriate for Oktoberfest. In each of the outdoor dining areas, a few dancers, some of whom wore lederhosen or dirndls, laughed while keeping up with the polkas and waltzes.

We agreed on the place to have dinner and found a table under the trees closer to the sidewalk than to the spitting rotisserie. I wanted to be sure to get pictures, so I started having each of us take turns photographing the other three.

People who live in Vienna sometimes avoid Grinzing because so many tourists go there. But at least a few natives enjoy it and gave us some of our most outstanding memories. The time we spent in Austria was almost like a fairy tale of friendship, adventure, and a little romance.

When it was my turn to take the shot, a young man from the next table walked up to me and, in German-accented English, said, "Excuse me, Fraulein. May I take the picture for you so you can be in it too?" Since I was the designated Mother Hen of the group, I immediately thought of guarding our purses and cameras. He must have sensed my hesitation because he continued, "Don't worry. We have our own cameras. We won't steal yours." I looked him in the eye, smiled, and pulled out a fresh flash cube to attach to my Instamatic.

"Please. That would be very kind of you."

He snapped the picture and immediately extended his hand with the camera in it toward me. "Any more?"

"No, thanks. I'll share with my friends when I get the prints made."

His friends followed his inviting wave over to join the conversation. The photo-taker said, "I am Gerhard. This is Peter; this is Paul, and this is Franz. We call him Fifi."

Fifi was shorter than average with a wiry build, curly dark hair, and a big, shy smile. He said, "No French poodle; nickname."

If any social ice existed, Fifi's sense of humor shattered it. We all laughed and pair by pair, eyes connected in conviviality.

"My name is Sue. This is Virginia; this is Chris, and this is Chris' sister, Cathy."

"Okay we join you?"

I looked at the others. Virginia gave an enthusiastic nod. Chris shrugged, and Cathy shook her head. Three out of four *yes* or *almost-yes* seemed close enough for me to say, "Sure."

They brought their steins with them and pulled up their chairs. I asked, "Have you had dinner?"

"Yes. We're here for beer."

"But I thought this area is known for wine."

"Yes—the new year's vintage—they keep beer for locals."

We exchanged banter back and forth. Despite the language limitations, the universal linguistic *tells* of laughter, eyes and eyebrows responding when words were understood but not available for response, and gustatory sounds bridged vocabulary gaps.

Dirndl-clad waitresses soon brought the half-chicken portions to us, along with generous servings of pommes frites. We offered to share with the young men, but they declined.

Paul said, "Ketchup?"

Chris and he had already seemed to make a connection. She said, "How did you know?"

"You are American. No Mayonnaise, always Ketchup."

I tried to practice my minimal German. Gerhard, whose English was the best, said, "Your German sounds funny because your English sounds funny. You live in the South of the OOO-ESS-AAH (USA) right?"

"Yes. And when I live around people with an accent, I tend to pick it up."

"Okay. We speak English. I need practice. My friends understand a lot of English, but they have not studied as long as I have. I travel often to Washington, DC and New York City."

When we finished our meal, I looked at my watch—the one my principal called my *hippy* watch—with the wide leather strap and double buckles attached to a man's Timex. "It is almost 23:00. We need to walk to the bus stop to catch the last bus." Gerhard called the waitress over and insisted on picking up the tab. Each of us thanked him for paying for our dinner and drinks.

Gerhard said, "We are *Das Team*. We have a van and plenty of room. Let us take you back to your room so you can stay out longer. We even have *Das Team* painted on the side of the van." It didn't take long to see that the van was a vintage Volkswagen straight out of *Hippyville*.

Cathy was already shaking her head. I saw no signs from Virginia or Chris to indicate that they wanted to accept the invitation, and I also did not want to venture into the van. Getting acquainted out in the open was one thing, but accepting a ride with strangers in a foreign country was a stretch, even for an adventurous spirit.

"It would be fun to stay longer, but we really do have to get back because we have only one more day in Vienna before our course begins. Thanks for your generosity and for the offer."

He did not pressure us, but said, "Remember *Das Team*. May we walk you to the bus stop? The van is parked across the street from the stop."

"Sure. I recall it is just around the corner." If any of the four men had shown a different tone or if my skin had crawled, I would have thought, *Here comes the abduction.* But I felt no apprehension based on their behavior, only common sense in need of exercise. We paired up on the sidewalk and set out for the bus stop—Gerhard and I in front, then Virginia and Peter, Paul and Chris, and Cathy and Fifi in the rear of our double line.

We saw the bus at the stop as we turned the corner and ran the last few yards to jump on the steps just in time to board, thinking we had seen the last of *Das Team*. We hadn't gone far before the bus had to stop at a traffic light. The blast of an insistent horn startled us. We looked out the window and saw Gerhard behind the steering wheel of the van, smiling and waving. I thought, *Oh, no! They're following us and will find out where we are staying.* Cathy said, "I knew you shouldn't have been friendly with those strangers." My faith in my own judgment was under serious question.

Virginia said, "Peter is so handsome. I really enjoyed talkin' with him."

Cathy said, "Talking? Seemed to me like you just gooney-eyed each other. I'll admit he is cute, though. But we don't know anything about them except what they say. How do we know they really are architect students and that Gerhard's father owns the firm where they will apprentice?"

Chris said, "Cathy, I know you've never liked to talk to strangers, but these young men really seem nice. They were courteous and fun."

Virginia said, "I was hopin' to see some of my boy-friends over here, but I sure didn't expect to meet anyone like Peter."

Cathy would not be placated. "Well, I just hope we don't have a big problem when we get off this bus."

I said, "Don't worry. We'll be in a well-lit area where there's plenty of traffic all hours of the day and night, and I'm sure there will be policemen not far from wherever we are walking. Keep your Mace handy, though, just in case."

At every traffic light between Grinzing and the Ring Strasse, *Das Team* reminded us with the horn that they were right there. Gerhard tried waving his arm as if to tell us to get off the bus and get into the van. I thought they would turn toward wherever they lived when we got close to the city center bus stop.

As expected, the bus went into an underground parking area to let us and a few others out before the driver parked the bus, punched out, and went home. Now the dilemma became real. Rather than following my assumption and parting ways with the bus, Gerhard followed us into the underground. I do not know whether it was supposed to be used exclusively by buses or if it was legal for a van to enter the area, but there it sat, full of four nice young men in hopes of taking four young ladies to their pensione. We stepped off the bus and stood in the parking garage trying to figure out which exit to take.

Das Team stayed in the van. Gerhard said, "Now may we take you to your pensione?"

Cathy, who was a parole officer and knew how to deal with persistent types spoke up. "No. We have a short walk and will not ride with you."

"I understand. I have a sister," Gerhard said. "If Sue and Virginia and Chris want a ride, we can drive slowly while you walk on the sidewalk. I would not let you walk alone even if it is a short distance."

My feet were killing me. Chris was tired, and Virginia welcomed the chance to gaze into Peter's eyes a little longer. Remembering that my Mace was in my pocket, I said, "Okay. But you must be sure that Cathy does not have to walk too fast."

"Agreed. And once you see that the van and we are okay, would you agree to let us take you to the amusement park tomorrow?"

"You mean the one with the huge prater wheel?"

"Yes. You know it?"

"Yes. I went there when I was here four years ago."

"Okay. Let's get you three and Cathy home for the night."

The other three men moved into the back seat. I sat up front, and Chris and Virginia sat in the middle seat. Gerhard kept his word. We kept the windows open so that we could talk with Cathy along the way as the van crept the 3-4 blocks to the pensione.

I don't know how I managed those directions when my sense of direction is so limited. I must have just given him the address from the confirmation letter. I told Gerhard that we were going to visit the Schoenbrunn Palace the next morning, but we could go to the amusement park in the afternoon.

Back in the room, we came close to a heated debate about the ride in the van but eased the tension by talking about visiting the Palace. We got up the next morning early enough to tour the Palace and attend a noon-time concert. A string quartet played some of my favorite pieces in a room fit for Mozart. We made it back to the pensione just in time to connect with *Das Team*.

They arrived right at 2:00. Cathy agreed to go to the park with us. We went straight to the park and spent the afternoon riding rides, playing games, and chatting. We kept the same pairings just like when people keep the same seat after selecting it on the first day of a class. I felt sorry for Fifi because Cathy was preoccupied with her camera and was almost distant to him. The rest of us continued to enjoy each other's company.

I was 31, claiming to be 25; Gerhard claimed to be 21 and may have been younger. Virginia was 22, Chris 26, and Cathy 24. I don't know how old the other men were. But they all were mannerly, fun, and generous.

When they took us back to the pensione, Peter said to Gerhard in German, "Can we take them dancing tonight? I really like Virginia and want to dance with her."

Gerhard asked, "Do you want to go dancing tonight? There are a lot of discos here. All of us like to dance."

Three of us nodded. Cathy said, "I'll be working on my photo diary. Count me out." She had apparently made up her mind regarding spending any more time with *Das Team* and would not budge. I almost felt sorry for her but reminded myself that she was used to living alone far away from her family and probably preferred to be alone much of the time.

"Okay. Chris and Virginia and I would love to go dancing tonight."

"We'll pick you up at 7:30."

Fifi said, "Okay I come? I find dance partner."

We all said, "Sure."

A little before 7:30, we preempted and went down to the first floor so that they would not have to climb the four flights of stairs and wait at the desk for us. We stopped at a Chinese restaurant before we arrived at what seemed to be *Disco Lane*. All the men were very good dancers, but Peter and Paul outshined Gerhard under the disco globes. And Fifi had no trouble finding dance partners everywhere we went.

When they took us back to our room, as we said our goodbyes, Virginia said, "I'm sort of sad to leave Vienna. I know I came over here to go to this course, but I'm going to miss you new friends, especially you, Peter." Gerhard gave him the translation. Peter gave Virginia a long hug and walked her toward the door.

Gerhard said, "What time does your train depart tomorrow?"

"About 9:30."

"Okay. I hope you have a wonderful course and learn a lot."

Chris and Paul were the first to get to the door. We all said our final goodbyes, and the three music teachers who had spent most of the day with three architecture students (or perhaps apprentices) dragged ourselves up the four flights of our pensione in Vienna for the last time. I wished I had followed my own advice and packed lighter, dreading lugging everything down the stairs the next morning.

Cathy had spent the evening happily on her own. She did some hand wash, wrote postcards, and worked on her photo diary. Other than her initial disapproval of our trusting strangers, she did not resent the time we spent with the Viennese gentlemen.

Virginia was a mess. "I don't know what I'm gonna' do now. I think Peter and I might be falling in love, and I almost don't want to go home."

I said, "You do seem to have a very strong attraction to each other. You look good together—so similar in appearance, about the same height, and so content to just be together with no concern about limited language exchange."

"I know. I'm usually such a chatterbox, but now I'm just tunin' in to how I feel and thinkin' of what I would say if he really knew English. We do pretty well with pointin' to words in dictionaries, and that little phrase book you told me to get comes in handy."

Chris said, "Guess that old saying is true—'Where there's a will, there's a way.'"

"Yeah—I just don't know if I'll ever hear from him after we leave here tomorrow."

I said, "Don't worry. Once we are in the course, you'll be so preoccupied with the musical fun and growth that thoughts of Peter will not consume you."

"Guess it's time for sweet dreams now."

When we were ready to board the train, Gerhard, Peter, and Paul came running up. "You forgot to tell me which Bahnhof. This is the east one. We went to the west one."

"I didn't know there's more than one station. How did you figure out where we were?"

"Easy—checked the train schedule for Salzburg and saw that the 9:30 departure was from this station. Your course is at the Mozarteum, right?"

"Yes, but it is held at Schloss Frohnburg, and the Gasthof where we are staying is a 45-minute walk from there."

"Don't be surprised if you hear from us."

"Okay. But don't be surprised if we have homework or projects to do."

Gerhard handed each of us, including Cathy, a long-stemmed red rose. Peter gave each of us a box of Mozart chocolates, and Paul added a bag of nuts for everyone. Paul said, "Fifi wishes you safe travel and good time in Salzburg. He stayed with van so it not be towed." They helped with our luggage, gave another round of final hugs, waved as the train found its momentum, then headed to where the fun-loving van was parked. It seemed like the last time we would see *Das Team*.

CHAPTER 4
DAS TEAM IN SALZBURG

*Travel—it leaves you speechless,
then turns you into a storyteller.*

Ibn Battuta
(1304-1369)

On the second or third day of the first week, the leader of the course gave me a slip of paper. She explained, "A young man called the office of the Mozarteum and told them he needed to get a message to you. He would like you to call him at this number."

I knew it had to be from Gerhard, then saw his name. When we got back to the Gasthaus after class, I placed the call. "Hi, Gerhard. This is Sue. I received your note."

"Peter and Paul and I have checked our work schedule and would like to come visit you and Virginia and Chris this weekend. Would that be okay?"

"So far as I know, sure. I don't think we will have homework or projects—at least not this week. I'll tell Virginia and Chris."

"We'll get a room where you are staying and will be there in time for dinner on Friday evening. Could you give me the exact address?"

I retrieved the confirmation from my purse and gave him the address. "They seem to be quite busy. I hope you can find a room here or close by. It is not in town and is somewhat isolated. We take a shortcut through a cow pasture on our way to and from Schloss Frohnburg. The bull has been angry with us only once so far. You won't have to go through the pasture, though." He chuckled.

"Take care, please."

"It will be fun to see you. Thanks for calling."

Virginia slipped right back into the loop of love when I told her.

Chris had met a different Paul from Belgium in the course and was not crazy about the first Paul coming over. But she did not want to go through the steps to tell German Paul to stay home. She would play both cards dealt to her, confident that the chances of running into Belgium Paul while she was out with German Paul were slim.

Das Team arrived on time. Gerhard knew where he wanted to take us for dinner and dancing and had already made a reservation. It was one of the older, classic hotels on the Salzach River. His dancing skills shined with ballroom dancing more than in disco style. I got so dizzy when he twirled me to the *Blue Danube Waltz* that I had to sit down. It was a magical evening for all of us.

He sat down with me. "Are you okay? Are you sure you want to dance?"

"Yes, I'm fine—just a bit dizzy because I have not danced much lately."

"You should never do something you don't really want to do. Be sure you are ready before we go back out on the dance floor. If you really do not want to dance, it is okay."

"I'll be ready after I rest a couple of minutes and sip some water."

The Gasthaus owner managed to get them into a room on our floor. The next day, after breakfast, we got in the van and headed for the salt mine tour in Hallstatt. I had done that on my previous trip but was eager to do it again because it is so unique and iconic to the area. After getting tickets, each participant must suit-up in coveralls for the trip down into the salt mines. The funicular train descends at a rather steep angle over 450 meters into the longest operating salt mine in Austria. Along the way, there is an observation deck where salt-slathered vistas stretch where an underground ocean once flowed. While it has been a source of salt since long before the common era, it has operated continuously since 1100.

A guide narrates the history of salt trade in that area and makes the point that the *silk road* existed in order to allow trade between distant lands, but the *salt route* existed, and still exists, to provide a necessity of life. It would be possible to simply read the history of salt production, but the point is to feel the damp and smell the salt air without waves lapping a shore and to know what it is feels like to be that far down into the ground dependent on manmade equipment to transport you back onto the crust that protects the salt mines where *white gold* is the ore of currency.

After the tour, we visited the town of Hallstatt—still only a small village beside a lake so beautiful that it is the subject of picture puzzles of all sizes—and whose patina has polished away all of the grime of tourism tarnish for thousands of years. The texture of the ancient stone buildings retains as much charm as the sparkle of the lake itself with every piece of the jig-sawed image a jewel of indescribable worth.

We visited the small parish church that is a part of the town's image. I thought about the stark difference between this small house of worship with a notable organ, rich hand carved hardwood in the pews and altar, and the industrial steel and concrete of many mega churches in the United States. I understood at a deeper level why I instinctively seek out small churches to visit on back roads rather than buildings brought to fame by the numbers game.

When we returned to the van, Gerhard was the first to pull out of the pensive mood we all had slipped into inside the church. We had been on the road only about 10 minutes, and everyone was quietly absorbing the sights, lost in our separate reveries. With the van's windows down and our hair echoing the flow of the phrases from a slow song on a cassette tape, Gerhard looked toward me and said, "You want to eat fish?"

I assumed he was thinking ahead to dinner plans. Virginia said, "Oh, my goodness. I have not even seen a scale since we left South Carolina. I'm afraid I've already put on several pounds. Is it time to eat already?"

Gerhard said, "The fish is smoked, not fried. It comes right out of this lake. Families set up stands beside the road and sell their smoked catch."

Chris spoke up. "We have family fish camp restaurants in North Carolina, but not smoked fish and no stands by the road. Sounds like fun."

By then, we were at risk of passing the first stand. Gerhard whipped the van to the right and slammed on the brakes to stop right in front of the stand. It looked like pictures I had seen of drying fish hung on what looked like a clothesline in Alaska. He bought one fish for each of us. It was an impromptu roadside picnic, or was it a *fishnic*? I licked my fingers and noticed that everyone else did too. I could have eaten another fish, but the consensus was to get back on the road.

Once again, when we parked at the Gasthaus, we had to go through assumed final goodbyes. It was time for *Das Team* to go back to Vienna and time for us to remember that we were there for one more week of coursework in Orff-Schulwerk.

At the Gasthaus, Gerhard said, "When do you have to leave?"

"We'll take the train to Florence on Saturday."

We went to the room and found Cathy taking a nap. She roused up and said, "Hi, everyone. Ya'll hungry? I wasn't sure when you'd be back, so I haven't had lunch."

I said, "We had a snack of smoked fish not long ago, but by the time we get to town, I think we'll all be ready for a meal. Would you like to go back to one of the beer gardens or try something else?"

Everyone said at once, "Beer Garden!"

Chris said, "I know we are in Austria, but the Hungarian Goulash is so good, and it's cheap."

Virginia said, "Just don't let me have so many Zimmel rolls. They make it seem like they are free, so I keep eating them and forget to keep track of how many to tell the waiter. I don't know when I've eaten so much bread."

Cathy said, "Just use less butter and jam and enjoy the rolls with the goulash."

"If only I could!"

We walked to the bus stop with much more confidence than we had felt a week earlier. We had learned the hard way that there was more than one Gasthaus with the same name as the one where we were staying. Now, we knew to specify the exact address so that we wouldn't get off half an hour away from the correct stop. We felt comfortable walking the streets in Salzburg and knew how to find several of the large beer gardens. Our favorite was the Augustiner Brewery.

Not only was the food good and inexpensive and the beer tasty, but the atmosphere almost required communal singing, dancing, and mixing at long tables like the brewery's oldest location in Munich. We had no desire to acquire a taste for the turnip slices that many locals enjoyed along with their beer, but the other dishes we tried were delicious. Even though our budget allowed one splurge per week for a special dinner, we were happy that night to have the humble Hungarian goulash, wash it down with steins of Augustiner beer, and limit our splurge to a shared Salzburger Knockerl, a sweet souffle, for dessert. One of the dirndl-clad waitresses explained that the Knockerl was made to be served in three mounds to represent the three mountains that overlook the Salzach River.

Virginia said, "Well, count me out. Ya'll can each have one mound. I'm really gettin' scared to get on the scales when I get home."

"Okay," I said, "but you should take one bite because it is such an iconic dessert to Salzburg."

Chris said, "Just leave off one of the rolls and you can have a little bit of the Knockerl from each of our servings."

"That's a hard choice, but I will at least taste it."

The next morning, we were back into our routine of classes for the three music teachers and photography for Cathy. Chris said, "I hope I don't have a guilty look on my face when I see Belgium Paul. I do enjoy talking with him and working with him on in-class projects, but I have to admit that German Paul knows how to show a girl a good time."

Virginia said, "I still haven't figured out how I can go home and never see Peter again."

I said, "I enjoyed spending time with Gerhard and appreciate all his and the others' generosity, but I have to say I look forward to seeing the dentist I've been dating for a couple of years."

Chris said, "It will be interesting to see if any of us hears from any of them."

On Thursday, I received a note to call Gerhard. I called him from the Gasthaus.

"Would it be okay for Peter and me to come see you off when you leave for Italy?"

"I think we will be in too big a hurry to have time to spend with you. It is very kind of you to ask, though."

"Okay. Peter says to tell Virginia he will write and hopes to see her again. I will write to you and hope to see you again also."

"Thank you for calling and for all the good times you gave us. I will look forward to hearing from you and will practice German when I write to you." We hung up, and I turned to Virginia. She was standing near me and heard my part of the conversation.

"Are you sure we won't have time to see them again?"

"Yes. It would delay our train departure, and we really need to be on that train so that we don't have to make changes along the way."

"It's probably better if I don't see Peter again, but I wish I could."

"I know. Leaving a person and places of great joy always stands a chance of causing tears of both sadness and joy. Now let's get to work on that project the instructor wants us to share tomorrow."

By then, we all were challenged by the skill level of the instruction. We saw classmates develop skills beyond what they came with and hoped they saw the same in us. We especially enjoyed the folk-dance classes and hoped the instructor's child would not make its debut before the course ended. There were about 50-60 classmates from over three dozen different nations, and instructors came from about six different countries. Although the course was taught in English, the mix of accents and languages was a delight within the universal language of music being taught as Carl Orff, composer and founder of the Orff-Schulwerk approach to music education, intended.

On that Saturday, we attended and participated in the final program of the course. We said our goodbyes to new friends and returned to the Gasthaus to retrieve our luggage and get a cab to the train station.

I stayed in touch with Virginia long enough to know that she and Peter corresponded frequently for about a year. In time, they each found and married someone else, but the last time I corresponded with her, she said she still thought of him at times and wondered if he was happy.

Gerhard and I exchanged letters for almost three years. The last time I wrote to him, I told him I was getting married (1976). His answer to that letter informed me that he, also, was engaged. Although I did not feel a romantic attachment like Virginia did toward Peter, I enjoyed my time with Gerhard and the letter exchanges that followed and have thought about him from time to time. I hope he is still enjoying life and feels content.

Out of all my travel memories, these experiences in Vienna and Salzburg are among the most outstanding for me. Good times shared with strangers who quickly became friends made the lure of travel sink even deeper into my soul and set my resolve to follow that lure as much as possible for as long as I can. So far, no recollections have upstaged the ones set in Vienna and Salzburg.

CHAPTER 5
FROM SALZBURG TO ITALY AND ZERMATT

Improvement makes straight roads; but the crooked roads without improvement are the roads of genius.
William Blake
1757-1827)

We took a nine-hour train ride to Florence. Because of the late hour, there were many empty seats, so each of us had the luxury of sleeping in the fold-out seats without trying to coordinate sleep habits. No feet-filled faces that night.

Although our intent was to sleep to avoid a night's lodging expense, we didn't sleep much. There were several really friendly conductors (or perhaps some other job description) on the route, and they took a shine to us. We had been warned about the possibility of Italian men pinching our butts, so we did not immediately encourage their banter. One of them was especially taken with Virginia's blond hair and blue eyes. He offered his hat to her, and she tried it on. That brought on an offer to Chris by one of the other train employees. Another one offered his hat to me. They left their hats with us and came to our seats every time they had a lull in duties. They wanted to chat and practice their English, but their English skill level was not as advanced as the waiter's in Salzburg or Gerhard's.

Despite the lack of a common language between us, we managed to make them understand that we were going to Florence for two nights before we headed for Paris with a couple of stops in between. They tried to make a date with us for dinner and sightseeing, but we all declined. We returned their hats when we left the train in Florence. I don't recall how they found out where we were staying, but after we checked into our pensione, we heard the one who liked Chris calling from the street, "Chrrrreeees!" The windows were open because it was oppressively hot, and there was no air conditioning.

After several of the troubadour-like calls, we went to the window and looked out. They saw us, and the calls started again. We finally decided for Chris, Virginia, and me to go down and tell them to go away and for Cathy to stand ready to inform the manager if something looked threatening. When we stepped through the door onto the sidewalk, Chris' admirer threw out his arms as though he had been expecting a long-lost love to appear.

"Chrrrreeees! I want see you."

"Virginia! You bellissima. I buy you food."

"Sue, you look good in hat."

Chris spoke up because her admirer was the most insistent. "We thank you for the good time on the train. We will sleep now because we did not sleep on the train. You need to go. The manager is angry because you disturb others. Please go to your place now."

We turned and went back up to our fourth-floor room, feeling how easy it was to climb the stairs without luggage to lug along.

One more try. "Chrrrreeees!" Cathy closed the curtains with a flourish, and we each crashed for a long nap before beginning our sightseeing later that afternoon.

I had avoided buying walking shoes because when I travelled in Europe in 1969, I bought my first pair of Keds—not walking or running shoes—just cheap tennis shoes that caused long-term painful corns to sprout on my little toes. One of my nieces used to call the corn pads I wore for years *cheerios*. I walked mile after mile on the 1973 trip in sturdy sandals with chunky high heels—just the right look with hip-hugger bell bottoms and stretchy body suits.

While we were in Florence, one of the sandal straps broke. We found a shop where it looked like I could afford to buy a pair of shoes. They were less comfortable than the ones that I had worn for about two years but were acceptable. They swallowed half of my souvenir budget for Florence.

After two nights there, we took the 2.5-hour train ride to Venice. We were lucky to be in St. Mark's Basilica when a choir gave a concert. The acoustics were just as we had studied in Music History courses, and the choir was placed to take advantage of the antiphonal effect in 17th-century choral literature. We climbed the steps to see the four horsemen, then sat at an outdoor table in the piazza. Tired after the stair-climbing, we ordered a pastry and coffee. I usually have a strong stomach, but almost gagged when I cut into my pastry and flies flew out. I knew where flies gather, maggots soon arrive.

That sight wreaked havoc on our appetites and sent waves of queasiness from stomachs to throats. We almost made the chairs flip over as we left the fly-filled food and tepid drinks on the table. With no specific plan in mind, we walked over to the taxi stand on the Grand Canal and were soon on a gondola going wherever it was scheduled to go. We didn't ask or care where we would end up—just any place where we could find a snack without flies once our tummies settled down. I had hoped to go to the Murano glass factory, but we ended up at a beach village for more walking and incidental shopping.

We stayed about an hour, then boarded another water taxi to return to St. Mark's Square. There were dozens of various types of artists displaying their craft along the edge of the canal walkway. I bought a charcoal painting of the view of the opposite side of the canal from the Square. The painting still hangs in my guest bathroom. Our pensione was within an easy walk from the Square, so it was our hub as we ventured out with suggestions from Frommer's book.

We walked and shopped and visited museums for hours. I bought a set of tomato red table linens with white embroidery that I still treasure and use. I also bought one tray that still sits on the dresser in the guest bedroom.

We had dinner in a small restaurant away from the Square. It was an out-of-the-way place, highly recommended by Frommer—nothing fancy or expensive, but delicious food and wine served with family pride. We appeared to be the only tourists there. Chris choked on wine when one of us said something that made her laugh. That was the only time on the trip that I felt really scared. It just seemed that she would never be able to catch her breath and stop choking. The waitress came over, patted her back, and offered a glass of water. Slowly, the coughs calmed, and sporadic gasps quieted. Despite Chris' getting choked, that was our favorite red wine of the entire trip.

It was well past dark when we walked back to our room. I tried to read a small map the desk clerk gave us, but the street/canal markings were confusing and hard to see in the dim light. Feral cats skirted from one garbage can to the next in narrow alleys where ancient buildings blocked distant lamplight and the day's laundry still flapped on clothes lines strung between windows overhead. We all noticed an unpleasant odor but could not determine its source. I said, "As long as we see cats and not rats, I won't worry."

We wandered into what seemed to be a rather seedy street and passed a dimly lit bar. Two men came out of the bar as we passed and fell into step behind us. I assumed they would hassle us, but they were almost silent except for the footsteps. It would have been less scary if they had pestered us with attempts at conversation. Their silence made us assume the worst and triggered us to pull our Mace out of our pockets. If someone had said, "Are these men bothering you," we would not have known how to answer. They certainly were following us, but we did not know why.

I fleetingly wished we had let the Italian train employees go to dinner with us. We kept walking and tried not to say anything to indicate that we were as lost as we were. For all we knew, at least one of the men spoke English. Finally, we saw some light that had to be coming from St. Mark's Square. We clicked along on the cobblestones faster and faster until we were almost jogging. The footsteps behind us kept pace with our tempo but did not accelerate beyond our speed. I wondered, *Why are they keeping up with us but not trying to catch or pass us*?

Once we entered the Square, we knew how to get back to the room and slowed our pace as we caught our breath. The footsteps slowed and grew distant. We were glad to be back in the neighborhood where the Grand Canal and massive St. Mark's Basilica defined our location and led us to the spacious room we shared that night. Open windows invited the cooling breeze, and the gondola traffic's rhythmic lilt ushered in our dreams.

We left our luggage in storage at the pensione and spent most of the morning exploring Venice. It was so hot that our energy level sagged easily, and we sat for rest and gelato frequently. I was glad we had not tried to go any farther south. Now as I complete this book in 2023, I am preparing to visit Rome in May. It should still be cool enough to enjoy walking and sightseeing even that far south.

We returned to the pensione around noon, picked up our luggage, and headed for the train station for a 7-hour trip to Zermatt, Switzerland on our way to Paris. We wondered if we would see the friendly train personnel. We didn't.

The final leg of the train trip into Zermatt is on a cog railroad line because automobiles are not allowed into the town. Beyond the thrill of seeing the magnificent scenery, we were enthralled when a group of about a dozen Swiss Guards apparently on holiday sang folk songs in four-part harmony.

It was time for dinner when we arrived at the youth hostel, but not too late to see and feel the breathtaking beauty of the town and surroundings. We checked in and went to the room just long enough to leave our luggage in a locker before we set out for a hearty meal of Swiss fondue.

We noticed that the hostel was pristine, like the entire country, but it was less than rustic—more like primitive in style. There were no individual beds, just one long slab of what we thought was plywood in a dorm-like room with thin pads that passed as mattresses and equally thin pillows spaced so close together that a standard twin mattress would have seemed luxurious. That was it—a slab and perhaps two dozen would-be beds with no partition of any sort.

It looked like we would have the space to ourselves, but the desk clerk had instructed us to use consecutive spaces unless we wanted to pay for extra spots. We left a book or something on each of the four spaces at the far end on the right-hand side of the slab and almost skipped in the crisp air as we looked for a place for dinner.

When we returned to the room after dinner and a stroll along the streets, we discovered that a couple had checked in and were in the two spaces on the opposite end. Our presence made no difference to the exuberance of their passion.

We four young women had no complaint about sleeping so close together. If we could sleep while trying to keep our feet out of each other's face on the train, we certainly could manage a clean, but primitive youth hostel in one of the most beautiful towns in the world. But the passionate couple at the opposite end of the single slab may have felt a bit resentful at our intrusion into what had been exclusively their space. Just us—four single women and an amorous couple who had no *off* switch. Virginia got a case of the giggles. I'm sure she was blushing too. Cathy whispered, "Looks like they'd have enough courtesy to call a halt to things after we came in."

Chris whispered back, "You get what you pay for, and tonight you're paying for a wooden slab, a thin pad, and a tin trough to brush your teeth in. Do you know how much a real room costs in this town?"

"No, but I can't wait to photograph the Matterhorn. I'm glad we're here—just wish Romeo and Juliet had more common sense or discretion."

Chris and I fought the urge to join Virginia's fit of giggles. I thought about how I would describe the scene when I would tell my mother about it, never thinking at the time that I would ever write about it.

The ubiquitous sound of cowbells woke us up early the next morning. When we went to the communal restroom with the trough for brushing teeth and washing hands, we saw the room-sharing couple. They looked very young and were friendly in the light of a bright Swiss morning. We found a place for breakfast, then wandered the few streets again before hiking in the meadow toward the Matterhorn. Cathy was in photography heaven; Chris was figuring how big an Alphorn she could buy; and Virginia and I were wondering how many cowbells would fit into our suitcase without triggering a fee for overweight luggage.

As we searched for a shop that specialized in instruments, I thought about the singing Swiss Guards in the cog railroad car and asked, "Why can't Americans sing *Happy Birthday* on pitch? Every one of those Swiss Guards sang on pitch *a cappella* in harmony and apparently really enjoyed it. There's got to be something about the music education systems over here compared with ours that accounts for at least some of the difference."

Chris responded. "That's true, but I think it's also because of the difference in cultural values. At home, singing *Happy Birthday* off pitch is not only tolerated; it's almost glorified."

Virginia said, "At York Road Elementary where I did my student teaching with Sue, the kids—boys and girls—sounded great. Something happens in adolescence, I think. It isn't that they can't sing on pitch or aren't being taught, but our culture teaches boys that singing is *sissy stuff*."

Cathy said, "If anyone in our family had sung off-pitch when we were growing up, our mother would have sat us down at the piano for a lesson. Good singing was expected in our home."

"Mine too," I said. "When I was in the second grade, I discovered that scooping (you know how you can slide your voice from one note to the next rather than change the pitch cleanly) from one note to the next toward the end of *Silent Night* really irritated Mother. She was always in charge of the Christmas program at church. I had heard some classmates sing *Silent Night* with a scoop at school and took malicious delight in irritating Mother."

I continued, "After tolerating my scooping as long as she could, Mother said, 'Remember to count the beats on each note where you are scooping. Count to three before you go to the higher note.' We practiced it a time or two, but I went back to the scooping just to get a reaction from her. She finally resorted to a threat, 'If you don't stop scooping, you will not be able to be in the singing group. I know you understand the correct way because you just showed me you can do it.' Once I saw that she was at the *I mean business* point, I complied. All of us sang, including Daddy. His voice sounded a lot like Bing Crosby's."

Cathy brought us back to the present. "Are we going to walk around and philosophize about singing all day, or shall we see about the Alphorn and cow bells?"

Chris spotted a shop with a decorated Alphorn on the sign. We went in and saw several rows of cow bells in various sizes alongside the family of Alphorns. She bought the biggest one she could afford, and the shop owner agreed to ship it home for her. Since she played

French horn, it was a special addition to her collection of instruments and a singularly appropriate souvenir. I bought a medium-sized hand-painted cow bell to use in my classroom and a few other items for family gifts. Virginia bought two smaller cow bells. "Just think—my first two instruments for my collection are from Zermatt, Switzerland. I hope my students will enjoy them as much as I do."

I said, "Students always like a little personal story added to the lesson. They will certainly appreciate your special cow bells."

CHAPTER 6
FROM ZERMATT TO PARIS FOR BASTILLE DAY

I never travel without my diary. One should always have something sensational to read in the train.
Oscar Wilde
1854-1900)

Before boarding the train for the eight-hour trip to Paris, we bought cheese, a loaf of bread, fruit, and bottles of water for yet another indoor European picnic. Curve by curve, tunnel by tunnel, and peak by peak, we gradually left the Alps. We vacillated between inevitable sadness for leaving the places, people, and pedagogy that had given us such ebullient joy, adventure, and musical growth in the course in Salzburg and the excitement of anticipating being in Paris on Bastille Day. We replenished energy reserves while we absorbed the natural beauty and relished recent memories.

We arrived about 8:00 PM, but the management knew we would get in after 6:00 PM and was ready for us. Virginia made her first acquaintance with a bidet. As would be expected for a beauty pageant contestant, she was taller than average. Mistaking the bidet for a second sink, after filling the regular sink with water and liquid Woolite, she tossed several garments in to soak. She knelt down and proceeded to try to wash her delicates in the bidet. I soon heard, "Hey, Sue, could you come see about somethin'?" I made a mental inventory of sanitary products in case she had run out. When I opened the door, I saw her squatting on her long legs in front of the bidet.

"How come this little, short rinky-dink sink won't hold water? I brought enough liquid Woolite to wash my undies and new clothes before I pack them. I've got 'em all soaped up, but I can't rinse 'em."

"Oh, no! I'm not sure the drain will handle all that soap."

"Why not? And why is this sink so short? Am I that much taller than French people?"

"It's called a *bidet,* and it's made for personal cleansing after using the regular toilet."

She jumped up and thrust her hands onto her slim hips. "You mean I have my best undies in a butt-washer?"

My sides split with the heartiest laugh of the entire trip. When I could finally talk, I said, "I see you have the regular sink full too. Let's try to get that batch rinsed and out of the way so that we can transfer what's in the bidet to the sink."

"I can't believe it. And the French are supposed to be so hoity-toity! I've heard about the *pissoirs* in the streets, but I never expected a butt-washer in our room! I want to just throw away these clothes, but my mother would kill me."

I told Virginia that I was sure the chamber maids cleaned everything thoroughly and again suggested that we get the main sink emptied so that she could transfer the delicates from the bidet to the sink.

"I hate the idea of dirty clothes in my suitcase and know my mom thinks it's awful when college kids come home with bags full of laundry. I wanted to show her I'm not like that."

"Don't worry. She'll get a kick out of the story when you're ready to tell her. If I were you, I'd rewash everything when you get home because I doubt if you can get all the soap out in this small sink. Rack it up to a memory and a small mistake you will never make again. I knew about bidets but have never used one, so didn't think to mention it to you. I'm sorry I didn't think to say something about it."

Garment by garment, we got everything rinsed enough to hang up to dry overnight. A few minutes later, Chris and Cathy knocked on the door. When they saw all the clothes hanging all over the room, Chris said, "Looks like somebody just did a lot of wash. Why didn't you just ask the desk clerk where to find a laundromat?"

I said, "This is Virginia's story to tell."

Cathy said, "What was all that cackling about? Sounded like we were missing a party."

Virginia said, "Well, you know, I went to college at Winthrop, and my hometown's just 15 miles north of Rock Hill, right at the state line. So I never was guilty of bringing home loads of laundry because I never lived in a dorm."

Chris and Cathy nodded their heads and said, "Oh, yeah. We know that scene."

We all joined in a fit of laughter and talked about how we had wanted to join Virginia when she had her fit of giggles when the couple in the hostel in Zermatt were going at it, with no concern about sharing their sounds with strangers.

The next day was Bastille Day—one of the biggest days of our trip. The desk clerk warned us to be up and out early to get a place to sit for the parade. He gave us a tube guide and outlined several routes we could take. We opted to head for the Place de la Concorde. There was plenty of space for us to claim our area to sit on the stone wall—a perfect spot to see the majesty of military might and tricolors flying in every direction.

We must have waited about an hour before the parade began. As several units of military personnel passed by singing in four-part harmony, we all but saluted the French flag. Cathy said, "Sue, you need to quit taking so many pictures. Those flashcubes are expensive. You'll never remember what branch of the service each group is, and the pictures won't let you hear the four-part patriotic songs. Just put the camera away and enjoy the parade."

"But these pictures will at least remind me of this event on this day with these friends."

Virginia eventually became fidgety. "My butt's gonna look pockmarked from the imprint of these stones pressed into it forever if we don't jump off and do some walkin'."

I said, "Okay. It's about time for lunch anyway."

We had been walking only a few minutes when we heard, "Virginia! What are you doing in Paris?"

Two of the childhood friends Virginia's mom had told me about had found Virginia in Paris. Seeing her other friends in Salzburg was surprising enough. This time, Cathy said, "Virginia, do you know someone in every city over here?" Virginia just laughed, caught up in seeing the boys she had known all her life.

"Hey, Paul. Hi, John. What are ya'll doin' here?"

"We're stationed at a different base from Bill and Bob. They called and told us about seeing you in Salzburg and that you were gonna' be here today. We just got lucky when we saw ya."

"Well, come on, now, and keep us comp'ney for a while."

We exchanged introductions and blended in with the swarm of humanity filling every inch of sidewalk.

We walked to the area of the Arc de Triomphe and continued to soak up the atmosphere of French patriotism. Pungent unfiltered cigarette smoke swirled with mixed aromas of food, sweaty bodies, and other earthy smells probably better left unidentified.

The finale to the parade was an acrobatic fly-over by military jets streaming tri-colored contrails. Members of the various armed services broke ranks at the end of the parade and joined the diverse melee of French-flavored spectators. Virginia's American soldier friends turned around to reconnect with their buddies. We four walked almost shoulder to shoulder as we looked for the perfect café for lunch. Finally, a menu board with prices in our budget grabbed our attention.

I remembered being introduced to a sweet cocktail when I was there in 1969—something flavored with mint—roughly translated as *Double Mint*, I think. I suggested we order one to go with our lunch—not because it was the right flavor or the right time of day for a sweet cocktail, but because it was the only faint clue I had about a French menu. The waitress finally figured out what I meant and brought the drinks.

Chris almost spit out the first mouthful she took. "This is just mint-flavored toothpaste mixed in water with a fancy name and a high price."

It seemed a little better than that to me, but not as delicious as in my memory. Since Chris was the only one of the four who had taken French through college, she was the designated spokesperson. The waitress apparently overheard her remark about the cocktail and wrapped herself in the cloak of stereotypical *ugly American* attitude toward us. Even though Chris did not make the remark directly to the waitress, she seemed to take personal offense at Chris' response to the taste of the drink.

Chris attempted to place our lunch orders. To my non-Frenchy ears, she sounded like a Parisienne. The waitress looked at her with scorn and said in English, "Your French is not very good."

With rueful humor and a big smile, Cathy defended her sister, "It may not be very good, but it's the best we've got."

When we left the café, a tsunami of uniformed men walked toward us, four of them angling our way. The tall one came up to me and, with putrid breath right in my face showed off his English skills. With a leer, he said, "I want to fuck you."

Similar remarks bombarded my friends. Was it a dare, a prank, or alcohol-enhanced impulsivity? A bad cocktail of all, I suspect.

Through the corner of my mouth, I said, "Just keep walking. Don't look back. I think they're already drunk. Walk fast."

After losing the would-be fuckers, I realized I had left my raincoat on the back of the chair in the café. "Oh, no! I left my raincoat."

Cathy said, "Don't worry. I have an extra jacket you can use. We need to get out of this crowd."

I've often wondered if the waitress claimed the raincoat and if she turned us into her *tourist of the day* story when she got home that evening. Her snide remark and the sidewalk assertions flavored the memories to keep them real and to make sure time would neither dilute nor delete them.

We spent most of the next day together. We climbed the Eiffel Tower, shopped in the stalls along the left bank of the Seine, visited *Les Invalides* and *Notre Dame*, and enjoyed a final lunch at a café before Chris and Cathy left to catch their train to Germany. Virginia and I retrieved our luggage from the hotel and caught our train around 2:00 for the 3.5-hour ride to Amsterdam.

Our reservation was at a youth hostel, but I expected it to be much better than the one in Zermatt. It turned out to be a multiple-bed floor, but the beds were reasonably far apart. I felt a little dubious about security but cautioned Virginia to place all cash and any valuables under her pillow and to keep her Mace handy. Nobody made us feel uncomfortable; it was just the idea of sharing a sizable room with strangers, some of whom could have been desperate for cash or objects that could be turned into cash.

The only unfortunate thing that happened occurred when we went downstairs after leaving our luggage in the secured storage area. Virginia stumbled on the steep stairs. When she started falling, she grabbed the rail where a piece of sharp metal was loose. She gashed her hand deeply enough to warrant a stop at the front desk and to ask if they had a first aid kit. They were competent and concerned and washed the wound with hydrogen peroxide, applied an antiseptic cream, then wrapped it in cause and an Ace bandage. While we were out on our city exploration tour, we bought a box of Band-Aids and a tube of antiseptic cream. She was a good sport and didn't let the discomfort slow her down, but I knew it was painful and shared my Excedrin with her.

At my suggestion, we headed out to see St. Bavokerk in Haarlem. I had visited it in 1969 and felt an attachment to it because Paul Jenkins, my organ professor at Stetson University, often took students over for the Summer Organ Festival. Several of my Stetson classmates had been there for extended study. What I didn't know was that there are two St. Bavokerks—the one I wanted to see and a smaller one. We got off the bus when the driver told us we had arrived. I looked around, expecting to see the magnificent church that housed the equally magnificent organ, but saw only small buildings. I finally saw a steeple about two blocks away. It didn't look right, but we walked toward it. The closer we got, the more I knew it couldn't be the church I intended to visit.

We retraced our way back to the bus stop. In about half an hour, another bus showed up. We asked if his route would take us to the large St. Bavokerk. "Yes, but it won't do you any good to go there now. It closed ten minutes ago." It was one of the few disappointments of the trip. I told Virginia she would just have to visit again some time and hoped that I would do the same.

We did as much sightseeing as we could by walking and taking the city bus tour. We had our big splurge dinner the second night at what was reputed to be the most famous Indonesian *rijsttafel* restaurant. I had eaten there in 1969 and thought it was worth the extra money for the unusual experience. Rijsttafel means *rice table,* and always refers to a restaurant where multiple courses are served at a leisurely pace—a place where memories are made both because of the cuisine, the presentation, and the experience of eating so many different courses with no concern for the time it takes. It's all about savoring the evening course by course, moment by moment, with no time-checking. A sip of Dutch Jonge Genever—sometimes called *Young Gin*—helped re-set the palate between courses, and an Advocaat apéritif substituted for dessert.

Our flight left the next morning with a layover in Philadelphia. Every aspect of the flight was smooth and pleasant.

Brenda met us at the airport in Charlotte. Chattering every minute on the way back to Rock Hill, Brenda said, "'Scuse me, Ya'll. I have to tell you 'bout somethin' that happened right before I drove to the airport."

Without seeing what she was talking about, I said, "Oh, my God, that big building burned!"

"Yes! How'd you know?"

"I don't know how I knew; it just came into my head. Was it arson?"

"They don't know. It just happened this morning. We're going to pass it just around this curve. They barely have the fire put out; it's still smolderin'."

Virginia said, "Sue, does that happen often?"

"You mean knowing about something before someone tells me about it?"

"Yes."

"No. That's a first. It's an odd feeling. I just knew that a large building had burned but didn't know what business it housed." To myself I wondered if I had smelled the smoke before it was obvious to the others, but it felt like more than that—something that made my insides feel unsettled. Brenda explained that it was a warehouse where one of the textile mills had stored excess equipment.

We soon pulled into my driveway, and I was placing as many items as I could onto my arms. "Don't you worry, now. Virginia and I will help you get all your stuff up the stairs. I thought you told everyone to pack light." We all chuckled.

"Okay. Thanks for the ride and for making sure that Virginia was able to go. We all had a lot of fun, and she did really well in the course in Salzburg. You'll get a kick out of all her stories."

"Hope she behaved herself. I've already heard that the boys really enjoyed meeting up with you all."

"Be sure and ask them about the chicken dinner."

"Will do. You be sure to come see us now ya heauh?"

CHAPTER 7
KINDRED SOLES ON INTERSTATE 10

Courtesy is the shortest distance between two people.
Anonymous

After a restless night, I pressed the snooze button and rolled over. Two hours later, mildly irritated with myself for oversleeping, I set out on the drive from Houston to Spruce Pine, North Carolina to attend a writer's retreat and workshop in the summer of 2016. Trying to be efficient, I had loaded the car the night before. It was stuffed—trunk, back seat, and front passenger side—with just enough room to see over the piles.

My plans included stops along the way, making the total time for the trip a little over three weeks. With no baggage limits, when in doubt, I tossed it in—electronics (even a small, new printer), office supplies, snacks, cooler, minimal utensils and dishes—all squeezed into the Camry. And just in case, two carryon suitcases—one for the road and one for the retreat—both on top of the large suitcase for the workshop.

I had expected to hit the road within minutes of the alarm's ring. But nights before a trip typically bring more excitement than rest, and that night was no exception. I planned to drive to Lake Charles, the first sizable town in Louisiana, before stopping for breakfast and perhaps allowing a short test of my luck at a craps table at the new Golden Nugget. But the nagging discomfort I recognized as a probable bladder infection forced a stop in Beaumont. I fretted over losing more time for frequent pit stops. Biloxi, Mississippi was my destination for the first two nights.

The web site for the retreat center, Wildacres, instructed attendees to "meet on the mountain." I was familiar with the area and looked forward to spending time near the Blueridge Parkway not far from Little Switzerland. In the late '60s and early '70s, I had spent a few weekends in one of the cabins near the Little Switzerland Lodge, and hoped I would have time for a brief visit to the lodge for hot tea beside the massive fireplace before heading up the mountain. I recalled how true it was to the style of a typical Gasthaus in the *real* Switzerland, except for the difference between elevation levels.

At a little over 400 miles from Houston, Biloxi was an easy drive, and I knew the road well. But it had been six years since my last stop at the Beau Rivage on the way to a composer's workshop in Pennsylvania. I anticipated the frenetic rush of energy at the craps tables; the pinging bounce of the ball jumping to its new home on a roulette wheel; the familiar jingle of the *Wheel of Fortune* slot machines; and the rapid slap of the deal of Blackjack hands all waiting for me if I could just get rid of the nagging discomfort urging me to stop almost hourly.

I had a reservation for a half day in the spa, including a hot stone massage. Two nights at the resort would give me plenty of recreation before going on to South Carolina where I had begun my teaching career in 1968, to visit friends.

Knowing I was leaving Houston's sultry heat for the Blue Ridge Parkway's lush coolness pulled me through the barrage of showers on I-10. The rain was almost constant and ranged from light drizzle to full-speed windshield wipers working hard to maintain visibility.

As usual, when I take road trips, I had an oversized shoebox full of favorite CDs to make my perception of time behind the wheel pass more quickly. But this time, the front seat shared the shoebox space with a large jar of cranberry juice. *If only I had rolled out of bed on time.*

As I approached Lake Charles, I resisted the steering wheel's urge to pull toward the back side of the lake toward the casinos. I crossed the high bridge and stopped at a service station, but not for gas—just a pit stop for me. As I projected approximate times for going through Lafayette and Baton Rouge, it appeared likely that I would hit Baron Rouge during afternoon rush hour.

I recalled the first time I made the trip across the Mississippi as an adult when I was a 19-year-old bride suffering from my first case of cystitis, although I had no clue as to why I was so uncomfortable or why it seemed that my bladder would burst, or my urethra might spurt blood when I saw all that water. On that trip, the pavement served as a massive parking lot while rain pounded and the mighty Mississippi's wide swath of Gulf-seeking current followed its compass south. My internal plumbing felt clogged and tortured me with an urge to urinate that was the most intense pain I had ever felt. And all the young groom had to say was, "Guess you'll just have to hold it for a while. Girls must have more problems than men."

Decades later, I knew exactly why I felt the way I did and hoped that water and cranberry juice would buy enough time to get to my friend's house in South Carolina and that her doctor would write a prescription for me before it flared into a serious infection. The discomfort was far less than on the 1961 trip, but I knew if I didn't get it under control soon, it would probably get much worse. I had to make time and not run the risk of a repeated experience on the Baton Rouge bridge. I could not outrun the dark clouds and constant drizzle, but I could maintain forward momentum except for short comfort breaks and, if necessary, adjust the timing even if it meant spending the night somewhere before crossing the Mississippi.

Usually heavy-footed on the accelerator, I tried to maintain the speed limit, but stayed in the righthand lane. About the same time as I spotted the first exit sign for Lafayette, I saw headlights on the pickup truck behind me flash. I wondered if someone was trying to tell me to slow down because they knew a patrolman was in the area.

The lights flashed again. I thought, *Oh, no! It's an unmarked patrolman, and he's pulling me over. I must have nudged over the limit.* Tales of Louisiana patrolmen pulling out-of-state cars for minimal provocation raced through my mind. At the same time, it felt like the car was trying to steer itself. I turned off the CD player and listened but heard only the whiz of vehicles daring a trooper to catch them.

I wondered, *Am I hydroplaning? Is the pavement slick with oil?* Since the car had just passed a safety inspection, my catalog of possible reasons for the apparent problem was a mix of circumstance and weather with no thought of a mechanical issue. Simultaneously, I heard a bumping noise and noticed the tire pressure warning light come on. Everything happened so fast that it seemed like a swirling blur of realization gripped me in a flashing red sign that screamed "Stop!'

Taught well by both my father and the driver education teacher in high school, I pumped the brakes gently and gradually pulled over, hoping I was not becoming a target for those behind me. The rain had slacked off to a sprinkle but was still persistent enough to soak clothes when standing outside the car. The pickup followed me onto the shoulder.

I watched in the rear-view mirror as the man in the truck jumped down and came up to my window. I rolled it down, still thinking he was a patrolman, expecting him to ask for my license and registration papers. Before I could say, "Is there a problem, Officer?" he said,

"You okay?"

Bewildered, I said, "Yes."

"I smelled it 'fore I saw it."

"Saw what? What smell?"

"The smoke from your left rear tire. Do you mind if I take a look?" I looked at the outside mirror and saw the smoke swirl just as the smell of hot rubber made my stomach lurch. He was not in uniform and did not wear a badge.

"Go ahead."

He came back and said, "The blowout must be on the inside wall of the tire. The outside looks okay. You have a spare? You can't drive on this tire."

I said, "I'm sure there's a jack and a spare, but they're buried under luggage and a ton of other stuff."

"That's alright. We just need to take everything out and put it in the back seat." His eyes darted between me, the tire, the water-splashing 18-wheelers, and then at the back seat. "You'll have to pull over as far as you can 'cause I need more room. These truckers are crazy now, tryin' to make up time they lost when the rain was so heavy." Using hand gestures, he guided me as close to the edge of the shoulder as possible because it was narrow with a steep embankment beyond the pavement. The Great State of Louisiana had not wasted any money on guard rails.

Still in the car, I thought that if he threatened me in any way, I could drive off, even if it ruined the rim. *Stranger danger* lessons were common in schools, and I recalled my parents' warning when I first started driving at age 14, "Don't pick up any hitch hikers; always keep your doors locked; and be sure you've got enough gas to get home." But I couldn't just sit there like a wannabe princess and let him do all the work.

When I got out of the car to help him unload the trunk and get the jack and spare tire out, I noticed that he looked like a typical dad of any number of my students—khaki shorts, checked short-sleeved shirt in shades of summer teal and salmon, clean shaven, and confident. His voice was resonant with a lyrical southern charm. He probably was exactly what he presented himself to be—a kind and thoughtful young man who was willing and able to help me. When face to face, I felt no vibes of concern or anything but gratitude that he bothered to stop and help.

What set the seal of my trust, though, was what I saw on his feet—a pair of Birkenstock sandals in the same style as mine. My mind rationalized, *anyone who wears Birkenstocks can't be a rapist or murderer.*

He extended his hand in introduction. "M' name's Mark. I live 'bout 40 miles from here but went to school right here in Lafayette. I know this little city well." I introduced myself and told him where I was heading.

We put the new printer, lamp, and fan on top of everything else piled on the back seat and put the luggage on the shoulder. As he pulled the jack and spare out of the trunk, he said, "I won't be needin' any help with the tire, but could'ja watch the traffic and give me a warnin' if I need to jump? These fast trucks really scare me. Just bump the fender with your fist if I need to move."

I kept traffic vigil as he worked quickly to change the tire. When he started to put on the spare, he said, "Ya' know this is what they call a *donut tire*, don'tcha? It's safe for a little bit—maybe 50 miles at a slow speed—but you have to get a new tire 'fore you get back on the interstate."

He went on to say that he knew where there was a reputable tire shop that he would recommend. He cautioned, though, "It's hard to find. Wou'ja be okay followin' me to the shop?"

"Sure. Just don't let me get separated if a traffic light catches me."

When the spare tire was in place and the jack was back in the trunk, we replaced the luggage and adjusted things in the back seat so that I could see through the rear-view mirror. We juggled small items to wedge the bad tire on the floor of the back seat.

Mark said, "Stay right on the shoulder, but go ahead and exit here. Pull into the first parkin' lot you see so's I can get ahead of you. I know these fellows will treat'cha right."

As soon as I turned off the shoulder, I spotted a parking lot, pulled into it, and let him take the lead. He jumped out of the truck and again approached my window. "It's kind'a out of the way, but it won't take more'n about 10 minutes to get there." I never would have found the shop without following him. I had a smart phone but had not yet learned to use the maps app. And my sense of direction is far from reliable.

When we got to the shop, I rushed inside to use the restroom and took a couple of Tylenol capsules, hoping to minimize the discomfort. Mark wheeled the blown tire into the shop. The owner came up to the counter. "Hey, Mark. What brings you this-a-way today?"

When I returned to the counter, I noticed the cast on the owner's right arm. He caught the question mark on my face and said, "Don'choo worry, Ma'am. My manager's here and he has two good arms and a couple 'a helpers." Sounds of tire hammers and air compressors coming from three bays beside the office comforted me.

Mark said, "This lady here, Sue, had a blowout right at the first exit off-'a I-10. I was behind her and smelled the rubber even 'fore I saw the smoke. She's lucky she didn't have a wreck. Can you fix it up for her?"

After looking at the tire, the owner said, "Ma'am, you better take pitchers of this and try to get a refund from Toyota. There's no sign of a nail, so it must'a been a factory defect."

"I'll try. The odometer has less than 17,000 miles on it."

"Just leave the car where it's at 'til we can get the right size from another shop. Shouldn't take too long"

I took pictures of the raggedy hole before Mark and I headed outside. He was on his way to his truck, and I wanted to thank him away from the shop guys. The sun was peeking through, but there were still plenty of clouds in various shades of gray overhead.

In the banter as we walked, I mentioned that I had travelled that route many times, including the time when I had attended a composer's workshop at Lehigh University in Pennsylvania.

"You mean you're a composer? And'ja write too?"

"Well, I do compose choral music, but mostly just for my students. I'm more serious about writing creative nonfiction now."

"Well, I sang in my high school and college choirs and now I sing in my church choir."

"I thought I detected the resonance of a lyric baritone in your speaking voice."

"Well, I don't know about lyric, but baritone for sure."

I had already planned to give him some cash to show my appreciation, but when I heard how involved he was with singing, I reached into the front seat of my car and pulled out a copy of the only piece of music I've published, along with a CD. I said, "You really came to my rescue today. Here's a token of my appreciation," and placed some cash on top of the CD before handing the two items to him.

He accepted the music and CD but handed the cash back to me. "I sure do appreciate the music, but you don't owe me a penny. I only hope that if my wife or one of our three daughters ever has trouble on the road, someone will stop and help'em out. My oldest girl will be gettin her license this year. Can't believe she's old enough to do that."

"Yeah—they do grow up fast. Your kindness not only got the job done, but also deepened my level of trust. I'm a little curious, though. Did you notice that we wear the same brand of shoes—even the same style?" His eyes glanced toward our feet and danced with amusement. I said, "I guess that makes us the 'kindred *soles*' of I-10.' I was sure I could trust you once I saw your Birkies."

He smiled and chuckled. "Guess so. I gotta get along now. You'll be okay here 'til your car's ready to get back on I-10. Be safe now."

I waved as he pulled away, then retrieved a spiral notebook from the car and went back inside where there was a chair near the restroom. I sat there and jotted down the points I wanted to recall about this part of the trip while I waited for the tire delivery. Close to an hour later, the driver of a truck rolled a tire to one of the bays. "Hey, Joe. Here's that tire you called about."

"Thanks, Mike. Jus' leave it right there where it's at."

The owner turned toward me. "Time to pull your car into the first bay. We'll have you all fixed up 'fore you know it."

"Alright. You can get rid of the old tire. I've got the pictures."

I returned to the chair after using the restroom again and recalculated the ETA for Baton Rouge and Biloxi. The delay of the tire replacement would put me on the bridge after rush hour. I knew I would make it to the Beau Rivage in time for a late supper and a little gaming before crashing into bed with hopes of getting more rest than the previous night. I called the reservation desk.

"I'll be late, but I will be there, probably around 9:00 PM."

"Don't 'choo worry none, Honey'. Your reservation's firm, and we'll be ready whenevuh ya pull up. Drive careful, now, ya heuh?"

I left the tire shop in Lafayette and headed for Biloxi, anxious to stock up on cranberry juice and to get to my friend's house in South Carolina to see about getting a prescription. But the most prominent feeling was gratitude for the kind Southern gentleman who helped me and took me to the right tire shop to get me back on the road in a safe car.

CHAPTER 8
FROM FOOTHILLS TO CORN FIELDS

Why not go out on a limb? That's where the fruit is.
Will Rogers
(1879-1935)

After staying in Rock Hill for three years beyond my time as a graduate student at Winthrop, I was on my way to Indianola, Iowa to teach Music Education and Piano at Simpson College, living my dream of teaching in higher education, even if I did have to compromise on the climate.

In late summer, 1974, I heard the lumbering moving van as it inched its way down my street. Trucks of any sort seldom disturbed the street's quietude or scraped low-hanging limbs of the oaks that shaded front porches. It sounded as though the van stopped a house or two away from where I lived. Looking out the front window in the living room, I wondered if the driver was confused about the address—626 ½. The motor stopped briefly, then choked and churned again as the big box slowly rolled my way. My pulse raced as I flew down the stairs.

When I saw the van in front of the sidewalk, I thought it was foolish for the company to send a huge truck for my meager furnishings. The driver soon explained that they would pick up two more loads of household goods to fill the van to capacity before heading west.

Of the three different places I had rented during my four years in Rock Hill, South Carolina, 626 ½ Milton Avenue was my favorite. Every time I wrote the address on a form or as the return address on an envelope, I thought of the Koechel listing of 626 for Mozart's

Requiem, his 626th and final composition—the one he was still working on when he died.

I often thought of the presence of the number, 26, in my life. The number of my high school choir robe was 26; my Stetson University Concert Choir robe number was 26; my father's birthday fell on the 26th; and my parents were married in 1926. I saw humor in the 1/2 as an indicator that I rented only half of a house. While 26 had shown up often as a random selection, I later found it was also my favorite number at a Roulette wheel. Many years later, when selecting a lot for our dream home, my husband and I were given a choice between #26 or #27. No hesitation—our house would be built on lot #26.

The owner of the house I was leaving, Dr. Elizabeth Johnson, lived in the lower story. Four years earlier, when I had entered graduate school, she had allowed a friend of mine, Jackie, to sub-let the upper story from the couple who held a long-term lease. They would be visiting their family in China that summer. When Jackie found out I was looking for a place to rent, she offered to sub-sub-let the extra bedroom to me for the summer, provided Dr. Johnson approved. That would give me enough time to find a place before the fall semester began. I was eager to meet Dr. Johnson and hoped that she not only would allow me to sub-sub-let from Jackie, but also might know of other rental options for the next 12 months.

Jackie had completed her undergraduate degree at Winthrop a few years earlier and returned to her hometown, Gaffney, to teach. She taught children with special needs in the same school where I taught music. Rock Hill was about 40 miles east of Gaffney, and Jackie knew it well. She did not know the rental market, though, since she had lived on campus during her undergraduate years. She expected to complete her master's degree that summer. I planned to begin the Master of Music degree and, by going full-time, to graduate at the end of the following summer (1971). Jackie had been taking one or two courses each semester and completing residency requirements in the summers.

She knew Dr. Johnson because she had taken two years of German with her. She saw the notice of the sub-let opportunity on a bulletin board in the graduate student lounge and was delighted that Dr.

Johnson was looking for someone to sub-let the apartment for the summer. Sharing the upstairs of a Victorian home just a few blocks from campus seemed to be the ideal way for me to get to know the town and to adjust to being single again.

When I pulled up into the narrow driveway, Jackie was already there and had moved her essentials into the upstairs apartment. She had already told me that she would spend most of the weekends with her parents in Gaffney and promised that she would help herself to their vegetable garden and smokehouse. She also told me a little about Dr. Johnson.

"Dr. Johnson (everybody calls her *Lady J*) is one of the strongest women I've ever known. She never married and treated her students as though they were her own children. She is a trail blazer—around 80 years old now—but still travels. She is also the only certified floral judge in South Carolina. You will love her flower garden—over 300 varieties in her back yard. She's picky about who she rents to, but I'm pretty sure she'll be okay with you using the second bedroom upstairs while I'm there this summer."

"I look forward to meeting her and hope you're right about her letting me use the extra bedroom."

"Her place has basic furniture. What do you plan to do with your furniture?"

"The faculty apartment in Gaffney (My husband taught organ at Limestone College) had only one bedroom, so I'll bring just a small dresser, a large steamer trunk, and kitchen supplies from there. When I find a place for the rest of the year, I'll buy a bed. The dining table will have to wait for a while. I'll add to the furnishings as I can, but most things will have to wait until I graduate and am on full salary again."

"That's good. It makes it easier to make this arrangement happen. Lady J does have a one-car garage, but I think she uses it as a garden shed."

"Her yard must smell like a big bouquet."

"Yes. And you'll also love her accent. She came from Manassas, Virginia, and has never lost that beautiful lilt in her voice. She was head of the modern languages department at Winthrop from 1922-1955. She had already retired when I was here, but she still taught German as an adjunct faculty member for a long time after she retired. Everyone knows her. I took two years of German with her. One of the first assignments she gave was to figure out what *Schlaffen Sie mit mir, bitte* meant." (Sleep with me, please.)

"I know enough German to translate that phrase. She must have stirred up a lot of curiosity as well as motivation."

Jackie continued, "Oh, yes. When she gave us that assignment, she said, 'Practice saying this, and translate it, but never say it to a man in Germany.' That certainly motivated us to work on the translation. Winthrop is still coed only at the graduate level, you know. Her early translation assignment almost became campus lore. Many first-year German students knew to expect it, but they played along with the supposed mystery. I think her fun-loving spirit helped many long-term friendships develop among her students."

"I wish I could have studied German with her."

"By the way, you're Episcopalian, aren't you? I think that is her church too. She has never owned a car, so maybe you could take her to church with you."

Dr. Johnson readily agreed for me to use the extra bedroom for the summer and explained that the couple who held the lease had taken their child to meet her grandparents in China but would be back before the fall semester began. She said, "I guess they want their parents to meet the first grandchild while she is still very young. If you like Chinese food, be sure to go to Kit Chen's Kitchen. My renters own it. Some of their family will run it while they are gone."

When I asked Dr. Johnson if she knew of any other rental properties that might be available for the next 12 months, she referred me to an agency. I was excited to find that a small duplex unit would be available at the end of the summer. It must have been less than 400 square feet—tiny—but two bedrooms and just right for someone with so little furniture and such a limited budget.

My second divorce was final at the end of the summer, and my ex-husband, Allyn, helped me get settled into the duplex after he returned to Gaffney following summer study in Oregon. He passed on a sofa that someone had given him and a few other items that made the duplex functional and reasonably comfortable. He went with me to buy a mattress, box springs, and frame. There was nothing wrong with our friendship, but it was not enough to support a marriage.

I was enjoying an active social life along with my graduate work, which included responsibilities of a graduate assistantship at Winthrop. Allyn and I had split our savings equally, but it was a modest amount. After I added a position as Organist/Choirmaster to my workload, I bought a picnic table with benches for inside dining. The big splurge was a large print of *Guernica* and a poster that said, *Make Love, not War*. I loved the way that the fine china and crystal set on crisp linen from my first marriage elevated the redwood picnic table to elegance when I hosted small dinner parties in the tiny duplex. One of the men I dated said, "This place is so like you—earthy and elegant."

When I saw Lady J from time to time at church, I reminded her that I would like to move back to her place if it ever became available. It was larger, was on a quieter street, and closer to campus and to the school where I taught. I also liked the advantage of having her downstairs and occasionally talking with her and sometimes taking her to church with me. And the fragrance of her garden was so much better than the car fumes at the duplex.

Dr. Johnson endeared herself to Jackie and me that first summer when she proved she was not an unreasonable prude about young adults having parties. Not only was her mind nimble and her petite body strong enough to push a mechanical lawn mower, but her spirit was a bit mischievous with a sparkling patina that reminded us she had not always been in her 80s.

I had completed the Master of Music degree and remained in Rock Hill to open a new school when she finally said at church, "You know, that couple who have been renting ever since I first met you are still there, but I'm a-boot to conclude I may have to let them know I won't be renewing their lease. They are nice and are very smart, but they don't seem to know how to stop having babies. They already have two and another one is on the way. Would you like to move back toward the end of this summer (1972)?"

"Would I like to!? I've been hoping this would work out for almost two years now. I have a roommate now but will tell her that she will need to get her own place. She has already been planning and saving money toward that option. I'll be so happy to be back in your place. Let me know an estimate of the date so that I can give notice to the professor I've been renting from. He's on sabbatical, but I'm sure he wouldn't mind if I move out sooner than planned. The dean is handling the property for him. I'll let him know about the plans. "

"By the way, Sue—how's Jackie? I haven't heard from her lately."

"She's fine—engaged and will be getting married in a few weeks. She's asked me to play for the wedding."

"Well, I can say that I knew she liked someone quite an awful lot. I just couldn't figure out which one she liked the most. My bedroom is directly under the one she used, you know."

Her eyes danced with the delight of gossip and female camaraderie.

In a few days, I got the call from her. "You're in luck. The couple already decided that they need more room. They'll be out in two weeks. I'll have the apartment professionally cleaned and painted; then it will be ready for you."

"Great! I've already mentioned it to the dean. He assured me that they always need housing for grad students and that my moving out now would not be a problem."

After I moved back to the upstairs apartment and the back bedroom was mine and the one I had used that first summer became my piano studio, she commented on my coughing when seasonal allergies brought on multiple sinus infections. I made sure that she would not wonder about who I might *like the most* by making sure my personal life evolved almost entirely off-site. Air conditioning was rare then because it was needed only a few weeks each summer. Otherwise, the windows were almost always open, and there was nothing wrong with her 80-something-year-old ears.

I was eager not only to get back into that apartment, but also to start my piano studio. When I talked with the dean again, I told him I could spend about $1,000 on a piano and asked him for a recommendation in that price range.

"No question—the Yamaha studio upright." The Dean went on to tell me that it was known for being sturdy and holding up well both musically and mechanically. He explained that the factories still used quite a lot of hand work on the lower end models, but that with the worldwide demand for that model, more and more of the workmanship was going the way of mass production.

I went straight to the bank to check on pre-approval for a loan. After getting the go-ahead from the loan officer, I drove to Charlotte to select the piano that would stay with me from 1972-2011. Soon, I was packed and ready to move the few blocks to the address I loved and to welcome my piano a few days later.

In a couple of years, when I received the notice that Simpson College wanted to interview me, I again asked the dean for advice. I was anxious about how to answer questions and handle issues such as salary, office hours, and committee assignments. It felt like I was headed into another round of oral exams with an additional depth of quagmire to wade through.

The dean said, "Sue, you need to stop worrying about answers and consider what questions you will ask. You need to show genuine interest in their program and offer solid examples of how your preparation relates to their needs. Think about how you could build upon what they already have."

"You mean the questions are more important than the answers?"

"In my experience, yes. By the time we invite a candidate to interview, we know enough about their qualifications to feel confident they are prepared both academically and musically. What we don't know, though, is how they will fit into our offerings and what they will add to our personnel and programs. Every department or school of music must strive for balance and generally has a gap or two that needs to be filled in order to maintain that balance. Now do some thinking about how your preparation and personality will make their department even stronger. I've written a fine recommendation for you and expect to hear an exciting report when you return."

As I stood in that empty living room feeling a mellow speed-recall of fun times and reminiscing about Lady J's quick wit, her spunk, and her skill at being an unobtrusive landlord, I broke the reverie when I ran down the stairs to meet the moving van. It had stopped on the street in front of the house. I thought, *Don't they know they have to pull in close to the stairs?* I stopped at the edge of the porta cohere and yelled, "Just back into the driveway." The motor again sputtered several times, then died. I called out again. "Get as close to the door as you can."

The driver called out, "Sorry, Ma'am, we're outa' gas. Thought we had enough to load and then gas up on the way outa' town."

"Do you have a gas can?" I asked, trying to keep incredulity out of my tone.

"No, Ma'am. Do you?"

"No, and my phone is already disconnected. I can't even call your company to let them know. There's a gas station right around the corner. They'll probably have gas cans." I asked if they wanted me to take them there. The driver glanced at my overloaded Datsun hatchback.

"No, thanks We'll walk."

They returned in a few minutes, each carrying a can of gas. I hoped that would be enough to get the van to the station. After pouring the gas into the oversized tank, they backed into the driveway and parked with the back of the van almost touching the roof of the porta cochere and the cab blocking half of the street. On their way to the stairs, the driver noticed my bumper sticker, *Take an autoharp player home to dinner*. He said, "You play the autoharp?"

"Not really, but I use it occasionally in my elementary school music classes."

The assistant spoke up. "My granddaddy used to play the banjo. He shore could make folks tap their toes and wanna dance."

"I know what you mean. Before I was born, my paternal grandfather played the autoharp and sang ballads in the bandshell in my hometown in Florida. My mother plays piano and she and my dad sing together."

After they came upstairs and surveyed everything to be hauled on the truck, the driver said, "What about that guitar in the living room? Did you mean for us to take it?"

"No. It will go in the car with me. I don't want to risk the heat in the van warping the neck. The piano will need to be tuned after the trip, but that's routine maintenance. It's too hot to put the guitar in the car right now, so please just leave it where it is, and I'll get it before I leave."

"We'll take real good care of everything for you."

Once they got the upright piano down the stairs, loaded, and tied into place, I quit trying to supervise and went back upstairs to take a few more swipes at the kitchen and bathroom. I was caught in cross currents of nostalgia, anticipation, and exasperation. I recalled moving out of 626 1/2 and into the tiny duplex where I had to sublet the extra bedroom to Jane. From there, I had moved into a one-story house and shared it with the same housemate. Returning to the upstairs of Lady J's house closed a small circle, but the moving van opened the circle, and I was about to redefine the circumference by more than 1,000 miles.

I thought about the time when Lady J unintentionally caused quite a stir at church. We were sitting together, and during one of the prayers, she slid off the kneeler and slumped over onto my left shoulder, her head resting on her chest. I slipped my left arm under her left arm pit to keep her from falling onto the floor and turned toward my right to tug the jacket sleeve of a man sitting behind me. I stage-whispered, "I think she has a heart condition. Get an ambulance."

I was surprised and relieved when he said, "I know. I'm a doctor. Make room for me." She was the third person in from the center aisle. As the two parishioners on her left got up and headed for the back of the church, the doctor, who had already climbed over the back of our pew, said to one of them, "Go to the church office and call for an ambulance. Tell them a parishioner known to have a heart condition has fainted and Dr. Smith is already here." By the time the kind doctor checked Lady J's pulse, helped her get back onto the pew, and scooted her toward the aisle, the ambulance attendants were there with a stretcher in the narthex. She seemed to be more asleep than awake, but occasionally responded to questions.

While the priest, the choir, and the organist kept the service going, the responders wheeled the stretcher to our pew. The attendants easily lifted Lady J's 110 pounds of fierce determination onto the stretcher while the doctor supervised.

After the siren's fading blare punctuated the organ's introduction, we sang *Awake, Awake to Love and Work*.

I talked with the Good Samaritan after the service ended. Speaking more as a fellow parishioner than as a doctor, he explained that Dr. Johnson was prone to fainting spells because of a heart condition. "It's a good thing we were kneeling when she passed out so that she didn't suffer any injuries. She'll probably be okay and won't need to be admitted. It's been a while since the last episode."

Less than two weeks later, I saw her out in the yard pushing the mechanical lawn mower—as always, wearing a cotton house dress with a small floral print and a white apron. I marveled at her stamina and thought about how it had served her well in her pursuit of education and a career as a single woman at a time when women seldom gained admission to PhD programs or were granted tenure at universities. She earned her terminal degree at Johns Hopkins University in 1916, a year before a woman was hired as a professor in the School of Medicine there.

With the apartment almost cleared out, I recalled how I had transformed it from the barely functional grad students' pad to the comfortable space with a piano studio, a quadraphonic stereo system, and customized economical décor. During the summer when I returned to Lady J's upstairs, in addition to the church job, I was moonlighting in a carpet and wallpaper store. My job was to help customers select carpet or wallpaper and to go to their house or apartment, measure, and calculate the amount of each product they would need. I enjoyed the work, even though the pay was minimal.

With an employee discount, I was able to buy the thickest black carpet made and had it installed in the studio space—in hindsight, an imbalance between taste and concern for acoustics. I hounded textile mill outlet shops until I found just the right fabric for creating a sofa and draperies for the studio. I found an upholstery shop that would make a custom cushion and a wooden structure to serve as a studio sofa. A second matching, but thinner cushion, had tabs to hang on a black wooden curtain rod, forming the back of the sofa. The print on the fabric covering the cushions was a large black and off-white houndstooth pattern. While the upholsterer worked on the sofa, I used yards of the same fabric to make lined pinch-pleated drapes for the two windows.

I also had the upholsterer reupholster the passed-along sofa. It sat in the living room near the wood-burning fireplace, and the old trunk still held treasures inside and drinks on top. That fabric, chosen because of its sale price, came a little short of my favorite color, green, but had a mixture of floral teals, some leaning toward green, some toward blue.

At the street end of the central hall that separated the studio from the living room, there was a large window where I used a *hippie* cotton bedspread from India as a curtain. It picked up the teals from the living room sofa in its peacock-colored paisley print with the motifs outlined in black. The hall was wide enough to accommodate the sewing machine cabinet and a small chair.

The bathroom was at the opposite end of the hall with corner built-in cabinets on either side of the door. When I finished teaching a Music Appreciation course at Winthrop, I cut out black and white pictures of instruments, scenes from operas, and examples of music themes from the textbook to make a collage on a swath of black wallpaper. The wallpaper was barely tacked to the hall wall, though, so that I could take it with me. It lasted many years before it became so brittle that I finally had to discard it.

I found an old fern stand at the same lakeside antique shop where I had bought the round oak table that I still have in my breakfast area, along with a Singer sewing machine base that now holds the silver chest my late husband bought. The marble slab I found in a warehouse fit the Singer base exactly and still anchors it.

After stripping layers of dark stain from the fern stand, I painted it primary yellow and found a couple of small throw pillows to echo the color. For a desk (of sorts), I bought two wooden cubes to support a slab of plywood. The cubes had one side open so that I could store music and vinyl LPs in them. I painted the inside area the same color as the fern stand and the outer surfaces off-white. The cubes were not high enough to function as a standard desk, but the structure served a purpose and gave me a sense of accomplishment. One of my young piano students said, "Ms. Orrell, is it okay if I call this the bumblebee room?"

"What makes you want to call it that?"

"You know—the colors are the same as bumblebees."

I chuckled. "You're right. That would be a great name for this room." It wasn't long before most of the other students caught on to the unofficial name of that cozy room with the jet-black carpet and ebony piano, black and off-white upholstery and drapes, and splashes of sunshine yellow. I knew I would miss the bumblebee room and the students who gave me joy. I hoped that the furnishings would fit into the faculty housing in Iowa. About ten years later, I thought about that room when I heard Paul McCartney and Stevie Wonder sing "Ebony and Ivory," and added splashes of yellow to complete the images in my memory.

The bathroom that I was cleaning for the last time had also been fun to decorate. Always looking for economical options, I used two thick tomato red bath towels with black tiebacks made from hand towels to cover the window. The pop of color against the white walls and white hexagonal floor tiles with black grout shattered the norm of placid pastels used in many bathrooms of the day. Plush black bath towels hung on the towel rack.

My second favorite perfume back then was Maja by Myrugia, a Spanish fragrance packaged in black and red with a flamboyant Flamenco dancer in the logo. The free spirit of the dancer called to my own spirit in what felt like a mutual celebration of life. Maja appealed to me as an alternate to my forever fragrance, Chanel #5, because of the popularity of Musk at the time. Musk alone overpowered, especially in drugstore brands, but mixed with some florals as in Maja, it fit the color scheme and me. Now, almost fifty years later, Maja soaps still sit on some closet shelves, and the only fragrance I use on my skin is Chanel #5.

When the van's driver and his assistant were almost ready for me to sign the papers, Lady J brought up a covered Chinet plate full of warm cookies. As she offered the cookies, she said, "These will come in handy on the road. I'm going to miss you and hope your travels take you everywhere you want to go. Always remember to learn at least the basic phrases of greeting and courtesy in the language of every country you visit. That will help build bridges and ease some of the *ugly*

American images that many Europeans have of us."

I thanked Dr. Johnson for the cookies and recalled the anti-American posters and anti-Nixon statements I had seen in Europe the previous summer. The aroma of chocolate chips melting against brown-sugared pecans made me salivate. But I knew the movers were ready to close the doors on my years in Rock Hill and that I needed to sign the paperwork. "I know I'll enjoy the cookies, and I will always remember your wonderful flower garden and your melodious Virginia accent."

"Yes, even now, I still get a lot of comments when someone hears me talk for the first time. You'd think it's a-boot time I blend in a bit more." We hugged for the first and last time.

The only time I ever asked Lady J if I could pick a few flowers and she had to decline my request, she suggested that I use some greenery from the front hedge with just one camelia blossom. The fragrance did not equal the roses, gardenias, or daffodils from her back yard, but when placed into a crystal bud vase, the lustrous greenery and clustered symmetry of salmon-colored petals added a touch of elegance to my budget-friendly dinner of spaghetti and marinara sauce.

Balancing the Chinet plate in one hand, I slung my purse onto my shoulder, grabbed my guitar and followed Lady J down the stairs. I gave her my key at the foot of the stairs. She dropped it into her apron pocket and went toward the front door as I went toward the van driver. After I signed the sheaf of papers that listed everything I owned that was not crammed into my car, the driver said, "You be careful now, ya hear? See you in Indianola in four or five, maybe six days."

"Will do. And you be sure to stop at the gas station around the corner."

"Yes, Ma'am." I held my breath as he turned his key in the ignition. Full-throttled fumes left the tailpipe as the cab led the trailer out of the driveway and away from 626 ½ Milton Avenue. I almost prayed to the two cans of gas, *For my sake, Get them to the pump in time.*

I got behind the wheel of the Datsun, placed the cookies on the console, and laid the Atlas beside my purse. Lady J waved me off, then eased a strand of wispy hair back into the bun at the base of her neck before I lost sight of her. I thought about how I would miss having 626 1/2 as my street address. I pondered how a move could simultaneously be both the happiest and saddest ever.

Once on the interstate, my wondering shifted to how long it would take to swap the Piedmont's proximity to Blue Ridge foothills for the flat plains where fertile fields cradled the nation's breadbasket. Driving from South Carolina to my parents' home in Missouri was a familiar trip, but beyond that, I had not driven in the Midwest. I thought of the lyrics to "America the Beautiful" and felt certain I would find beauty wherever I was.

When I arrived after an uneventful trip from the Blue Ridge foothills, through the Smokey Mountains, across the Mississippi, and then angling northwest through endless miles of corn fields, wheat fields, and hog farms, I parked my suspension-stressed car and wondered when the moving van would appear. Fields of grain filled the horizons but left space in the air for pungent smells to blow in from adjacent acres dotted with miniature wooden structures larger than dog houses but roomy enough to welcome Yorkshire hogs when temperatures nosedived, and winds whipped skin.

The first couple of days in Indianola mostly blur in my memory, but I recall staying with the Professor of Organ and his family. It would take several more days for the van to arrive and unload my furnishings into the downstairs of the house across the street from the music building.

Once the van left with only my new tape recorder missing, I went to the music building to see what I needed to do to settle into my studio. The department chairman greeted me and said, "You might have noticed that you have the choice studio on the ground floor, just down the hall from my own office and studio. I'm sure you saw it when you were here in the spring, but it is empty now and ready for you to settle in. You'll probably want to leave both pianos where they are, but you can place whatever small items you may have wherever they will fit. I understand that a few students will be helping you bring over your books and music."

He barely left enough opening in his monologue for me to acknowledge any of his remarks. He continued to give suggestions. "Just give the maintenance department a call and make an appointment to pick out a paint color for the walls. Might I suggest a nice, muted gold or perhaps a pastel yellow for the paint? You might also consider getting window coverings."

I thought, *Pastel or muted, when I'm used to ebony, ivory and primary yellow--we'll see about that.*

There were, of course, adjustments, but for the most part, everything fit in the downstairs of the house as expected. One of the interior living room walls was just right for the piano, so the second bedroom became the sewing room. I sold the living room sofa before leaving Rock Hill, but the studio sofa and other items from the studio fit the living room.

The department chairman invited me to his home for afternoon tea not long after I saw him in the music building. We reminisced about the good time we had in New York City when I had interviewed with him. He had been on sabbatical and was working with the Metropolitan Opera Company. Once he approved it, the acting chairman called to invite me to interview on campus. The interview in NYC took place during spring break, which included St. Patrick's Day, and the campus interview with the rest of the faculty, retiring professor of Music Education, and some students took place the week after.

While sipping tea, the department chair called attention to the rich texture of his draperies. "You may not notice, but these draperies are made of heavy corduroy with a substantial lining. In candlelight, they can almost pass for Renaissance velvet." I was much more interested in presenting a youthful vibe with a print that made a statement than creating an atmosphere of faux-Renaissance heaviness of color saturation and thick texture. Expressing my own taste was much higher on my list than complying with his *suggestions*. Even though I was to play in and conduct the recorder/early music ensemble, I did not want my studio to reflect that historical period. I understood that appearance and self-expression mattered to him because they mattered equally to me. I was neither prepared nor willing to become a sponge for his preferences regarding studio décor.

As I did more unpacking that night, the more I thought about his remarks about the paint color suggestions, the more I realized that *might I suggest* coming from him should have been translated into something like *this is what I expect you to do. Period.*

The calendar did not allow time for me to make draperies, and I knew that even if I could afford to purchase ready-made drapes, they were not available for such huge windows. The feeling that the department chair and I were on a collision course to butt heads threatened to dampen my excitement.

I went to Younker Brothers Department Store in Des Moines to look for possible solutions to the window covering dilemma. On a whim, I went to the bedding department and found exactly what I thought would be right for the room and for me. Since it was the end of summer, there was a deep discount on Marimekko bedspreads. I didn't know the designer's name but recognized the oversized print design and vibrant colors because I had seen some of her designs in a store in Sweden in 1969.

It worked out so that a twin size bedspread would be just right for each of the four windows. When I told the sales associate my idea, she said, "That's a brilliant idea. You're in luck. We have exactly four left." The weight of the fabric was right—heavy enough to hang well without a lining, but light enough to launder easily and to respond to the breeze when the windows were open.

When I got back from Des Moines, I went over to see how the print would look in the room. Thinking the painter would still be working, I was surprised to find the door locked. There were no students or faculty in the hall. I then saw a note near the doorknob. It read, "This is the number for the painter. Call me as soon as you see this note."

I went back to my apartment and made the call.

"I just saw your note. Do you know why my studio door is locked?"

"You will not be able to enter it for at least two days. I discovered a huge hive of bees in one of the outer walls. I heard them when I started working in the room."

"Oh, no! I hope you didn't get stung."

"No. I've already called the exterminator. He's a buddy of mine and agreed to come on over after he gets off work to get the hive before it gets too dark. I'll meet him there in about half an hour and let him in. He'll take the hive to one of the professors who takes care of bees on his farm. They probably are native to Iowa and won't attack unless the hive is attacked. I'll have to be careful for a few days, though, in case some are left behind and are mad about the hive leaving."

"Okay. Please be careful and keep me informed."

My time to get ready for the semester to begin was shrinking, and my new studio had taken on the reality of the Rock Hill studio's nickname—honeybees instead of bumblebees, but close enough to fit the moniker.

After the exterminator and the painter finished their work, the painter called to let me know I could claim my studio. "It's all done; the bees are gone; the paint color looks good; it's all yours now. Do you have curtains to hang?"

"Yes, but no ladder."

"Just bring them on over. I'll be glad to hang them for you before I leave."

"I'm on my way."

I was glad I had bought the rods and stitched the rod pockets in all four bedspreads the night before.

With minimal effort, the painter got the colorful curtains up and seemed to share my joy in being ready for students to help haul boxes of books and music from my apartment across the street to the corner office with the four boldly draped windows.

The next morning, the department chair came to call. When he stepped into my studio, he almost went ballistic. "Sue, I thought I *suggested* a pale yellow or muted gold for the paint and drapes. This paint is neither muted nor pastel. And that bold print will be seen clear across campus."

"I know. That's why I like it. Also, it was easy for me to sew a pocket seam for the curtain rods. It was the most practical solution I could find. I think the wall color complements the shades of yellow, orange, and green in the print." While he puffed himself up with exasperation and blood rushed to his face, I mused to myself that perhaps the window coverings and the paint color would remind me of Florida sunshine when grey Iowa days shortened, and snow rose deep.

He wanted to have the last word. "Maybe your sewing skills could be more properly applied to the madrigal or opera production costumes." With his typical dramatic flair as though he were the powerful villain in an opera, he stormed off and slammed the door to his studio.

A student approached and knocked on my open door. "Rough day?"

"No. The day is fine. Just a strong difference of opinion."

A few more students joined the first, ready to haul my boxes and help me unpack.

In the chatter while hauling boxes, I mentioned that my brother had come up from Kansas City, Missouri and had made sure that all the mechanical systems in the apartment were up and running. One in the group asked, "That's faculty housing, right? Seems like the maintenance department would be sure it's ready for you."

"I'm sure they either had or would have, but it felt better for Richard to be here and give his assurance that the house was as ready as I was for my first semester at Simpson. He even showed me how to light the furnace in the basement. I knew to expect severe winters, but I was surprised when I had to turn on the furnace this weekend (Labor Day weekend).

The students made good-natured suggestions about my need for winter clothes and boots.

As spring approached the next semester, when I first opened the four windows and let the bedspreads wave to students crossing campus, I heard a sharp knock on the door. With clenched jaw, the chairman said, "Will you please close your windows? I just came back from a rehearsal in the theater, and your so-called curtains are flapping out the windows as if this grand dame of the campus were a barn."

I corralled the curtains, closed the windows, and wondered about my prospects for staying there. Full tenure required a doctorate, but a terminal degree was the least of my worries.

Even though we disagreed about issues that were peripheral to our profession, he never expressed any doubt about my qualifications and had complimented me on the student evaluations.

He knew that the lab class I established for my Music Education students to observe and have hands-on experience with Orff-Schulwerk with children was filled, mostly with children of professors. My private piano students had placed well in the Des Moines Christmas recital and Piano Guild Review. He knew I had received a grant to purchase a set of instruments for the lab class, and the students in the early music ensemble let him know that they enjoyed the rehearsals. He heard the results of those rehearsals at the big madrigal dinner. I assumed he was confident that I would represent the college well, even if I didn't decorate my studio in a style he admired.

Academically and professionally, the year was all I had hoped for and more. But when fine leather shoes wear blisters on your heels, it is time to consider different shoes and let the blisters heal. Both he and I were wearing band aids on our heels, but his blisters were filled with numbing authority and seniority while mine were filled with stinging saline fluid.

Shortly after signing contract for the next year, my father's diagnosis of terminal illness threw all considerations into revision. I knew the music supervisor in North Kansas City. She encouraged me to interview there. Like me, she was a specialist in Orff-Schulwerk. She offered me a position before I left her office. I returned to Indianola, turned in my resignation, and started packing, ready to return to the elementary school music classroom to be near my father as he and my mother spent much of his last year with my brother in Kansas City. My metaphorical blisters disappeared in a vapor of irrelevancy.

CHAPTER 9
MILE-HIGH SURPRISE

The paradox of courage is that a person must be a little careless of his [or her] life even in order to keep it.
G. K. Chesterton
(1874-1936)

I knew to expect severe winters when I moved to Iowa to teach at Simpson College but was shocked when I had to turn on the furnace on Labor Day weekend. When I told a group of students that I had already turned on the heat, one of them said, "You know you will have to buy winter clothes, don't you?"

"Oh, I have winter clothes. I had to buy them when I moved from Florida to South Carolina. The first thing I bought with a credit card was a reversible red tartan Pendleton wool cape with tartan skirt and black wool beret to match." I smile when I think of how much I still enjoy wearing the 55-year-old cape, especially for Christmas Eve services—classic vintage and aging well.

The student said, "Sounds kind-a fancy for around here. What you need to do is wait a couple of weeks, then go to one of the department stores in Des Moines and get yourself a real winter coat. If you already need heat in your apartment, you'll certainly need a heavier coat."

Rather than waiting to shop, I ordered fabric from a designer fabric outlet in New York City and set out to make my own winter coat. A simple Vogue pattern that looked more like a bathrobe than a coat was the exact style I needed to make construction as efficient as possible. With the right fabric, I thought it would be perfect because I could use an unconventional lining and make it reversible and heavy enough to declare war on sub-zero temperatures. And I would not have to sweat over buttonholes.

The outer fabric was 100% wool—a creamy ivory and milk chocolate brown tweed—heavy and bulky even before adding the lining and interlining. I chose a blend of wool and polyester for the ivory lining and nubby lamb's wool for the interlining. I would have bet that the stores would not have a coat any warmer than what I was making. Later, when I finished it and attempted to hang it in the closet, wire hangers behaved more like wet noodles and dropped the coat to a pile on the floor. Plastic hangers snapped under its weight. Only heavy-duty wooden hangers could handle its heft.

My job interfered with getting the coat finished in time for the first wave of bitterly cold air and snow. I layered up with the warmest clothes I had and waddled across the street to class and piano lessons. Snow boots soon had a spot in my closet. When neighbors informed me that I was responsible for keeping the sidewalk in front of my apartment cleared, I talked with the upstairs neighbors. We soon had a shovel rotation schedule.

Once I got the outer fabric, the interlining, and the lining stitched separately and ready to assemble into the final garment, I discovered that my sewing machine was not up to the task. After several broken needles and loss of my patience, I gave up and bundled the entire project to take with me when I visited my family in Missouri for Thanksgiving. My oldest sister, Margaret, was a seamstress for some of the Branson entertainers, and I knew she would come to my rescue with her industrial sewing machine. I wrote her a note to give her a heads-up about the Thanksgiving visit. She assured me that she would have her machine set up and that it would not take long to complete the coat.

Margaret was right. Her machine hummed across the multiple layers of bulky fabric worthy of Iowa winters. With the right equipment and her expertise, it took only about an hour to complete the project.

One of the first things I did after getting settled in Indianola was to check journals for Orff-Schulwerk-based workshops. I was thrilled when I saw that Grace Nash would be a keynote presenter at the national American Orff-Schulwerk Association conference in Denver that November. I had met her at a conference in Atlanta my first year teaching (1968) and had followed her, studied with her, and taught with her in summer courses since then.

As soon as the semester began, I requested approval to miss two days of classes to attend the conference in Denver. Despite being miffed at me because of a difference of opinion regarding the décor of my piano studio, the department chairman supported the request and encouraged me to maintain ties with my mentor. He said, "Missing class for two days won't be a problem. Unlike teaching music in public schools, you won't need to get a substitute, but you will need to make sure you assign enough work to keep your students busy while you are gone."

"Thank you for your support. I know the conference will be outstanding."

"You also need to set high expectations for your piano students. Since they are voice majors taking the piano proficiency requirement, they may not yet have developed sufficient discipline regarding piano practice."

"Some are quite enthusiastic, but I think I know the ones you may have in mind. I'll be sure they know what I expect them to accomplish, especially if I have to miss their lesson that week."

I made reservations for my room and flight and let Grace know I looked forward to seeing her. She reminded me that she would be busy with her presentations but would plan to have breakfast with me that Sunday before we left Denver.

While checking in at the front desk of the hotel in Denver, I struck up a conversation with a woman who had just started her teaching career. Her personality brimmed with effervescence. I suggested that she put one of Grace Nash's sessions on her schedule.

"You mean you know her personally?"

I told her about my initial acquaintance with Grace and why I had been following her workshops and using her materials for over five years. I had first met her at a national conference in Atlanta and then took a three-week summer course with her and was her assistant when she taught two summer courses at the school where I earned my master's degree.

"We studied her work in one of my classes. It will be exciting to meet someone important enough to be mentioned in Music Education courses."

"You will love her, and her workshop will inspire you."

We chatted a few more minutes about the conference agenda, agreed to have dinner together, and set the time and place to meet. Less than an hour later, we met at the hotel's main restaurant. She was interested in the possibility of setting up a private studio for Orff-based music lessons. I talked about having a private piano studio and encouraged her to talk to one of the clinicians who had experience with a private Orff-based studio.

She was eager to get the most out of her first professional conference and was equally excited over her life in general. She had completed her undergraduate degree that year, married right after graduation, gone on an extensive honeymoon, and started her first teaching job all within 5-6 months preceding the conference.

Rebecca gushed over all the milestones she had experienced so recently. Conversation topics frequently veered from professional brainstorming to the addition of details about her personal life. It was almost as if her mind flitted between the 50s and the NOW consciousness-raising of the 70s. And I kept thinking, *I hope she doesn't expect a long account of my personal life. All she needs to know is that I am divorced and am focused on my career and new job.*

Rebecca and I splurged on a steak dinner. While enjoying the taste of tender midwestern beef cooked exactly as requested and sauced with a gravy of mushrooms simmered in red wine, we talked more about the private studio idea. I said, "I had a piano studio in Rock Hill for several years, but never thought about teaching Orff-Schulwerk privately. It might work, though, especially if you are the first in your city to offer it."

"Maybe, but I don't know what my husband will say. He supports my career but makes the decisions about money. It would be expensive to rent a place big enough for the instruments and movement activities and to buy at least one set of the instruments."

"One of the things that Grace Nash often says is, 'If you don't invest in your career, then who will?' If you get your own credit card, you can do it on your own with only your husband's emotional support. Think about it this way: if you would do it if you were single, why not do it now?"

"I just always thought that the man should make decisions about money."

"It seems to me that big joint purchases such as a house should be a joint decision. But for a relatively small investment in your career, I think it is primarily your decision."

"I just don't know. There's so much to think about."

"Yes, but that's the fun of having options."

Rebecca said she would talk to her husband after she had done some research and had a better idea of the amount of investment it would require, along with the possible advantages over other options. For the next year or two, though, she said she would concentrate on improving her own skills in using Orff-Schulwerk in her classroom at school.

After splitting a dessert described on the menu as a *mile high* chocolate concoction, we paid the bill and left. Out in the crowded hall, we headed toward the elevator. The congestion of well-dressed bodies was so thick that it was easy to overhear others' conversations. The mixture of fragrances reminded me of the entrance at an upscale department store. I thought about my favorite perfume in high school, Avon's *Persian Wood*. I didn't feel dressed without it and even used it to spray envelopes for the letters to my high school sweetheart, who was in the Army then. My mother sometimes reminded me, "Honey, your fragrance must whisper, not shout." Most of the people were apparently oblivious that their fragrance shouted and stifled the air with *fragrancitis*.

I said, "Would you like to stop at the bar for a night cap?"

"Yes. My husband told me to have a good time while I'm here."

A couple of men standing near Rebecca and me apparently overheard our remarks about the night cap. One of the men touched my elbow to get my attention and said, "Excuse me. My friend and I are heading up for a nightcap. Would you two ladies like to join us? Tables will be hard to come by with so many conferences going on at the same time. I've never seen this hotel so crowded."

Rebecca and I looked at each other with raised eyebrows, both of us uncertain about an answer. I recalled the time a friend and I had met a couple of men at the hotel bar in Charleston and the social debacle it led to—no real harm, but something I didn't want to repeat. I also thought about Rebecca's story of being recently married but expecting to enjoy attending a national professional conference for the first time. Those fleeting thoughts thrust me right between curiosity and caution.

The men were dressed in dark suits and light blue dress shirts with ties slightly loosened. They carried themselves with relaxed confidence—no phony bravado. They appeared to be old enough to be established in their careers, but not a lot older than Rebecca or me. During the chaotic rush to the elevator, everything happened so fast that there was not much time to think beyond a cursory assessment and reaction—about the same amount of time it takes a parent or teacher to calculate whether a child is being honest or not.

Neither Rebecca nor I responded with a knee-jerk answer of "No, thanks." She spoke first.

"It might be fun to share a table, but I've got to let you know that I won't be sharing anything else besides a drink. I'm barely off my honeymoon. My husband did tell me to have a good time, though."

"Of course. We just thought it would be fun to chat over nightcaps. It's probably going to be easier to get a table for four than two tables for two."

I said, "Ok, we'll join you for a drink. We'll need to excuse ourselves after that, though. Our first session is at 8:00 a.m."

The one who had touched my elbow said, "I'm Travis. This is my friend, Sam—a couple of Texas boys here for an oil and gas conference. We control our own expense accounts, so adding guests to the bar bill won't be a problem." The words he spoke sounded a bit boastful to me, but his tone was nonchalant. It made me wonder if he was a bit of a bragger or simply being kind and generous. I certainly wasn't naïve, but my experience in bar settings without a date was limited.

Sam said, "Our conference begins tomorrow, but we don't have to be early birds."

When we passed the closest elevator and veered off toward another hall, it became obvious they were headed in a different direction from the bar Rebecca and I had in mind—the one we saw advertised in the marketing brochure. When I spotted a different elevator, a lump of uncertainty swelled in my throat. Was this the elevator to their floor? My internal image of myself as a young single professional out on my own, "foot-loose and fancy-free," collided with equally strong images of myself as a person with at least a fair amount of common sense. I assumed that they were trying to charm us into their room(s). I asked, "Is there another bar on a different floor?"

Travis smiled and said, "There sure is. You two ready to visit the Playboy Club of Denver?"

Rebecca was as giddy as a child finding the prize Easter egg. She clasped both hands to her cheeks and said, "Are you kidding? My husband has a subscription to Playboy magazine. Uhm—for the articles, right?"

They both nodded their heads and chuckled. Travis said, "Oh yeah. We know about the articles. Mighty fine writin'."

Still thinking it was probably just a ploy, I reminded myself that we didn't have to enter their rooms and that if we did end up at the Playboy Club, we could leave anytime we wanted. The spirit of adventure outweighed caution.

Sam pulled out a large old-fashioned keychain with one key hanging on it. He dangled it as though teasing or entertaining a baby and said., "This is how you get a table for four when the hotel is swarming with thousands of people looking for a good time."

Travis said, "You still have that old thing? Put it away. You know it hasn't worked since '66."

Sam put away the old-fashioned key, and Travis pulled a plastic key the size of a credit card from his wallet. "This is all we need now," he said as he gave it a flourish while aiming for the slot.

I was almost numb—not because of anticipating seeing voluptuous women in form-fitting costumes, but because the serendipity that placed the four of us in that hallway was such a remote possibility. Reassurances I had given myself melted in the wake of far too many questions. Would the men go back on their word and expect sexual favors for taking us there? Would they hook up with a Bunny and leave us stranded? And just exactly how would the evening end? My sense of adventure whiplashed back into control. No need to bail out.

I had a vague recollection of hearing about Gloria Steinem going undercover as a Bunny in New York City. But that happened in 1963, and we were there in 1974. Steinem gave a speech at Winthrop while I was there. Her sense of humor combined with pinpoint articulation kept the mostly female audience riveted. One of the points she made was that the women's movement offered benefits to both women and men because it meant that men no longer would be valued primarily for the size of their (long pause as she panned the audience)-----paychecks. I admired her cleverness and courage not only to be hired as a Bunny, but also to write about what she observed and learned.

Once inside the club, my eyes adjusted to the dim light. Several patrons stood at a pool table in one corner, happy to stop shooting when a Bunny offered shots in a glass. I recall seats of different types on several different levels—almost like a formalized bleacher structure, but round. Bottles and glasses on the bar shone like mirrors and sent glimmers of light in all directions from the lower center level. Clinks of ice cubes, long lacquered nails on goblets, and smooth jazz joined the shards of light to make the entire room buzz with hyper-charged frivolity. I speculated that the room had been designed to maximize sightlines to the abundance of cleavage hanging out of every Bunny's costume (or was it a uniform?).

There were other female guests. More than a few could have passed for a niece out with a favorite uncle. Some seemed to be trying to imitate the Bunnies' attire. But most were as normal looking as Rebecca and I. Seeing that we were not the only female guests who would not attract undue attention on the street eased my sense of caution, letting me feel a little less like an intruder.

The Playboy logo had not escaped a single surface or item. Even the cocktail glasses were adorned with it. But what made my eyes bulge were the live Bunnies' bulging boobs. I knew about the costumes but was not prepared to see them in person. So far as I know, I had never seen evidence of breast augmentation. To me, augmentation was a musical term indicating that the rhythmic value of a note was to be increased, usually doubled.

It wasn't that I hadn't seen girls and women with large breasts, but the big-breasted bodies I had seen were much more likely to have waists in proportion to the bra size along with thighs that made ample laps for children or pets. The combination of overflowing cleavage atop disproportionally tiny waists grounded by long, firm, fishnetted legs gave the atmosphere the feel of a fantastical playground of sensuality. The blusey harmonies, scented candles, and encompassing aura of permissible naughtiness set just the mood that Hugh Hefner's hype promised.

I noticed that the heights of the bar stools and chairs also were calculated to put the eyes of most people sitting on them right at cleavage level. The benches in the waiting area were so low that if drinks were served, the Bunny had to lean over, giving patrons and guests a clear sightline that left little wonder as to whether her navel was an in-y or an out-y.

The mountain range of Enhanced Boobs would have distracted the Pope himself if, by some bizarre circumstance, he happened to accept an invitation for a night cap there. Yet I didn't see *dirty old men* ogling—looking, yes—noticing, yes, but not leering. Perhaps most of the men in the room were frequent customers and had become somewhat inured to the sight. Or maybe they believed an air of nonchalant cool would score more points with their companions. I wondered if members had a reward system for frequency of visits and if the frequency had a specificity to the "mile high city"—perhaps a "Mile-High Playboy Club" designation.

I couldn't help but feel somewhat awkward, though—not so much from what I was experiencing, but from the realization that a woman I had just met that morning and I were with two strangers in a notorious den of titillation with no knowledge of the layout, the expectations, or even appropriate etiquette. Did we have to have a key to get out? Was there some sort of secret exit that only the members knew about? The worst of my *what ifs* intruded on my thoughts. What headlines would be written if we never made it out? Another bout of doubt about our judgment.

Meanwhile, conversation maintained a light, nonaggressive pace. Rebecca took over the lead and turned it into a personal monologue about her wedding, honeymoon, and ecstatic thrill of being inside a Playboy Club. Sam was patient with her demeanor.

Our small table for four fit nicely into the space two or three levels up from the center area where the Bunnies picked up the loaded trays. The layout was not nearly so tight as when I saw Frankie Valley and the Four Seasons in Las Vegas many years later. There was enough space between tables for Bunnies and patrons to walk easily without bumping tables or boobs.

Rebecca punctuated her monologue with, "I just can't believe how jealous my husband will be when I tell him that I went to the Playboy Club of Denver."

After I answered Travis' question regarding what conference we were attending, he probed further. "What's so special about how you teach music? I was in band in high school, but I have no recollection of a music teacher in elementary school. And why do college students need to learn how to teach this special way?"

"It would take hours to fully answer those questions. For the sake of brevity, though, I will just say that elementary music instruction is the most important level of music education. If students are not turned on to music in the early grades, then secondary band, choir, and orchestra teachers will have a much more difficult time recruiting members, and the ones who do choose to be in performing groups will have a much longer learning curve to build skills."

I went on to say that the most important aspect of the particular philosophy, materials, and teaching approach held by AOSA (American Orff-Schulwerk Association) members was that it was most likely to build self-esteem and to bring joy to students of all ages and ability levels.

"You seem really passionate about your work."

"I can't help it because it's so fulfilling."

The pace of the swirling apprehensions that had filled my head gradually slowed, and I felt my shoulders ease into relaxation. Perhaps the Bailey's Irish Cream in the Irish Coffee was winning out over the caffeine. The men didn't seem to be hitting on us, but just wanted some company. I wondered if it was even possible that they really were simply doing us a favor by assuring we would not have to wait an excessive amount of time to be seated at the regular bar. I presumed that if they were suffering from false expectations about how or where the encounter might lead, they would have applied pressure by then.

When our glasses were nearly empty, Travis offered to buy another round. I said, "No, thanks. We really do have to get to bed and be prepared for a long day tomorrow. This has been a lot of fun, but it's time for us to go."

Sam said, "Don't forget to take your souvenir swizzle stick. The management expects everyone to take one." Both men gave their swizzle sticks to us so that we would have two each. Now, almost 50 years later, one of the swizzle sticks is among a collection that sits in a mint julep glass from a Hyatt Regency revolving restaurant in Atlanta, the site of the conference where I first met Grace Nash. The second one disappeared long ago. No other swizzle stick brings back such unique memories as the tallest one with the Playboy Bunny perched on top.

When we got up to leave, Travis and Sam stood and walked us to the exit. Right before Travis opened the door for us, Sam looked at me and said, "Sure you're not interested in one more nightcap?"

"Yes, I'm sure. Thanks for the drinks and the experience of visiting a Playboy Club. Good night." The two men who had shared their access to a table for four turned and walked toward the table we had shared. I wondered if they would find two others to fill our seats. Rebecca and I found the elevator and headed back to the real world, average breasts and all.

I said to Rebecca, "Do you think they hope to get lucky with one of the Bunnies when they get off?"

"I don't know. I'm not sure if they were just being nice or were really looking for a playmate. I'm glad they didn't pressure us."

"I doubt they would have complained if we had encouraged them. Maybe they just decided to hold out for greener pastures. If they're night owls, their night is still young. I guess we'll never answer all our questions."

Rebecca summed it up, "No, but I will smile whenever I remember the first night of the first national conference I ever attended."

CHAPTER 10
FROM MANCHESTER TO EDINBURGH

Only that day dawns to which we are awake.
Henry David Thoreau
(1817-1862)

On my way to the Murphy Writing of Stockton University course to be held in Dundee, Scotland in 2019, I flew into Manchester, England. I knew the city somewhat because the previous year, after the same writing course concluded in Wales, I made Manchester the hub for several day trips, including a visit to my father's ancestral village of Orrell. Being a fan of trains, I went directly from the airport to Piccadilly Station and booked the earliest and most direct departure for Edinburgh. I even requested a front-facing table seat near the baggage bin, proud of myself for remembering details that would minimize the bother of the oversized suitcase and smaller bags.

With ticket in hand, I went out to the outdoor waiting area where the train would stop and sat down on a damp bench to enjoy a coffee and breakfast roll. Pigeons scavenged for morsels but were more polite than the sea gulls I had met on previous trips. Accustomed to crowds of hurrying ticket holders, they tried to stand their ground when children several benches away tried to turn them into playmates. I put on a second jacket and hoped that the warmth of the coffee and the rising sun would soon warm my damp-chilled bones.

There were empty benches near the one I was on, but a young man who could have passed for an American high schooler came up and said, "Mind if I join you?"

I gestured to the bench, said, "Please," and moved over to make room for his backpack. He pulled out a thermos jug of what I later learned was tea along with a bag of what appeared to be a homemade snack. He offered me some of his snack. I declined but opened a bag of biscuits and offered the open bag to him. He politely took out one biscuit, thanked me for it, and settled into checking his phone.

In just a minute, he looked up and said, "Are you on the one to Edinburgh with only one or two stops?"

"Yes." He put his phone in his pocket and seemed to be ready to chat until the train arrived.

Turning toward me, he said, "My name is Rhys."

"I'm Sue." We shook hands. I told him that I had known only one person named Rhys—a student in one of the classes in the school where I had taught music for fifteen years. "He was an excellent student and was in the instrumental ensemble and choir."

"Can't say I'm especially good at music, but I do enjoy listening and dancing."

We waited less than thirty minutes before the train pulled up right in front of us. After those bound for Manchester disembarked, we both grabbed our baggage and started walking toward the coach. He rushed ahead of me, but came right back empty-handed and said, "Here, let me help you with that big bag." He was quite small, but wiry, strong, and fast. Quiet self-confidence bred from extensive travel seemed to be second nature to him. I told him that my reservation was at a table near the baggage bin. "Yep. I already spotted it." I assumed he had been scouting out his own seat number.

He moved quickly and almost invisibly—by my side or within sight one second and nowhere to be seen the next. Thinking he had gone on to his seat, I scanned the seat numbers as I walked from the end of the coach past a couple rows of seats, then spotted the table with my seat number. My big purple suitcase was secure in the bin. There he sat at my table with a wide grin, sitting on the opposite side of the table so that he would be facing the back of the coach. Seeing the question mark on my face, he said, "I can keep an eye on the luggage bin from here."

As I took my seat, he continued, "I changed my seat number so that we could chat. Hope you don't mind." I surmised that he had made the change online because he hadn't had time to do so in person.

"That's fine. Are you going all the way to Edinburgh?"

"Just to the outskirts. You see, I am from Wales and have been working in China for over a year. My mom and dad are on holiday near Edinburgh, so I am going there to see them."

"I was in Wales last year for a course in creative nonfiction. It was held in a retreat center called Trigonos not too far from Bangor."

"I've heard of it; never been there, though. My family lives closer to Cardiff."

"What kind of work do you do that would take you to China when you must have just finished school when you left for your job assignment?"

He gave the Welsh equivalent of an *aw, shucks* look and said, "I'm a little older than I look. I got the job assignment in China right after I finished college. It might seem boring, but I sell big metal containers to large companies." He continued and explained with more detail about his job, but jet lag was setting in and clouding the part of my brain that processes new information.

I closed my eyes for a few minutes, but as soon as I opened them, he pulled out his thermos jug again and asked, "Do you drink Chinese tea?"

"I suppose so. Doesn't a high percentage of all tea come from China?"

"I mean genuine Chinese tea that the Chinese people drink. Here, I'll show you what I mean."

He took the lid off the thermos jug and said, "You want to taste it?" I took out a straw I had stashed in my purse and took a small sip.

"It has an unusual taste, but I like it. What type of tea is it?"

"It is the most popular tea in China. Everybody I met drank it. Here. Take this home and enjoy it."

He handed me a small plastic vial of the tea. "It isn't instant, but once you make it, it will last for a long time. Just add a little tea and more water when you have almost finished it. You can reuse a tea strainer's worth of tea for several servings. It doesn't have to be strong to taste good. And it is good hot or cold. I like to start with it hot in the morning and let it cool throughout the day."

I took the vial and looked at the fine print. Finally, I knew what the tea was made from—black Tartary buckwheat. I asked, "Do you think I could get this on Amazon?"

"Yes, but it is pricey. It is worth it, though, because it tastes so good, it helps with digestion, and may lower blood pressure."

"I will get some from Amazon so that I can share it with my man-friend. He usually drinks white tea with jasmine, but I think he would like this."

"Here. Have another packet for him."

The young man was an outstanding conversationalist and seemed genuinely interested in whatever we happened to talk about. He said, "Did you know they have wine bars everywhere in China? The young professionals gather either in wine bars or tea houses. They are so friendly. I was studying Mandarin, so tried to practice my lessons when I was out in the wine bars or tea houses. People I met there encouraged me by helping me learn more vocabulary along with grammar and pronunciation."

"I found that was true in southern Germany and Austria many years ago. In a *gasthaus* or *bier garten*, it seemed that if you knew one word of German, someone would teach you two more. I only knew a few words, but by the time I left, I could understand a lot of what was said if it was said slowly."

I told Rhys that I had met a young woman in Houston who taught Mandarin. She had never been to China, had worked in a non-college-degree field prior to learning Mandarin, and had a thick Texas accent in her native speech.

"Yes. Young people are catching on that Mandarin is the language of the future, especially for commerce."

About half-way between Manchester and Edinburgh, Rhys said he was getting tired and was going to doze for a while. "I want to be fresh for my mom and dad, you know." He pulled his cap over his eyes and slid down in his seat. I pulled out a small notebook from my purse and made a few notes so that I would not forget the conversation.

It was remarkable to me that such a young man had spent a year in China and that he was so excited about meeting up with his parents—a combination of sophistication and primal attachment. While he obviously was highly intelligent, I got the impression that his job assignment might have been based more on the type of person he was than primarily on his intelligence and education. I guessed that the company for which he worked had spotted his personal characteristics that allowed him to be placed in a country vastly different from his own, without knowing the language, but able to function in the international business world despite the obstacles he would have to overcome.

Considering what he had been doing for the previous year, traveling from Wales to Edinburgh to meet up with his parents seemed inconsequential. Yet when combined with his enthusiasm and apparent love and respect for his parents, it was monumental.

When the train slowed and stopped on the outskirts of Edinburgh, Rhys woke up, took off his cap, and got up to retrieve his small suitcase from the bin. I thanked him again for the tea, his help with my luggage, and the engaging conversation. "It's been a pleasure for me too. Cheers."

I smiled and said, "Be sure to tell your parents that you talked with an older lady on the train, and she told you to tell them that they did an excellent job with you. Enjoy your time with your mom and dad."

He chuckled and almost skipped down the aisle. I wanted to see him hug his parents, but lost sight of him when he exited the opposite side of the coach. I hoped that he had absorbed my appreciation for his treating an older woman with respect with no ageism in his demeanor, his comments, or his attitude. While young enough to be my grandson, he had made me feel special by relating to me simply as a fellow traveler open to exchanging stories and ideas that helped to fill my bank of indelible memories—a friendly extrovert with no ulterior motives—who shared an encounter on an efficient train ride through beautiful countryside.

I was embarrassed that I had thought he might be looking for a handout when I first saw him and wished I had been as generous in attitude toward him immediately as he was toward me. He was simply a fine young man eager to see his parents after he had been working for a year in China and who did not hesitate to extend assistance and friendship to an older female train companion from the United States.

CHAPTER 11
MY BROTHER'S HANDS

To see a world in a grain of sand
And a heaven in a wild flower,
Hold infinity in the palm of your hand
And eternity in an hour.
William Blake
(1757-1818)

My brother's hands are large on his 6', 2" frame, both palms zigzagged with scars, knotted and gnarled, tough to the touch. The scars recall surgeries made to release the clasp of Dupuytren's Contracture. Being a guitarist, finger flexibility and control are critical not only to his comfort, but also to his musical expression.

It had been only two weeks since Richard's son, Rick, and his wife and daughter had spent a week with me in Houston, and two years since his daughter, Camie, and I had toured Ireland together. Since my brother also is a writer, I had wished that he could come to the workshop with me.

When I arrived in Edinburgh five days before the workshop was to begin in Dundee, I had been awake more than 24 hours. After unpacking for a five-night stay, the fresh air through the open window cleared my head of the jet's hum and mechanical thumps while the lilt of the Scottish gulls lulled me to sleep.

I awoke at about 1:30 a.m. in a cold sweat following a nightmare in which I had just signed papers to allow doctors in Edinburgh to withdraw life support from my only brother and to approve cremation of his remains. After sleeping about 10 hours, I still felt groggy and unmotivated, but knew I had to do errands and that I wanted to push myself to get out of the room and enjoy Edinburgh as soon as shops and tourist attractions opened. But I had to lie there until I processed the horrible dream enough to even get out of bed and use the toilet before trying to sleep even more while the city prepared for the next day.

I recalled the gist of something I had read many years ago, "The half hour between waking and rising has all my life proved propitious to any task which was exercising my invention." (Scott) In Sir Walter Scott's city more than a hundred years since his death, I was struggling with that twilight zone time between deep sleep and full wakefulness. As I fought the presence of the dreadful nightmare scene and the lure of the city, I became aware of a darkness overcasting my mood and energy. As I lay there, I could not release the hold the nightmare had on me—no sleep—just a tape loop of anguish that refused to rest or allow me to drift off again.

In the swirl of the dream's dark beginning, I was making arrangements to fly to Scotland. Rather than preparing for a writer's workshop, I was preparing to accompany Rick and Camie, my nephew and niece, to sign the unthinkably final papers.

I felt responsible for Richard's death, completely heartbroken, and that I must be strong for his children. In the stream of unconsciousness, his surgeon in Missouri had told him that the only additional relief for Dupuytren's Contracture would be the last resort of amputation. The ring finger on his left hand was locked at an angle that limited his guitar technique. Both hands were so full of scar tissue and gristle that the surgeon in Missouri could no longer do any surgery.

In the terror of the dream, I was the one who had told him that the most prominent hand surgeons in the world were in Scotland. He made an appointment and braved the trip alone, hoping to save his left hand.

When he arrived at the hospital for the initial evaluation, he stepped out of the taxi and collapsed. The taxi driver got out of the car and said, "Sir, are you alright? Can you manage to stand?"

When Richard gave no response, the driver called the hospital's emergency number. Medics arrived almost instantly, placed Richard on a gurney, and sprinted to the ER. Once in the ER, the attending physician diagnosed a massive heart attack. They documented a flat line on the EEG and notified his wife, Linda, of his condition. She requested that he be kept on life support until someone from the family could arrive.

Since Linda has limited mobility, she asked Rick and Camie to make the trip. Camie called me. "Aunt Sue, Mom just got a call from a hospital in Edinburgh. Dad collapsed with a massive heart attack when the taxi dropped him off. He's flat-lined, and Mom wants Rick and me to go take care of everything. I can't believe that Pop is on life support 'til we get there."

"My God, Camie! I suggested that he go there for possible treatment instead of amputation. I feel terrible."

"We all know you had only his best interests at heart. We are just so stunned that we hardly know which way to turn. I can take care of tickets for Rick and me, but we don't know what to do once we get there."

"I will go with you. I know that your mom is not able to go, so let me take care of the tickets. I will meet you in Newark so that we can be on the same flight from there."

The weight of realization that we would be forced to make the final decision, which would end his life—the life of the man we all adored—kept clouding every thought and left a taste of bile in my mouth as my stomach produced upward-climbing acid and my eyes refused to close for peaceful sleep. It seemed that I had wasted thousands of dollars to come to the workshop early and explore Edinburgh when I felt only like taking the next plane to Missouri to see my brother. In the dream, it took several days for Camie and Rick and me to make arrangements for the trip and to get the tickets.

When we landed in Edinburgh, we dropped our luggage off at the hotel, then went straight to the hospital and met with the doctors. The medical staff was kind and sympathetic and had already arranged for a chaplain to meet with us. She explained that the likely cause of the heart attack was blood clots from the plane travel—the trip I had advised my brother to take.

There were endless details and expenses, but the one thing that sent all three of us into utter despair was the need for our signatures on the medical release forms. We all agreed that Richard would not want to be kept alive artificially and would want to minimize expenses, but we did not want to issue permission for the doctors to *pull the plug*.

In the reality of a beautiful setting in a city not far from my paternal great-grandmother's birthplace, it took several days for me to shake the feelings of queasy sadness, guilt, and fear. The dream about Richard's need for hand surgery seemed to be more real than the ancient surroundings waiting for me to explore.

During times in my life when I was going through a difficult situation, my hand would get lost in Richard's as my only brother—my youngest sibling—shared his strength. His scarred palms reminded me of our father's calloused tender touch.

On the guided city tour, my thoughts began to turn to my reason for being in Scotland—to attend the Murphy Getaway to Write workshop in Dundee. But too often, the hovering presence of the nightmare interrupted my mood and thoughts, binding focus and creativity in a fog far denser than the wisps of haze on the horizon. Hearing that we were near Robert Louis Stephenson's home tempted my attention. But I kept wondering what would have prompted such a dream. Could it be a warning that I might have a blood clot? Was it an omen about my brother's health? Did I need to see a doctor? Did I need to warn Richard? Was there a way to get out of the obsession that threatened to smother my entire trip?

Days later, I gasped when Peter Murphy, the instructor, announced the writing prompt: *Write about a dream that has haunted you.* On a group excursion to the Victoria & Albert Museum in Dundee, I learned about the Hands of X work on prosthetic hands. How could my unsettling experience and the museum's prosthetic hand work be connected? How and why had I told my brother in the dream that the best hand surgeons in the world are in Scotland? As a Houstonian, the more likely scenario would have been to advise him to come to the world class Medical Center of Houston.

Perhaps these hand-related coincidences connected to the rightness of my being there, a type of prediction. Perhaps there was a hint of precognition regarding the Hands of X exhibit. I certainly was not aware of that work prior to the visit to the V&A. I have no objective explanation for the relationship between the writing prompt and its relevance to me, but I am thankful that the bone-chilling coincidence gave me the tool I needed to shake the grip of the nightmare and to be ready for the next prompt.

Before leaving the Dundee V&A exhibits, a small group had lunch together in the upstairs restaurant. Arbroath smokies—the fish delicacy that requires certification that it came from the town of Arbroath—had found its way to the menu. The aroma of smoked fish was the same as in Arbroath when we had first tasted it on the excursion to Arbroath a day or two earlier. The presentation of the fish was the same but with an addition of dark green spinach and poached eggs to add color to the plate. The lunch with fellow writers was the perfect way to allow the obsession with unreal events to complete its process in my mind and for me to release its hold after seeing the Hands of X exhibit. Writing about the horrific dream clarified the cloud in my mind and mood, but I will never forget the nightmare or its effects on me.

CHAPTER 12
DREAMSCAPE ON WRITING

*It has never been my object to record my
dreams, just to realize them.*

Man Ray
(1890-1976)

Looking forward to the final online class in a writer's course, I went to bed earlier than usual—before midnight. Tired with the satisfaction of being prepared to read from one of my assignments and to listen to classmates read their writing samples, I went to sleep without the usual tossing and turning. Three hours later, I awoke from a beautiful dream that seemed to be a mixture of history, hope for future far-distant writing retreats once COVID-19 loosened its grip on the world, and fantasy.

In the dream, I was near a place where I had participated in a writer's workshop in 2018, a place of quiet beauty at the foot of Mt. Snowdonia in Wales. But rather than boarding a small van at the train station to get to the remote retreat center, I was on a full-sized commercial coach filled almost to capacity. I was aware that there were two groups aboard and scanned faces as I found my seat, hoping to spot familiar faces from the previous workshop. No eyes met mine and no smiles of recognition registered on faces.

I found a seat by the window in the middle of the coach and wondered who would fill the aisle seat. When I looked toward the front, I saw a stunningly handsome man step into the aisle. He wore high-fashion shades, so I couldn't tell if he noticed the empty seat next to me. Not wanting to appear over eager, I tried to make a friendly wave and pointed to the adjoining seat and to two others across the aisle. He chose to sit in the first aisle seat he came to, just a couple of rows ahead of my row. I wondered if he was a part of the writers' group and if he might be in my section of the course.

Right after the man sat down, I saw another man behind him who had a service dog on a leash. Again, I gestured to show the boarder the two seats near me. He chose to sit right across from me and gave the command for the dog to sit at his feet. The coach full of people seemed abnormally quiet. I assumed everyone had jet lag and that conversation would liven up after a nap before orientation and dinner.

On the way to the writer's retreat venue, the coach stopped at a hotel and let off about half of the passengers. The man with the shades stayed on, letting me know that he was a part of my group. When the coach stopped at the retreat center, the man who was sitting across the aisle from me stood up before the coach had fully stopped, commanded the dog to get up, and started walking toward the front. Two rows up the aisle, the shaded man cocked his head toward them, got up, and led the way to the steps before he disappeared from my view.

When I found my assigned room, I was surprised to find it was a large dorm room rather than a private room like I had the previous year. There were two sets of bunk beds and a single bed in the room.

A woman had walked with me from the check-in table when we discovered we would be in the same room. She and I chose the bottom bunks, leaving the top bunks and single bed for our roommates. We were beginning to unpack essentials for the first night when the man who looked like Andre Bocelli and the man with the dog entered the room. Another woman followed them.

"Would you mind taking one of the top bunks," the man with the dog said to the woman just coming into the room. She told him that would be fine, but that she sometimes had vertigo and would have to take the mattress off and place it on the floor in case a bout set in. He assured her that he would help her. He said to the other man, "Go ahead and take the single bed, and I will be in the other top bunk."

The Bocelli look-alike pulled out something that looked like a lightweight foot-long round white stick from one of his pockets. With a snap of his wrist, he shook it to make two hinges release the folds. Once he placed the tip on the floor, the hinges locked automatically to keep the three-foot stick extended. He methodically tapped the tip as he paced out the room to memorize the steps from the door to his bed and to the door of the bathroom. I realized then that he shared Bocelli's disability as well as his looks. He accepted only minimal help from his assistant and the service dog. When the dog saw the blind man sit on the single bed, it lay at his feet, ready for a belly rub and a treat.

Once we had all claimed a dresser drawer and a few inches on the top, we figured out how all of us would be able to plug in electronic devices and extra desk lamps for those of us who needed extra light. The blind man's assistant set up his braille equipment.

The next morning, the assistant, service dog, and blind classmate were already out for a walk when I rolled out of bed. Later, during midmorning tea break, I talked to the blind man about the walk. "Where did you go on your walk?"

"We followed the road around the farm. My dog enjoys the smells of the country. It is a treat for him because we live in a large city."

"I live in Houston, which is very large, so it is a treat for me also. I love to smell the natural scents of the farm animals, flowers, cooking aromas, and clovers."

"My favorite part of the walk was the peaceful feeling of the lake breeze mixed with the sounds of birds and sheep. I was born with sight and still remember colors and can visualize places once I know the layout of the size and shape of an area."

"I once had a piano tuner who also was born sighted but suffered a childhood illness that left him blind. He was one of the best tuners and technicians I ever had. I would pick him up at the music store near my house and take him back when he finished working on my piano."

"Yes, many times, the loss of one sense makes another of the senses become hyper-developed. I look forward to getting to know your work in class."

"Likewise. Let me know if there's anything I can do to help you in class."

I wondered how he revised and edited his work. Later, he told me he had learned not to waste time on bitterness because his life was full as it was. He was grateful for the training available for him to learn to function independently. But when he travelled in a new place, he preferred for his assistant to be with him, especially to handle the electronic Braille technology. He enjoyed practicing adapting to new places with minimal help but didn't hesitate to accept help when needed.

At least two decades separated our ages, just as two rows had separated our seats on the coach, but we connected through our writing journeys and our mutual pleasure at the environment and the challenges we faced as writers and as fellow travelers.

When I woke up in my own bed, I wondered if there would be a man with this description in the next writers' workshop. With just a bit of regret, I have to say there were men who were handsome, who were talented writers with compelling stories, but none of them were Bocelli look-alikes.

CHAPTER 13
A MIGHTY GOOD TIME AND A STOP SIGN

Education is the ability to listen to almost anything without losing your temper or your self-confidence.
Robert Frost
(1874-1963)

Several years ago (pre-COVID-19), I was at my computer in the small home office in the front of my house at about 1.30 a.m. That was not unusual because I am an extreme night owl and often start writing around 10:00 P.M. While teaching music in public schools, I managed to function within everyone else's time frame, but once I retired, the biggest luxury was not having to set the alarm clock. Like most others on my block, I kept the porch light on all night. But only a few others kept interior lights on.

A shuffle of feet and a knock on the front door startled me so badly that I jumped off the seat of my chair. The knock was not just loud as if someone was eager to make me respond to the knock, but aggressive. Before I could gather my wits and decide what to do, he knocked again with even more intense speed and volume in the sharp-knuckled rap.

Feeling just a bit smug because of my phone's ability to view the one knocking, I took a few seconds to view the camera log. A male of undistinguished appearance stood just off the front patio in the grass—white tee shirt and rumpled black jeans to go with his topsy-turvy dark hair and dirty sneakers. His hands were empty—not even a phone. If he moved near the door again, he could see me if he was at the right angle because the faux wooden blind stood out a little on the bottom where it hit the dead bolt lock.

I swiveled and quickly turned off the hall and office lights and the two desk lamps. I had a flash of memory of active shooter drills and tornado drills at school, but this was neither an active shooter nor a tornado. I decided to face the situation rather than hide under the over-sized desk.

Since the top half of the front door had a glass panel with decorative diamond shaped wooden inserts, I got a better view of the man when I peeked out the blind. But I didn't want him to see me.

Thinking perhaps he had run out of gas and needed someone to make a call for him, I mustered my strongest voice of authority and called out, "Who is it?"

Speaking slowly, but not with slurred speech, he said, "It's Ronnie. I'm yore neighbor. Y'know where Joey lives at, don'tcha? My house is right next to his."

"I don't know any neighbor named Joey."

"Won'tcha help me? I'm only askin' for some Gator Aide. I just went to drink some and it's all gone. I don't know who drank it."

"No. I don't have any Gator Aide. I think you need to leave."

"Really? I'm only in my forties. I'm only askin'. And I could show you a real good time."

"No. You need to leave. Now."

He used a sing-songy chant, "You'll be sorry. I could make you feel real good. I know you're intersted. Like I said, I'm only askin'."

"I'm not interested. And I will call the police if you don't leave right now." If he knew the neighborhood, he knew that the substation was less than 2 minutes away.

"Okay, but I gotta' say, you're missin' out on a mighty good time."

I watched the making of my security system's video as he turned and walked toward the sidewalk. I made sure he was beyond my car, which was parked in the driveway, then sat down at the computer in the dark and wondered what to do. His gait was slow and less than steady, so I assumed he was pumped up on something that slowed his speech without making it slur.

After a couple of minutes of deep breathing, I called 911. "What's the nature of your emergency?"

'There's a prowler on my street. He just left my house headed East, but I can't tell if he's still walking or has stopped at another house."

"Did he threaten you or your property?"

"Only by inuendo, but he seemed to be under the influence of something. His speech was not slurred, but was slow, and he claimed he wanted me to give him some Gator Aide."

"Well, that's a new one. We'll send an officer right away. Do you want him to stop at your house to take a police report now, or come back during regular office hours?"

"I'd prefer to talk with him tomorrow. I just want some assurance that the prowler is taken care of tonight."

"Yes, Ma'am. I've already dispatched Officer Garcia."

"Thanks! I know him because he patrols my subdivision. He is especially careful about the four-way stop sign around the corner from my house."

The dispatcher signed off. I heard a car and peeked out the front door blind but did not see a vehicle. Then I saw that the car was going slowly and using only the streetlights—no headlights—to make its way down the street. For a second, I thought it was going to stop at my house, but it keep on crawling along. There were no markings on it, so I didn't even know with certainty whether it was a patrolman or a civilian.

About mid-morning the next day, I heard less obtrusive knocks on the front door. I peeked between the blind slats and saw it was a uniformed officer with a marked squad car in front of my house. I opened the door.

"Mornin', Ma'am. I'm Officer Garcia. I think I remember you. Piano teacher, right?"

"Yes. I remember you too."

Not long before "Ronnie's" visit, a piano mom, a grandmother, and I had all received a ticket from Officer Garcia for making less than a full stop where he had his favorite stakeout. When Officer Garcia turned on his lights and gave one blare of his siren, I pulled around the corner and stopped, truly surprised because I had seen him and thought I had made sure to stop. His favorite place to stalk stop-sign rollers was in the shallow cul-de-sac on the opposite side of the four-way stop from my turn.

"Hello, Officer."

"Good afternoon, Ma'am."

After checking my license and registration, he said, "Do you know that you rolled the stop sign?"

"I thought I stopped completely. I saw your car and tried to be extra careful."

"No, Ma'am. Not a full stop. I'm gonna' have to issue a ticket. You can go to court if you want, or you can take a defensive driving course, so it won't raise your insurance rates."

"Okay. I'll think about the options, but I have to get home now before my piano student gets there ahead of me."

"You take care, now, and watch yourself at this corner."

"Yes, sir."

The piano mom who also was ticketed there fully admitted that she routinely rolled stop signs and paid the fine. She said, "You know, my husband is an attorney and probably could get the ticket removed, but I decided to just pay it so that my daughter will learn a lesson from it. She'll get her license next year."

Not long after the Ronnie incident, I noticed that my friend, Nancy, was running late. I was about to call her when her granddaughter, Nora, came running up to the front door.

"Nora, what's wrong?"

"It's Nanna. She's really mad at the cop that just stopped her. She won't get arrested, will she? I think he's giving her a ticket because he thinks she didn't stop at that stop sign. But I was in the car. I know she's a good driver. She told me to run the rest of the way to your house so we could still have most of my lesson time."

"I hope she doesn't argue with him. That probably wouldn't be a good idea."

Though only in the fifth grade, she had picked up on her grandmother's dislike of Texas and was afraid that her Nanna might say something she shouldn't to the officer.

"He is a nice man, but he probably would not react well to a driver arguing with him."

"I know. But Nanna already told him that she stopped all the way and asked him how fast she was going. He said 'zero.' That's when she told me to run to your house. I'm afraid she didn't want me to see her lose her temper with the cop."

I hugged her and asked if she would like some tea or water.

"No, thank you. I just want Nanna to get here and not be in trouble."

Nancy soon was at the door. I opened it for her, and she came in on a wave of exasperation. Nora hugged her and said, "Nanna, are you okay?"

We walked toward the sofa.

"Yes, Dear, but I need to sit down. I'm shaking with anger. That officer stated on the ticket that I was going zero miles per hour. How is it even possible to run or roll a stop sign if you are going zero?"

Nancy and Nora sat on the sofa, and I sat in the rocker.

"Sue, I will never get used to being in Texas! And, by the way, how do you know Officer Garcia? When I told Nora to run along to your house, he said, 'Does she take piano from that lady around the corner?'"

Nancy continued to explain that she asked the officer why he was asking about piano lessons. He told Nancy, "Because this isn't the first time I've seen a car roll this stop sign on the way to her house."

Trying to lighten the mood, I smiled and said, "Guess I'm getting some free publicity for the studio. You are now the third person I know of who has been ticketed on that corner."

"You didn't fuss at him, did you, Nanna? I don't want you to be in trouble."

"No, but I think he read the expression on my face."

I said, "Did he give you the option of attending a defensive driving course?"

"Oh, yes. He was quick to list several right around this area plus an online option. He must send a lot of people to those outfits. Maybe he gets a kickback every time someone enrolls because of his ticketing."

"Shall we try to have a partial lesson, or would you rather reschedule?"

"Let's just count this as my therapy time with you. I need to decompress before I go home. It's so unfair. I think I might have screamed if he had called me 'Ma'am' one more time."

Nancy pulled out her checkbook. I said, "No charge for today."

"No. No, I insist. We're using your time." While she made out the check, she continued, "I can't believe it! I had a perfect driving record before Officer Garcia spotted me. Now I have to take one of those stupid driving courses. I wanted to ask him how he thought I got here all the way from Connecticut, but I held my tongue."

"Well, at least you and Nora and I will have a good story out of this. Nora, would you like to play your piece before you leave?"

"No. That's okay."

"Alright. We'll work on it next week."

The doorbell rang. They left as I ushered in the next student. The mom said, "Did you know there's a policeman at that four-way stop? I happened to see him and made sure I stopped completely."

"Consider yourself lucky. He has already ticketed me and two of my piano parents."

I looked at the student and said, "Let's get started. I would love to hear some music."

Once the officer knew what I did in the afternoons, anyone bringing students to their piano lessons became sitting (or rolling) targets. That week, I told all of them, "When you get to the four-way stop around the corner, you'd better not just come to a full stop, but look to the left and try to make eye contact with Officer Garcia before you make your turn. He is a nice man, but he is overly serious about his assignment as neighborhood watch officer. He wears the uniform with pride and commitment. I don't know if officers are on a quota system, but if so, he could earn the title, 'Stop Sign Roller Catcher of the Month' with little competition from his peers."

Officer Garcia stood in my front hallway the morning after *Ronnie's* visit and pulled out his tablet to take notes. He interviewed me for about 15 minutes. I told him every detail I could remember about *Ronnie*.

"I'm concerned that he may have been targeting me. Why would he claim to be in his forties and try to talk to me?" I also wondered if he had some idea of my age and had assumed I would be an easy target for bumming Gator Aide or whatever else he might have had in mind.

He never explained his (mis)perceived connection between Gator Aide and a *good time*. I continued, "Can you let me know if he really is in his forties and if "Ronnie" is his real name? I'd feel more comfortable if I knew whether he lives in this neighborhood or not."

Officer Garcia said, "Excuse me, Ma'am, but I can't say much. I'll let you know what I can after I do some work in the car. I'll be back as soon as I have more answers."

He left and sat in his car for 10-15 minutes, then knocked on the door. When I opened it, I saw a big grin on his face. He was all but dancing a jig. "They got him!"

"What can you tell me? Is he really a neighbor?"

"No, Ma'am. I talked with the arresting officer. The car you saw last night was an unmarked patrol car. They watched him approach two other houses on your block. He tried to run when they approached him, but they caught up with him when he tried to get a back yard gate open. He tried to tell them that he was in his forties, but when they told him they would take him to a halfway house since he couldn't remember where his parents lived, he came clean about his real age and address. They delivered him to his parents' home. It's in a different subdivision several blocks north of here."

I was relieved to know the prowler had been caught and that he had not singled out me or my property. The verification that his stated age was wrong was irrelevant but remained one of the many things I often pondered.

Officer Garcia continued, "They also told me they interviewed all your neighbors and found that the prowler had knocked on five doors, including yours, and told a BS (pardon my French, Ma'am) story to everyone he talked to. He was so high on something that he didn't know he was in the wrong neighborhood. You were not targeted in any way, except you were one of five with interior lights on at that time of night."

"Thank you, Officer. I feel much calmer now."

"Glad to help because I really care about this neighborhood. If something goes wrong, I want to make it right. Just remember to watch out for that four-way stop."

"Yes sir. See you around."

Glad to share the news, I called Nancy to tell her about the result of the investigation about *Ronnie*. She was still unhappy about having to take a defensive course but said that Nora was looking forward to her piano lesson the following week. I offered to pay for the course, but she would not take my offer. I said, "But Nancy, without my piano students, I would feel unbearably lonely. They fill in the gaps left by my retirement and give me both musical and personal joy. I'm really sorry that Officer Garcia's zealous concern for the stop sign caused you a problem."

"Don't worry. I'll learn the Texas way of driving and will watch for the officer." She reminded me that Nora looked forward to seeing me each week and that they would be back at their regular time the following week.

CHAPTER 14
CHILDREN'S VOICES

*A child's life is like a piece of paper on
which every passerby leaves a mark.*
                                Chinese Proverb

Over the span of more than thirty years, I taught Music in the states of FL, SC, IA, MO, TX, and MD. As is the case in all memoir writing, these mini stories are true. They reflect some of the joys and heart aches inevitable in the dynamics of teaching. These are the ones that took up permanent residence in my memory bank. Where strong regional accents were a part of the environment, I chose to spell words phonetically to give a sense of the aural flavor. This in no way construes a lack of respect for any person or for any region of the United States. My mind has always tuned into sound and remembers the dialogue as though it occurred yesterday. I cannot unhear them—accents, grammatical mistakes, and all.

Out of concern for individual's privacy, I omitted or changed names and other means of personal identification. I share these mini stories in celebration of the satisfaction of teaching and with recognition that the profession always has and always will need teachers who go beyond teaching content. My primary mentor, Grace Nash, said it best, "We do not teach Music to the child. We teach the child through Music."

GUN AT SCHOOL

In my first year of teaching, I was almost ready to leave the third-grade classroom where I had just finished the music lesson when the principal rushed into the room. I wondered if he intended to do an evaluation and got the times mixed up. Usually, the Supervisor of Music conducted evaluations, but I thought perhaps there was a requirement that the principal provide at least one because I was receiving academic credit from the local college for Student Teaching.

The principal pulled me aside where students could not hear him and said, "Lock the door when I leave. Do not let anyone out and stay here until you hear an 'All clear' on the intercom." He then explained that one of the boys in that class had walked home during recess. "His dad's on the police force and his mother's on campus with a gun. We don't know what her intent is." He didn't give me time to ask about the classroom teacher. I assumed she was in the teachers' lounge.

I later learned that when the boy went home, he told his mother he left school because he was angry with his teacher because she had made him sit in the hall outside of the classroom door during recess. Rather than comply, the student walked home. His mother said, "Why'd she make you do that for?"

"'Cuz she said I was fartin' on purpose. Said it smelt so bad I couldn't stay in the room. Said somethin' about learnin' me a lesson from missin' recess."

"Well, we'll just see who's gonna' get learned a lesson."

She left her son home alone and headed up to the school after loading her pistol and putting it into her purse. It took two policemen and the principal quite a while to get the gun away from the mother and to get her off campus. Her husband was not allowed to respond to the call due to the conflict of interests. So far as I know, she never faced any consequences for her action.

Rumors were that her husband convinced the principal that he could *handle her* and that it would never happen again. The boy was back at school the next day. It was one of the few times I have ever felt truly afraid. I realized that if the pistol-packin' mamma managed to get into the classroom, she might mistake me for the classroom teacher.

I usually tended to plan more teaching/learning activities than I expected to get through in one lesson. That day, I wished I had followed that tendency. I reviewed what we had already done but had to wing it for about half an hour while the students wondered what was happening and I was wishing for fewer windows on the back wall.

I AIN'T PREGANUNT

The two-storied school building was old and had neither a music room nor an elevator. I had a cart on rollers. Seeing my fourth-grade class coming in from recess, I asked several sixth graders to help me wrestle the cart up to the second floor. The two shelves almost overflowed with books, record player, albums, and percussion instruments. The worn oak stairs creaked as the cart bumped along. I kept the lower end level while two of the students pulled from the higher level and two on both sides did their part to help stabilize and push it.

At the top of the stairs, I thanked the helpers and pushed the cart toward the assigned classroom, relieved that I did not have to retrieve anything from the stairs. As I approached the doorway, I saw a girl standing outside the room, crying. Her arms encircled her forehead as she slumped against the wall. If she had not been crying, it would have looked like she was playing *Hide and Seek* inside the building. But her sobs and sniffles gave away her plight.

I asked a couple of students to push the cart into the room, then said, "What's wrong, Francie? Did you get hurt at recess?" She shook her head and lowered it trying to wipe her nose and eyes on the hem of her dress. I gave her a tissue.

Francie was thinner than most girls her age. Her unusually thin hair was caught up in a few braids that dripped with perspiration or splashes from the water fountain. Her small eyes lacked sparkle and darted from side to side as though she feared the bullies who caused the tears were in the hall and might start taunting her again.

She blew her nose, then answered, "No, Ma'am."

"Could you tell me why you're crying?"

"They talkin' nasty to me."

"Do you mean students in your class?"

"No, Ma'am. They them big boys."

"I'll talk to the fifth-grade teachers and ask them to be sure their students are not mean to you."

Starting to sob again, she said, "They sayin' I preganunt."

As a first-year teacher, I was caught completely off-guard and felt inadequate to respond in a way that could ease Francie's pain and give her some reason to hope that the situation would improve. I blurted out, "Well you're not, are you?" I was certainly not prepared to expect any such conversation with a fourth-grade student. I think I was trying to at least imply that since the accusation was not true, there was no reason to be upset, but I quickly realized that my implication was not only beyond the girl's ability to understand, but also irrelevant. Even if she had understood the clumsy nuance of my remark, she still would have been upset. She knew *nasty* when she heard it.

She responded, "Oh, no, ma'am. I ain't even started *ventilatin'* yet."

I tried to hide my gasp. Assuming she had not been *held back*, she was only nine years old. I was aware that she spent most of each day in Special Education classes but was mainstreamed in Music and PE, but I did not know her exact age. Aware of the facts of biology enough to know of the correlation between *ventlatin'* and pregnancy and vulnerable to the shame slung at her, I saw her as the most pathetically sensitive girl I could imagine. And if I had let myself, I could have picked her up and taken her home to safety from the playground taunts and whatever else already haunted her soul because I knew firsthand the same sting of verbal evisceration.

When I was about the age that I assumed she was, I had been aware that girls in my community occasionally *visited an aunt* for six or seven months before returning to their home and school, but it was not overtly condoned or discussed. It was what females whispered about and males tried to deny. It appeared to me that she had an expectation that becoming *preganunt* was not something that, in her thinking, might happen to someone else, but was a high probability for herself.

Aware that I needed to be in the classroom and to get the lesson started, my heart broke for her as I handed her another Kleenex and said, "Come on into class when you're ready. You probably will feel better when you sing or play an instrument. You may choose which instrument you'd like to play."

When I talked with the classroom teacher about the brief conversation, she let me know there was a high number of unwed mothers in the town and that a significant number of the births were from nonconsensual incestuous encounters.

Whether or not it was even possible for that fourth-grade student to get pregnant, her tormentors had no right to throw verbiage at her and laugh at her pain. This type of playground scene could have been the inspiration much later for Allen Shamblin and Steve Seskin to write the lyrics, "Don't Laugh at Me," particularly the line, *Don't get your pleasure from my pain,* so beautifully recorded by Peter, Paul, and Mary. I saw her tears as a combination of the playground taunts and what she seemed to intuit to be her future. Despite her limited reasoning ability, she already appeared to be defeated, grounded in the quicksand that statisticians could predict would devour her. And all I could offer was a couple of tissues, a talk with her classroom teacher, and a chance to play a classroom instrument.

YOU AIN'T A REDHEAD

Being a redhead did not always produce happy feelings. One day when I was in the third grade, I cried as I walked home from school. That was the only year my family lived close enough to my elementary school so that I could walk to and from school. The short walk from school to the house that day was not sufficient to soothe the hurt feelings I had been nursing since afternoon recess.

As always, when I opened the door leading from the front porch to the foyer, Mother met me with open arms and a warm smile.

"Hello, Darling. Did you have Music today?

"No. It wasn't Mr. Weber's Day to come to DeLeon Springs."

When she saw that I was beginning to tear up, she said, "Now, now, no need to cry. It couldn't have been that bad. Did you get to practice your piece for the talent show?"

Fighting the tears that I knew she would discount again, I shook my head.

"Then why do you seem so upset?"

" I got mad at that boy that comes down from New York every year. He called me a 'Redheaded woodpecker,' then everybody else started pointing and laughing."

Mother smiled, gave me another hug, stroked my hair, and told me that I should not worry about what any classmates said about my hair. Since I had her coloring, she understood what was going on.

With her typical gentle patience, Mother explained that only very special people were allowed to have red hair. "Anyone can be a blond or brunette, but you have to be very special to be a redhead." Years later, she admitted that her own mother had told her the same thing. I told my late husband, Chris, this story early in our relationship, and he frequently reminded me in loving ways that I was special, partly because I was a redhead. One of his pet names for me was *pelle rojo*, Spanish for *redhead*. By the time I went to junior high school in the seventh grade, I had embraced my hair color and felt it a compliment when someone commented on it.

Early in my teaching career, I noticed that a fourth-grade boy with bright red hair lingered outside the entry to my room as he tried to get his tears under control. It was common for Music to be scheduled right after recess, so it was not unusual for playground incidents to spill over into my classes. While the students settled into their chairs, I stood by the door and asked the child what was wrong.

"Neal, did you get hurt outside?"

"No, Ma'am."

"Are you sick?"

"Nothin's wrong 'cept what the kids are sayin'."

"What's that?"

"They been callin' me a 'redheaded woodpecker.'"

With memories of my mother's words of wisdom to me, I smiled at him and told him the same story she had told me. When I finished the story, he raised his head, scrutinized my hair as if he were inspecting it for the first time, then looked into my eyes, and, with a look of confusion on his face, said, "Ms. Orrell, you ain't a redhead."

Clearly, he wondered why I thought I was a redhead and, by inference, how I could possibly understand what he was going through. When comparing my hair color with his, I guess I would have to describe my hair color more accurately as medium auburn. Perhaps it was slightly lighter than in my childhood, but not enough that I would have noticed without Neal's comment. I understood his hurt feelings in response to the taunts, but I could not see why he thought I was not a redhead. I surmised that his definition of red hair was whatever matched his own flaming shade.

That day happened to be my thirtieth birthday and Friday date night. I vowed to myself that as part of my birthday celebration, I would make sure that he and everyone else would have no doubt that I was a redhead. At the risk of being late for my own birthday celebration, I stopped at the nearest drugstore on the way home that afternoon and invested in my first bottle of Clairol Loving Care. The picture on the box showed a slightly deeper shade of auburn.

While waiting the required twenty minutes for the chemical process to work its magic, I stood in front of a mirror and lifted the plastic cap every few minutes to check for any sign that the color was not right. I wanted the shimmer and sheen of a copper penny, but with the patina of a well-traveled coin, not the harsh brightness of a piece of newly minted metal. And I didn't want my use of the drugstore product to be obvious.

Clairol's over-the-counter product served me well for at least three decades before I finally had to resort to professional salon color treatments. I've had to correct several hairdressers through the years who incorrectly referred to my diminished red as gray hair. In my mind, red hair never grays; it just fades and fades, and then fades some more until the next chemical intervention restores the luster. *G-r-a-y* and *o-l-d* are two words I will never use or internalize if others accidentally use them in reference to my hair or to me.

That night, when the man I was dating arrived for the party, he eyed my black satin low-riding hip huggers and matching bra-type halter top and said, "Wow! That outfit really looks good on you! I do like your birthday suit! Got a new haircut too?"

"No—just a little change in how I fixed it."

LITTLE MISS MANNERS

During many years of my teaching career, I also had a church music job and/or a private piano studio. For at least one year, I taught full-time, was organist/choirmaster at a mid-size church, taught Music

Appreciation in Adult Education night school, and had a dozen piano students. At one point about two-thirds of the way through my career, I was not teaching in the schools for a while and had over thirty piano students. I especially enjoyed working with beginners.

The student who generated this story was a sweet little girl in the first grade. She was a good student and was always dressed in a very "girlie" style. Her voice was unusually soft, and she was unfailingly polite—a perfect *little miss perfect* already too well-practiced in that debilitating art.

When she started playing the assigned piece, she turned to me, stopped playing, and said quietly, "Excuse me."

Guessing that she had burped, I said, "That's okay; everyone burps sometimes. If that ever happens when you're playing in a recital, you'll need to keep going."

She leaned over toward me, cupped her hand over her mouth as though she were telling a secret, and whispered, "But I didn't burp with my mouth. I let a little panty burp. My mom says I always have to say, 'Excuse me,' when I do that."

"I understand. Now, let's see if you can re-start your piece and keep going no matter what happens."

Less than a minute later, she said "There! I did it." It was a perfectly played one-page piece.

BUT TEACHER . . .

Very early in my teaching career, I was assisting a classroom teacher in preparing the school's Christmas program. It was tender turf because during the long history of the school prior to my being hired as the first Music specialist, she had been in charge of all the special programs. I did not want for her to feel as though she had been pushed aside, but at the same time, I wanted to have some supervision over the program. I talked with her and came to an understanding that I would play the piano while she directed. With her permission, I made some suggestions for songs that would be appropriate for young singers and that she probably knew. Since I saw the students only once a week, this seemed to be a workable compromise.

I was there for the daytime performance in the auditorium. Seated at the piano, I had an angled view of the stage left wing. As the shepherd boys were waiting in the wing for their cue to come out on stage, one boy peeked around the curtain and frantically waved his arm toward the director. Even after the shepherds were center stage, he continued to attempt to get the director to let him speak. She tried to ignore him, probably assuming he just wanted a little extra attention. But he was not to be ignored. She kept using a stage whisper to try to get him to put his hand down and to do his part on stage.

"Quiet on stage."

"But Teacher . . ." (A stage whisper)

"Hush up."

"But Teacher . . ." (Soto voce)

He started doing the potty dance that all teachers recognize.

"You stand still."

"But Teacher . . ." (Heard a few rows back)

"Hush up, I can't be talkin' to you now."

Finally, with vocal projection like an operatic tenor, he shouted, "But Teacher, I gots the shits." Parents on the back row had no doubt of his dilemma. But the audience remained quiet.

"Oh, well, then go on. You may leave the stage."

He ran off, throwing off the brown bathrobe that identified his role, and shot out of sight.

I had to stifle my own urge to laugh out loud and try to keep a straight face. The classroom management at that school was so militaristic that the few audible giggles were soon shushed by the looks of scorn from the teachers.

The show did go on despite the interruption, and the shepherd boy with the emergency re-appeared in the wing a few minutes later, donned the bathrobe, and stepped boldly onto center stage with confidence brimming through his wide grin and beaming in his eyes, ready to do his part to spread Christmas cheer to school mates, teachers, administrators, and parents.

A MOTHER'S ILLNESS

Two brothers who were in the second and fifth grades where I taught the longest were exceptionally talented and excellent students. The older brother was in the instrumental ensemble I conducted. His mother was often late to pick him up following afternoon rehearsals, but I did not have the heart to tell him he could not participate unless he had reliable transportation. I knew she would show up eventually. He never complained and seemed to enjoy talking with me as we waited for his mother to arrive, usually about 10 minutes late. While he didn't appear to be in emotional pain, he rarely smiled or showed spontaneous joy unless he was singing or playing an instrument.

One day, as we waited for the mom, the student tried to explain the reason for her tardiness. I had already been told by a colleague that the mother apparently suffered from alcoholism and depression, which accounted for her lack of dependability.

As we waited for his mother that afternoon, he said, "Ms. Dr. Orrell, you probably never heard of this disease, but it makes my mom real sick. It's called menopause, and she has to sleep a lot."

"I'm familiar with it, and I understand that it might make your mom feel bad." That was the only time he mentioned it. From then on, it seemed that he trusted me to remember the reason for his mom's tardiness. If that were the correct diagnosis, it would have been unusual because of the mom's apparent age.

Close to the same time as the menopause story, his younger brother's class was in my room. He was so much like his older brother in looks and personality that I sometimes called them by each other's name. They both had a demeanor that made them seem older than they were and overly serious. It was a combination of utter innocence coupled with a sadness and lack of typical childhood joy that marked them as different from most of their peers.

In the younger brother's class, we were discussing the history of folk music before learning to sing a new song and to accompany it with classroom instruments. When he raised his hand, I called on him. He said, "My daddy's a complete virgin, but I was born in Texas, so I'm only half a virgin." My mind raced to wrap itself around that concept; then it clicked.

"Do you mean that your dad was born in Virginia? That would make him a Virginian."

A slight smile brightened his face. He said, "Oh yeah; that's it." There was no doubt of his sincerity.

When I let his classroom teacher know about the remark, she was relieved to know what he was talking about. She told me she was puzzled by his daily journal entry, which stated, *One of my sisters is a virgin, but the other one is only a half virgin.* The teacher said, "I wondered if I might need to mention this to his mom, but now that I understand what he meant, I won't bother her. It's sometimes difficult to catch her at a good time."

"I really enjoy teaching both of the boys."

"Their sisters are just as nice and also are excellent students. My daughters are friends with them."

"Virgins, half virgins, or Texans?"

We shared a moment of lighthearted educators' humor and headed for our respective hall duties during dismissal.

THE NEW INSTRUMENT

In the mid-late seventies, the state-adopted music textbooks began introducing the new electronic instrument, the synthesizer. It was my first year at that school, which meant that I would receive at least one unscheduled visit from the principal and supervisor of music each semester.

Early in the first semester, the principal stepped into my room and took a seat soon after a fourth-grade lesson began. Seeing the forms he was holding, I knew he was there for a formal evaluation. I expected the class to do well because I had introduced them to the new instrument the previous week, and they were enthusiastic about the music listening lesson that illustrated the synthesizer. That day, I planned to review the previous lesson and to extend it with movement activity.

There was a redhaired girl in the class who always knew the answer to any question I asked. Because of that, and because I did not want to appear to favor redheads, I tried to let someone else answer the question and name the new instrument they had just learned about.

I asked three other students, but no-one was able to remember the new word. Finally, I called on the redhaired girl. She said, "I know it; I know it; but I can't quite get it out. It's right—on—uh—uh."

I interjected, "On the tip of your tongue?"

"Yes!"

I hoped another second or two would make the word materialize. There were no more hands waving for attention, and eyes shifted downward or toward the windows when my head turned toward theirs—the classic plea that the teacher only call on someone who makes eye contact. It looked like she was my last hope to demonstrate for the principal that they had learned something the previous week and remembered it. I knew they had enjoyed the lesson; they just couldn't remember the word I was trying to pull out of their brains. Finally, the redhaired girl almost exploded with the answer. "I got it now! I got it! It's the circumciser!"

The young male principal almost lost it. His eyes locked on the clipboard of papers or anywhere that would prohibit eye contact with me. I tried to limit my facial expression to a smile and explained, "The correct pronunciation is 'synthesizer.'" I went right into the review of differences between acoustic and electronic instruments before playing the listening lesson and having them brainstorm a movement activity to go with the music.

After he completed the forms, the principal helped move desks to the sides of the room before he thanked the class for being good students as he left for his next adventure in another classroom, and we continued with the movement activity while the recorded synthesizer engaged the students' minds and bodies.

DRUMS

I was sitting on the floor *crisscross-applesauce* style with a kindergarten class for the first Music lesson of the year. After introducing myself and briefly going over classroom expectations, a girl near me raised her hand. I called on her. "Music teacher, we have a new friend, and we're supposed to try to help her. See—I'm sitting beside her to be her friend." Several in the class had been classmates in a pre-kindergarten class.

I noticed that the girl she was referring to wore large hearing aids behind both ears. I had not yet received the medical alert list, so did not know that I would have a profoundly deaf child in kindergarten Music that year. The child's friend did not want to stop her discussion of the situation. "See—it's really hard for her to hear. That's why she has those 'things' around her ears."

Trying to get the concerned child to stop talking and to get the class's attention focused, I said, "Thank you for letting me know about our new friend. We will all try to help her."

Not to be squelched, she shrugged her shoulders, slapped her legs, and with tears in her voice said, "But I feel so sorry for her. She has drums in her ears. Maybe that's why she can't hear."

I wondered if perhaps the girls were neighbors in their subdivision or if the informer's mom had talked to her about the person who would become her new classmate. I've never seen deeper empathy from anyone of any age than from the sympathetic kindergarten student who was baffled by her friend's sad situation.

ALL BETTER

In a different kindergarten class, a boy was sitting politely, was listening, and seemed to be enjoying the class. When I looked back at him after turning my attention to someone closer to me, I saw that he had reached inside his shorts from the hemline, pulled the fabric up, and had pulled out his penis. It appeared that he had forgotten to put on a pair of underwear.

He was bent over, gazing at it with the intensity of a first-year Kindergarten Anatomy student. He started brushing it off as if dust bunnies had gathered there. I tried to make eye contact with him, but he was too preoccupied to notice me. I cleared my throat to see if that would get his attention. Nothing worked. He was really focused, but not on anything I was saying. Thinking that he might have a rash, or even a tick, I finally said, "Bill, do you need to see the nurse?"

Too engrossed in his self-exam to hear me, he gave a couple more brushes like a final flick-off of lint, then announced to himself, "There now. It's all better."

With the problem solved, he gave his penis a few pats like he might give a puppy, placed it back inside his plaid shorts, and pulled the leg of the shorts back down. Not a single child seemed to notice Bill's fascination with anatomy, but I couldn't take the risk that someone would notice, and the distraction would cause more than one student to ignore me and the lesson I had planned. I started a rhythmic game of echo-clapping—gotta keep those hands busy.

DOING IT AGAIN

In a different state, I was teaching music in a Special Education class. The students in that room were diagnosed in the terminology of the day as *Mentally Retarded, Trainable*. Their academic achievement was far below grade level, but they were sweet children and tried to participate. They did best with movement and enjoyed modified square dancing. The class was housed in a room that must have been designed originally for kindergarten because there was a restroom in the classroom.

One of the students was a boy who was considerably older than most of the other students. One of the younger girls in the class told me, "I don't like that big boy. He has whiskers."

While it is not uncommon to see students of all elementary grade levels occasionally masturbate, that was the only time in over thirty years I witnessed it routinely. If the class was sitting, waiting for an activity to begin, George often placed his right hand inside his baggy pants and rubbed himself. In most classrooms, just a little eye contact curtailed such action. But for George, redirection had to be overt and precise. His classroom teacher used a code that he understood, "George, you need to go to the restroom."

I never tried to use that verbiage because invariably, if the teacher did not happen to notice it right away, George's tattle-tale friend, Tommy, would announce, "Teacher, he doin' it agin." Tommy apparently enjoyed telling on his friend as much as George enjoyed the activity that both boys knew would result in George's going to the restroom.

Learning that some things are meant to be private was a big part of the curriculum in his IEP (Individual Education Plan).

RHYTHMIC UNDERSTANDING

In a second-grade class in a high socio-economic area, I was introducing the concept of sixteenth notes toward the end of the school year. The main point for the class to understand was that sixteenth notes are used when four sounds are made on one beat. We had discovered that the names of many states have four syllables and would use sixteenth notes if the word were notated. Some examples are Alabama, California, and Mississippi. A cute boy with a twinkle in his eyes raised his hand to contribute to the discovery of words that have four syllables. His contribution was *Tally-Wacker*.

Knowing that it was a word that was used to mean *penis*, he giggled and looked around to see who else might be giggling. It appeared that he was almost daring me to either join the giggles or reprimand him. Only one or two other boys laughed. I treated it as though it were an everyday word used in the classroom and said, "You're right; it does have four syllables." By not laughing and by reinforcing the accuracy of his contribution, I defused the issue and maintained the focus and momentum of the lesson. He never tried to pull something like that again, but he always kept the twinkle in his eyes.

WEIRD KITTENS

In my final year of teaching, I taught violin as an enrichment class at the end of the school day. On most days, a few students showed up a little early to help me set up the room. They arranged the chairs and stands and placed the books on the stands while I set up my own stand and tuned the violin I used.

One of the students was a second-grade girl who was unusually responsible and enjoyed having an outlet for her abundant energy. Toward the end of the year, as she set up the stands, she stopped abruptly and said, "Ms. Dr. Orrell, you know how you're not supposed to make out with your brother?"

I held my breath and tried to think of how I would handle what I thought she was about to tell me. Very slowly, I said, "Yeeeees." Her lighthearted look and bouncy demeanor made me realize that what she was about to say probably would not alarm me.

She continued, "Well, my grandma's cats did that, and those are the weirdest kittens you'll ever see."

I laughed and said, "I once had a cat like that." But I would have been too embarrassed to admit to her that I named the cat, "Spaz."

I THINK I HAD AN ACCIDENT

The Child Protective Services Department of Texas rightfully takes failure to report suspected cases of child abuse quite seriously. Such failure is a Class B misdemeanor and carries a fine of up to $2,000 and/or up to 180 days in jail. As part of their orientation, new teachers are informed of this possibility and instructed to be forthcoming if they observe signs of possible abuse.

Educators know and understand that children sometimes stretch the truth. But I also realize that at times, their own sense of self-preservation demands they hide the truth. Part of the learning curve for new teachers is to fine-tune their own skills of reading body language so that they can interpret a child's nonverbal language that reflects mood and temperament just as well as they evaluate written and oral language. Each new student revs up the need and opportunity for teachers to refresh their ability to interpret each student's nonverbal communication signals.

I was in about the middle of my career when I noticed a fifth-grade boy's demeanor change from active participation to sad withdrawal. Uncharacteristically, he squirmed around and appeared unable to get comfortable. I wondered what was wrong, but didn't question him, expecting to see him in the choir rehearsal at the end of the day.

He attended the rehearsal, as expected, but still seemed uncomfortable and inattentive. He sang very little and didn't relate to those sitting near him. When we started learning a new piece, he held the music so haphazardly that it fell out of his hands. He let a neighbor retrieve the scattered score. His normal musical leadership was missing. I wondered if he might be sick.

At the end of the rehearsal, I entrusted the choir to parent volunteers for dismissal and asked the boy to stay for a minute. He complied, still withdrawn, but not surly. I said, "I noticed that you didn't participate in class and in rehearsal. Are you not feeling well?"

"No, Ma'am. I'm not sick."

"Is there a reason for this change? You usually sing so well."

"I just have this thing on my back. It hurts, 'specially when I have to sit so long."

"Is it where you could show me?"

"Yes, Ma'am. I already showed the nurse. She's gonna take me home today and talk to my mom."

He pulled up his t-shirt enough to show most of his back. On his fairly dark skin, the red line of a belt laid a diagonal path from his left shoulder all the way down his back and was still visible where it disappeared beyond the waistband of his jeans. I wondered if the buckle had hit his buttocks and if the bruise from it caused the discomfort when he had to sit. There were two lesser lines where I assumed he had tried to escape the thrashing. It brought up vivid images of the *Roots* series that had aired on television not long before this young boy suffered the blows of an angry father.

"Can you tell me what happened?"

"No, Ma'am. I'll get in trouble. I think I had an accident."

"Please tell the nurse exactly what happened so that she can help you. If this was not an accident, she will make sure that it does not happen again. Do you understand?"

"Yeah. She's a nice lady. She gives me and my family clothes so we look as good as the rich kids. She'll talk to my mom."

In those days, teachers were still allowed to hug students. I gave him a hug and told him that he could always talk to me. I walked with him toward the nurse's office. She met us in the hall about half-way between my room and the clinic. Concerned that she had seen the choir members leaving and that he had not come to her office yet, she was afraid he might have forgotten and headed home with a friend. One of the parent volunteers told her she would have to check with me because none of them knew all of the students and weren't sure they could give accurate information.

I said, "I'm sorry I made Jim late. I asked him to stay after rehearsal because he seemed to not be feeling well." I turned to Jim.

"Could you please sit here on the bench while the nurse and I talk for a few minutes?"

"Okay to just stand here? I been sittin' a lot all day."

"Sure. We'll only be a few minutes."

The nurse said, "Thanks for your concern. I've talked with him, and I'm going to take him home so that I can talk to his mother. She's not answering the phone; I wouldn't be surprised if her service has been disconnected. I've had other conversations with her and need to let her know it's time to act. She needs to be prepared to protect herself and her children once I file the report with CPS. I have a safe house plan for her."

I thanked the nurse for her part in helping this family and others in that school and let her know that I wanted to help in any way I could. She said, "Would you be willing to write up a report of what you observed in the student's behavior."

"Of course. I also saw the marks on his back when I asked him if he could show me what was bothering him."

"Just keep your eyes open for any other signs of possible abuse if he and his siblings return to this school. Since he is the oldest, he gets the brunt of the blows, but he is not the only member of the family who is suffering." She reminded me of the large fine for not reporting suspected cases of child abuse, which gave us leverage in dealing with parents who were either in denial, overwhelmed, or guilty with the enormity of what they were facing and needed extra help. Paying a large fine for failure to report possible child abuse would have been nothing compared to the guilt I would have felt if I had not reached out to the student and followed through with the nurse.

As we stepped out into the hall, the nurse motioned for the student to follow her. When they reached the door, he waved goodbye and gave a hint of a smile as he headed to his unsafe home sheltered by the nurse's caring professionalism. I couldn't help but guess that he was hoping the nurse would help his mother take him and his siblings away, which I knew was her plan. I also knew I would never forget him and hoped he would add his voice to another choir if he had to transfer to a different school. I prayed that he never would have to squirm in his seat to get through another class or rehearsal again.

BIRTHPLACE

I grew up in Central Florida. Because a large percentage of the population of my hometown was from the North, my accent was not what might be expected from the Deep South or other areas of Florida.

I began my teaching career in South Carolina. When I started a music lesson in one of the lower grades—first or second, I think—a girl raised her hand to get permission to say something. Rather than saying, "Where are you from?' she said, "Ms. Or-ray-yull, you a Yankee?"

Surprised by her question and verbiage, I said, "No. My home is farther south than South Carolina. I'm from Florida." With the naivete of a first-year teacher, I thought she could or would relate to me more positively if she understood that my home state was in the south, even if my hometown was atypical of the Deep South.

Her slowly drawled response was, "Ya' soun' jus' lack one uv 'em."

There it was: the community's continued *us vs. them* mentality that went with the Confederate flags and the *Jesus Saves* laundromat. All it took was a voice in noncompliance with the local accent for me to be lumped into the "outsider" category. In the context, I was proud to be *one uv 'em* and hoped that the girl and all the other students I taught there would notice that my treatment of all students was consistent, even with those who had different accents, different skin tones, and different family challenges.

GEOGRAPHY LESSON

In the school where I taught for the longest time period, there were over three dozen different languages represented among the students.

Being in the Houston area, any country that produced oil and gas had expats in local schools—Norway, Scotland, Nigeria, Qatar, Venezuela, India, Malaysia, Canada, Indonesia, Mexico, and more were represented in our school population. Those who were not native-born USA citizens were enriched by learning multiculturalism first-hand rather than from a book.

The classroom teacher told me when she brought her second-grade class to my room that there would be a new student coming into the classroom before the lesson was over. She asked me to be on the lookout for the new student and to introduce her to the class. If she knew, she didn't mention the new student's home country.

About fifteen minutes after the class began, one of the office personnel brought the new student to my room. She said, "This is Adamma, and her family has just moved here from Nigeria." I immediately thought of the boy in the class whose family also came from Nigeria.

After the new student was seated in the circle, I had each student introduce themselves by chanting their name in response to my chant to them. When it was his turn, the boy from Nigeria would not stop with mere participation. He felt compelled to talk to the class, especially the new friend. He became unusually animated.

Once he chanted his name, he went right on, "Ms. Dr. Orrell, can I tell everyone about my trip to Nigeria? I know all about that long trip our new friend had to make in a plane. We just got back from a visit to Nigeria. You have to flay all night, and the plane has to keep going and going—(long pause, big breath)—and going and going. When you finally get over land and you see that it's really, really dirty, you know you are about to land in Nigeria."

There were a few spontaneous *ewoos*, but I redirected the focus on making music together by starting a rhythmic echo game that led into an African folk song. This is one experience I will never forget because of the poignancy and the sincerity of the boy who told it. He was obviously happy to be living his life in America and delighted to welcome someone from his home country. Adamma appeared to be adjusting to the new environment as well as any second grader could react to such a milestone move.

YOU CAN'T GO TO SUNSET HILL

On the day of the choir's Christmas concert, one of the best singers came up to me in the cafeteria and said, "Ms. Orrell, me and my friends can't come tonight."

Concerned, but confident that I could solve whatever the problem was, I said, "What's the problem—transportation?"

"Yes, Ma'am. Nobody can bring us to school tonight. My daddy was gonna but his car broke down."

I said, "That's alright. I'll stop by your house and pick you up. Just tell your friends to meet us there.

The student looked at me with a pleading look on her face and said, "Oh, no, Ms. Orrell. You don't supposed to come to Sunset Hill after dark." I was appalled to see that a young girl would have to consider such a divisive cultural leftover. She seemed surprised that I was not aware of the unspoken rules concerning an Anglo person driving into an African American neighborhood after dark. I did not sense that she meant I would not be safe, but that it was so against social norms that I would be ostracized, and she might even be punished for allowing it to happen. It felt like she was taking on the responsibility of my well-being within the greater community.

I cherished her honesty and concern as she considered her need for transportation and the futility of my offer. But my reserves of courage and wisdom seemed horribly inadequate to bridge the divide outside of the music classroom and hallways of the school. Children should never have to feel compelled to teach adults societal norms of exclusivity, even if their intent is to spare the adult repercussions of their own *tribe's* making.

"I'm sorry I was not aware of that. Please try to find someone else who can bring you. We really need your voices, and I hate for you to miss the concert after you've worked so hard to learn your parts."

"Okay. We'll try. Can we still sing in the dress rehearsal this afternoon?"

"Of course! That will make the dress rehearsal even better than the concert will be if you can't find a ride. Thank you for letting me know about the problem. I hope you can find transportation, but if not, I understand."

NAME-CALLING

I must have really aggravated a fifth-grade boy. I was not able to verify that his written outburst was intended for me and, if so, what the issue was. But I knew from his note how he felt about someone.

As I was teaching, I noticed that he was hunched over, apparently trying to hide something he was writing. I walked over near his desk to see if he was writing on paper or on the desktop because the paper was too small to be seen from the front of the room. Once I did see it, I asked him to put it away since there was no need for him to be writing during the activity. He boldly said, "Here. You can have it. It's yours anyway." I could tell from the tone of his voice that it was not a love note.

Although he was in the fifth grade, the penmanship looked more like a second or third grader's writing. His written message was, "You is a got dam shit." I kept a straight face and calm demeanor as I tried to keep the class engaged and attempted to monitor his behavior and attitude unobtrusively.

When the class was over, I called him aside and asked, "Could you please tell me what I did to make you so angry?" His only response was a silent sulk. I turned the note over to his classroom teacher and asked her to let me know if he said anything about what had prompted the sentiment in the note. So far as I know, he never let anyone know what had triggered his anger.

As I reflect on the incident decades later, I wonder if perhaps he really intended it for a classmate and redirected it when I confronted him. Perhaps he thought the consequences would be less if he directed his anger toward me rather than to a classmate. Maybe he feared the intended recipient. Perhaps something had happened at home and the note was intended for a family member. All I know for certain is that someone had caused a strong response from him—a response not typical of his behavior when I taught his class—something that he needed help to process, and I was not able to help him resolve it. If it was intended for a classmate, his deflecting it to me may have helped keep him out of a playground fight. I wish I could know with certainty that it was a simple spillage of an inconsequential pique on paper but latching onto that possibility could only be a salve for my own ego's being under attack by a fifth-grade boy.

QUESTIONABLE FASHION

One of the things I have always loved about children is their honesty. During the early '70s, I still wore high heels to school and dressed as well as a teacher's salary would allow. It was a time for bodysuit fashion. They were like an infant's onesie with large snaps in the crotch. Using the restroom was an ordeal that required unfastening the crotch of the bodysuit, pulling up the garment before pulling panties and/or panty hose down, guarding against possible wayward sprinkles, and finally re-pulling under garments into place and re-fastening the bodysuit. Matching up the grippers was always a challenge as one hand pulled the back side of the crotch to the front side and tried to get the grippers to grip. Having the skills of a contortionist would have helped. But bodysuits were the trendy way to keep the hip-huggers low without having shirttails flowing or love-handles showing.

In those days, music educators' schedules typically allowed for five minutes of "travel time" between each class. In reality, though, one class was usually ready to enter the music room while the previous class was ready to exit, making restroom breaks hasty at best, and then only at the mercy of the classroom teacher who might stay for a minute to supervise the changing of the class. Classroom teachers were eager to begin their planning period.

I matched up a white-collared navy knit bodysuit with burgundy knit pants that rode low on the hips and flared wide at the ankles. A couple of the choir members came up to me as they exited the school bus one morning. They stared at me as long as they dared, whispered among themselves, then one said, "Hey, Ms. Orrell. We was just wonderin'—What you tryin' to BE?"

They apparently saw my fashion statement as a costume rather than an outfit for a young professional. I looked more closely at what they were wearing and realized that their clothes were likely hand-me-downs from older family members or friends and reflected outdated styles.

I smiled and said, "Does that mean that you like this outfit or not?"

"Nah—just wonderin.'"

I kept monitoring the buses unloading and the girls went on to their classrooms.

I SEEN HER

While on lunch duty, as I walked up and down the aisles in the cafeteria, I noticed two or three third-grade girls whispering as I passed by. One of them called me back and asked, "Ms. Orrell, ain't it true you drank?"

I said, "Well, sometimes I have a glass of wine with dinner."

The girl in the know gave an elbow punch to one of the friends and said, "Tole ya so. I seen her car at the licker store."

Never expect anonymity if you have a bumper sticker that states, "Take an autoharp player home to dinner."

NO PARTY GOING ON

I was aware that one of my younger students was on the list for frequent absenteeism. He was from one of the poverty-stricken families, and the school nurse had taken him under her wing in a mentoring role, hoping to help him find his academic footing.

The nurse was absent one day, and the person who was subbing happened to be British. When the substitute nurse saw a note regarding what to do in case this particular child was reported absent for the day, she picked up the phone and placed a call to the child's home. Because she assumed that the child was *playing hooky*, she was not surprised when she heard a child's voice answer the call.

With her crisp British accent, the substitute nurse asked, "With which party do I have the pleasure of speaking?"

To which the boy responded, "Huh?"

She repeated the same question, and the boy, still utterly confused, said, "Ma'am, there ain't no party goin' on. I gots the crud."

WATCH OUT FOR GOD

I had a first-grade class in my room and, as usual, I sat with them on the floor in a circle. We were playing a game toward the end of class. Because they loved to keep score, I asked a girl to show with her fingers the number of points the two teams were earning. She accidentally put up the middle finger in the score-keeping process. The entire class erupted with a gasp. Someone called out, "Ms. Dr. Orrell, she put up her middle finger."

I said, "It's okay," and tried to ignore their concern. Since this is such a big deal to first graders, they just would not let it drop. Remarks erupted with no thought of getting permission to speak.

"She's going to be in trouble with her momma."

"I'm going to tell my momma. She won't let me play with kids that do that."

"My daddy does that all the time, but my momma tells him not to."

I over-talked the melee. "It's alright. I can't play the piano without my middle fingers, so I think they are good fingers." I could tell they were not *buying* that, so I started demonstrating how I used each finger at the piano. They had outgrown the kindergarten song, "Where is Thumbkin?" and were in the know about the dastardly third finger.

With the buzz of concern still filling the air, one boy jumped up and shouted, "No! Ms. Dr. Orrell, don't you dare use the middle finger. God'll strike you dead and send you straight to hell, and I mean you'll be there in two seconds! Just like that! (Finger snap) Two seconds, tops!" He was so upset that he couldn't talk fast enough in his concern for my imminent strike-down by God and so earnest that I knew I had to acknowledge his feelings.

I said, "I appreciate your concern, but we do need to get on with the game. I promise I'll be careful with my fingers."

That experience made me wonder what sort of teachings he had been exposed to. I felt sorry that such an impressionable child was growing up to view God as a spy in the sky who would kill people out of anger over the middle finger. I wondered if his parents would be embarrassed or proud if they knew of his outburst. I fear they would have been proud.

JACK-IN-THE-BOX

In one of the years in the school where the balance between extremely low-income families and extremely high-income families was skewed, a second-grade class was in my room. One of the students in a different class had given me a jack-in-the-box for Christmas. Since I knew that several of the classmates were from families not likely to have a jack-in-the-box in their house, I wanted to share my gift with them.

I taught a game song in which the students act out the part of Jack while singing the song. After they were familiar enough to sing it and play the game, I showed them the gift and explained, "This jack-in-the-box is very special because the *jack* is a cat holding a fiddle. That lets me know that the student who gave it to me made sure the gift had something to do with music. The *jack* can be almost anything, but this one is a cat with a fiddle like in the nursery rhyme."

Several spoke at once and started tapping the beat and chanting, "Hey diddle, diddle, the cat and the fiddle. . ."

"That's right! You remember!"

When I asked for a show of hands from those who had seen a jack-in-the-box, several hands remained still. I held the box in my hand and walked around the circle as I talked so that each child could see it up close and touch it.

"I have a special shelf in my home where I keep things that children give me." Perhaps unwisely, I continued, "Since I do not have children of my own, gifts from students are extra, extra special to me. One of my favorites is a rock from a beach. The student was in the fourth grade and painted an *L* on the rock. She told me it would always remind me of love. This jack-in-the-box makes me think of how beautiful violin music is and how much fun we have when we chant the Cat and the Fiddle nursery rhyme."

After demonstrating the mechanics of the toy, I had the children practice acting out being a jack-in-the-box. We were about ready to sing the song and play the game when I noticed that one of the boys who usually was vivacious had a look of extreme concern on his face, a deep frown replacing his usual wide smile. The look of concern swirled with more than a tinge of sadness. For a second, I thought he was sad because he did not have a jack-in-the-box at home. He tended to speak impulsively, and that day was no exception. He said, "Ms. Orrell, you mean you ain't got no children?"

I answered, "No, but I have many nieces and nephews and hundreds of students."

He thought for a moment longer, then said, "Ms. Orrell, you got you a husband?"

Recently divorced, I shook my head and said, "No."

He placed one hand on his chin and looked like he was in even deeper thought, almost a caricature of *The Thinker*.

Another blurt. "Ms. Orrell, I just believe you could find you a man."

I thanked the student who was caught up in his perception of my well-being. I knew he meant it as a compliment. "Let's stand up and play the game and sing the song. Watch out for each other when you jump out of your pretend box."

I held the toy and tried to sync its jump with theirs so that everyone jumped into the air at the same time. The cat and fiddle jack-in-the box covered in fabric printed with roses and leaves still sits on one of the bookshelves in my home office. And now it will be hours before I can make the song quit ringing in my ears.

TAKING CARE OF A NEW SISTER

In the same school, I was using a variety of percussion instruments with a first or second grade class. Included in the group of instruments were many different types of unpitched, hand-held instruments such as drums, wood blocks, guiros, and triangles.

When part of the class completed the first round of playing the instruments, I noticed that a boy was sound asleep. I assumed he must be sick and walked over to him, gently shook his shoulder, and called his name. He raised his head and looked at me as though he wasn't even sure where he was.

It was a Monday, and I immediately presumed he had gone to bed late because of getting out of his regular routine over the weekend and watching TV too late. Having sufficient presence of mind to ask rather than to accuse him of staying up too late, I said, "Ray, did you stay up too late last night because you were watching TV?"

Deep resentment mixed on his face with the look of exhaustion beyond his years. He said, "No, Ma'am, Ms. Orrell. My new baby sister and my momma come home from the hospital. I had to stay awake to make sure the rats didn't get on her. I ain't been watchin' no TV."

My heart wept for him. I patted his shoulder and said, "That's a brave thing to do. I understand why you're so sleepy. Would you like to go to the nurse's clinic? Maybe you could take a nap on the cot."

"No, Ma'am. Music's my favorite class. Can I just listen?"

"Sure. You will be the best listener in the whole school today. Just let me know if you decide you want to play an instrument."

Even though I was an experienced teacher by then and viewed myself as a sensitive child advocate, the student taught me to extend my patience farther and to temper assumptions with facts before attempting to judge exterior symptoms that only hint at the internal struggle.

KEEPING A SECRET

After I retired in 2009, I worked almost full-time for several years, taking long-term sub assignments in Music. At one of the schools where I subbed, I became a mentor for a boy in second grade and continued the mentoring relationship through his eighth grade.

I had heard that I was nominated for *Mentor of the Year* and wondered why the principal came by the library and took a photo of the mentee and me during one of our meetings. I knew that most schools in the district had a mentorship program but did not know whether the possible recognition was within that one school or district-wide.

It turned out that there was one winner per school, not a district-wide winner, and there was a big Texas-size recognition gala. I was honored to be among those at the gala and to see the photo of my mentee and me on display.

On the day before the big event, I was playing a game with Tom. Completely out of context with our conversation, he said, "Dr. Orrell, you already know I'm good at games and with my pet snake, but if I knew a secret, I'd be really good at keeping it."

I said, "That's a very thoughtful thing to do because most people enjoy surprises and are disappointed if someone spoils them."

He knew more about the gala than I did. By then, I knew I would be attending, but didn't learn about his secret until I arrived at the mentor recognition party that included dinner and a silent auction. He had written a letter to me, as had all the mentees of those being recognized, and the principal had attached the photo she took to the letter. The final sentence in the letter stated, "I chose to use a pink pen because girls like pink." Since I was seventy years old then, I relished being viewed by a third-grade boy as a *girl who liked pink*. He had never seen me wear pink but had absorbed some cultural bias and applied it to me. And through it all, he kept his secret about the letter and picture *really good*.

REAL PEOPLE

At one of the schools where I taught a long-term sub assignment after retirement, there was no time on the schedule for restroom breaks for the music teachers. In most schools, there are at least five minutes between classes so that the music specialists can take a restroom break and not have to ask the classroom teacher to stay until they return. At this school, there were two Music teachers, which allowed one of us to take care of the double classes for a few minutes while the other took a restroom break. When the lunch period hit, we both made a beeline for the restroom before diving into our twenty-minute lunch in the music room.

The large teachers' lounge was on the other side of the building, so I usually used the girls' restroom right across the hall from the Music room. On one afternoon when I was hurriedly trying to use the restroom before the first class after lunch, I saw a first-grade girl down on all-fours attempting to crawl out of the first stall. It seemed odd because the door was open about six inches. Recognizing the child, I spoke her name and said, "Please come on out of the stall, wash your hands, and get back to your class. I have to use the restroom too." She complied.

By the time the girl got to the sink, I was in the stall she had left, the first one, with the door locked. Another girl was in the second stall. She and I heard the crawler say to herself, "I wonder why teachers have to use the bathroom."

The girl in the stall next to me spoke up. "Because they are just like us. And guess what? They're EVEN REAL PEOPLE!" By the time she finished her remark, she was yelling.

I had to bite my lip to keep from laughing out loud. I knew that young students often ask teachers if they live at the school, and when they see us out and about in a grocery store or gas station, they look at us as though we are aliens, but I had never heard questions about teachers' need to use the restroom.

When I later related the story to the classroom teacher, she explained that a girl from her class had gotten locked in that same stall the previous day and had to crawl out under the door. Apparently, the girl who was trying to crawl out of the stall even though the door was open just wanted to see what it felt like. Maybe she thought she should practice it just like all children practiced active shooter drills. I then understood her behavior, but still laughed when I told my teaching partner that at least one precocious first grader knew we are real people.

I GOTTA NAME
(apologies to Jim Croce)

In the early eighties, I took a few years off from teaching and worked in the business world. I sold life insurance annuities to teachers for one year and was a stockbroker the following two years. After those three years in business, I was ready to return to the music classroom. I applied to several school districts, but there were no openings in all but one of the districts to which I applied.

Finally, three weeks after the fall semester had begun, I was asked to interview. The interview with the music supervisor went outstandingly well. She told me that she wanted to hire me but did not have a *plum* position to offer. I was upfront with her about the type of position I hoped to eventually have and assured her that I was willing to take almost any position because I knew that in such a large district, if it was not a good situation, I could request a transfer when other options became available. With that understanding, I called the school that needed a Music teacher and made an appointment for an interview with the principal.

With my background of working in rural and small city districts and one large city district, I thought I was prepared for almost any situation. But nothing I had seen or been involved in could have prepared me for what I experienced in the setting in which the interview took place.

The principal was a large man with a linebacker's build, a courtly manner, and broad smile. He welcomed me in the front office and ushered me toward the library where he introduced me to the librarian.

"This here's 'Ms. Moosic Lady."

I tried to keep my eyebrows down as I looked at the librarian. She lowered her eyes. I could almost swear I detected a slight head shake as if she were embarrassed by the introduction.

He continued, gesturing toward the librarian, "She can tell you all about the strang program we had. She knew that moosic lady real good, didn't you?"

The librarian blushed and extended her hand. "My name's Laurie. I've been here a couple of years. One of the former Music specialists tried to start a strings program, but there was a problem with the funds that were allocated to help with instrument rental expenses."

The principal interjected, "Don't be 'fraid to tell her the troof. We gonna get that money back and teach these kids some strangs."

With his nod toward the door, we started walking toward the main exit.

"I guess that supervisor lady done tole you we have Moosic and PE in the portable."

"No, but I've taught in portables before."

"Can you teach strangs?"

"No. I have special training in an approach to Music Education called Orff-Schulwerk."

"Never heard tell of it. Do it use strangs?"

"No. I'm not certified in strings, but I believe the students would enjoy my approach. I also have always had a choir in schools where I've taught and would want to continue that as an extracurricular activity."

"These kids can't be comin' up here early or stayin' late. This schedule has some extree plannin' time in it. Maybe you could do choir practices then. I don't know if we could have a moosic lady that can't teach strangs, though. You know, we gotta find that money and make the parents happy."

"Could you tell me exactly what happened and what needs to be done about the funds? I definitely am not qualified to teach a strings program, but perhaps I could help with finding the funds."

"Nah. Only one that might can hep is the liberry lady."

As we entered the portable, the principal said, "You could share this with the PE lady, can't you?"

I perused the large room trying to spot equipment and materials.

"Is there a closet where things are stored?"

"Nah. Everwhat's here is what you see. This here's the PE lady. She's from up north, but she does a real good job with the kids."

Her face lit up. "I'm Janie. I'm very pleased to meet you and hope you'll stay a while if you're hired for this position."

"I know it's a little late in the year to be hiring but I'm not sure if there has been a Music teacher these first weeks of school."

"No. There have been several here to interview, but the position is still open."

"How do you split the schedule when you both need to use this space? It's adequate for one class at a time, but what about when it rains, and you have to have class in this room?"

"It usually works out so that the Music teacher takes that class to the auditorium when I have to teach inside."

"What about when lunch is being served?

"In this size school, lunch doesn't take too long. If necessary, one class can sit on chairs and one class can sit in a circle on the floor and the music teacher and I can handle it."

The principal was ready to get on with the official part of the interview and ushered me toward the exit door. The PE teacher and I said our goodbyes with a mutually cordial tone. Since the principal's back was turned toward us, she motioned with her hand, showing me 5 fingers, then pointing toward me. I read the message to be, "You'll be #5." I pointed to myself and showed my open palm. She nodded. Later, she told me that I was the 5th Music teacher in three years.

On the way to the main building, I again brought up the issue of classroom instruments. He said, "Since the money fer them strangs disappeared, we don't have no way to get them insterments you keep talkin' about. And don't even ask me about no PTA money."

"What about if I ask the Supervisor of Fine Arts about it? There might be some instruments at schools where the Music teacher is not trained to use them."

"Ask her everwhat you want 'cept about the missin' funds. We gonna git 'em back. Sure you can't teach strangs?"

"I'm certain. My certification is Vocal Music Education, K-12."

"Alright. I can let the liberry lady take care of the missin' funds and I'll be callin' the supervisor lady. But as fer as them other insterments is concerned, I can't even promise you a tangerine."

My laugh almost erupted, thinking he was trying to make a joke, feeling the need for some humorous relief. When I looked up at his face, though, I saw that he was serious—serious in his concern about the missing funds; serious in his concern for the students; and serious about getting the Music position filled. Despite his lack of polish and preparation for the responsibilities he was trying to fulfill, I felt sorry for him because I knew too well what it feels like to be in over your head with no lifeline in sight.

When I received the call from the Supervisor, I was happy to accept the offer and to get back into the Music classroom where I felt most at home. I asked her about the possibility of using some of the classroom instruments that might not be needed at other schools, and she managed to find two or three tone bar instruments that are used in Orff-based classes. They were minimal but helped to provide a fairly well-rounded musical environment for that school the one year I was there.

The PE teacher and I worked well together, and I felt pride in the musical strides my students made. The newly formed choir gave two concerts, and about half a dozen boys passed the audition for the Houston Boys Choir.

VALENTINE'S DAY CANDY

While I was at the first school I taught in after attempting a business career, a third-grade class had just come in and sat in the chairs. The PE class was outside, so I had plenty of room for dancing or other movement activities. I was not surprised to see one boy surreptitiously attempting to get candy out of his pocket. I simply reminded the class that we did not eat candy during class, even on Valentine's Day. He complied.

A different boy kept adjusting his shoe. I said, "Do you need help with your shoelace?"

"No, Ma'am. I'm just tryin to get somethin'."

I thought he must have a small piece of gravel in his shoe. After a couple of minutes of fidgeting and digging with his finger, he took off his shoe and sock and pulled out three or four small candy hearts and proudly came up to me and said, "Here, Ms. Orrell. I been savin' these just for you."

I had to keep a straight face and show appreciation while at the same time telling him to put his sock and shoe back on and to leave any other candy alone during class time.

"You gonna' eat 'em right now, aren't you?"

"No. Even teachers are supposed to eat only at lunch time."

I regretted being unable to give him the joy of seeing the recipient of his gift relish the treat, but was thankful that school protocol gave me a way to avoid eating foot-sweated sweet hearts.

BLACK/WHITE

I had a fourth-grade music class in the portable building. One of the boys entered with a snarly attitude, so I assumed he had been involved in some disagreeable situation prior to coming to Music. His bottom lip protruded outward; his arms were crossed across his chest; he slouched in the chair with his feet sprawled out, refusing to participate in any activity. He was really trying my patience, which ordinarily was in sufficient supply.

When I asked him again to sing with the class, he said, "I ain't gonna' sing for no white honkey."

Another student jumped up, planted his feet in front of the name caller, and said, "You can't call her that."

The first one said, "Can so 'cuz that's what she is."

The one taking up for me said, "Nah, she ain't like that. She kinda black/white. You better be nice to her too."

I took that as one of the most meaningful compliments I had ever received from a student. To me, it meant that he saw me as fair and that he expected to have a positive experience in my class. What puzzled me was that the snarly boy had been okay for several months before that incident. I wondered if perhaps someone he trusted had just found out that I was one of the few Anglos on campus and had said something that caused his withdrawal. There was no obvious explanation.

I NEVER KNEW A GENIUS

It was the last week of Music classes for the year. The classroom teacher had stepped into the room and was ready to take the students back to her classroom in the main building. As the students were leaving, I chanted, "Goodbye, _____." In the blank, I inserted the name of the student. They, in turn, chanted their goodbye to me. It made the classroom teacher have to wait for several minutes, but she seemed entranced by this simple dismissal technique. After the last child was in the line, she motioned me aside and with awe whispered, "I never knew a genius before."

Not realizing that she was talking about me, and puzzled by her remark, I said, "I think I've probably known a few people who deserve that distinction. They certainly were remarkable."

She said, "I don't mean nobody else. I mean you. You a genius because you know the name of every single child."

As I stood dumbfounded, she announced to the first child in line, "Go ahead, Little Girl. You may go now. Little Boy, keep your line straight."

The two lines began their precision sidewalk-following trek back to the classroom where every girl and every boy had to share the same moniker because with less than two weeks left in kindergarten, their classroom teacher did not know their names and thought I was a genius because I chanted each name without looking at the attendance list. Even after almost a full academic year on that campus, brain-freezing instances of reality still leapt into my senses. The roller coaster I was on vacillated between the high of the year's progress and the utter helplessness of attempting to climb the next incline with the gauge of hope skirting on *empty*.

CHAPTER 15
BUTTER PECAN DELIGHT

*Blessed be childhood, which brings down something
of heaven into the midst of our rough earthliness.*
Henri Frederic Amiel
(1821-1881)

  Children who are strangers frequently gravitate toward me. Little ones squirm in parents' or other caretakers' embraces, stretch out their arms, and lean toward me. Many times, their eyes connect with mine and seem to lock before their smiles beam. Some old enough to travel without parents have latched on for inflight reassurance, never suspecting that for many years, I would not fly at all, and then only with white knuckles except when a child or two needed me. But I have never had such a dramatic experience with children I do not know as I did that day at Ritter's Frozen Custard.

  With a promise to myself that it would be the final indulgence before resuming pre-COVID-19 dietary discipline, I walked up to the order window at Ritter's Frozen Custard located about five minutes from my house. There is only one other Ritter's in Houston, and it is about half-way to Galveston, a good hour and a half away. The number of weathered cement tables with blue and white striped umbrellas is limited, especially those under sprawling oak trees, so customers routinely share table space.

  The only people ahead of me were a young man and two girls who appeared to be his daughters. One of the girls still wore a diaper under her elastic-waist shorts. The other appeared to be a first or second grader.

  As soon as I stepped onto the 6-foot-apart marker, the younger girl turned around. Her eyes met mine and locked. She started jumping up and down as if her feet were bare and blistering on hot concrete. Her auburn ringlets bounced as though the air teased their elasticity. She could not have been more excited if it had been her birthday and she had just spied the present she wanted more than anything else.

Flits of light in her dark brown eyes danced with as much energy as tips on Fourth of July sparklers and seemed to be ignited by instant recognition. Squeals of spontaneous joy erupted while she waved both arms, showing tiny baby teeth in a face-wide grin. The radiance she exuded sparked a reaction in me I had not felt since my (step)grandchildren were that age. Instinctively, I waved to her and said, "Hi. Are you getting ice cream?"

She broke the eye lock to look at her dad, patted his leg with a toddler's urgency, pointed at me with her other hand, and said, "Look, Daddy, it's *Mommy*!" He turned toward me, nodded, and flashed a big Texas smile.

Racing questions ricocheted through my mind. *Has her mother died? Have her parents recently divorced? Is her mother away on a business trip? Does she identify all females as her mother? Is her mother a redhead?* Too jarred for my mind or emotion to process, I let go of the unanswerable questions and latched on to the moment. I laughed and said, "If it were possible, I would love to be your mommy." By then, her older sister had turned attention away from helping their dad with the order and waved.

Speaking with strong assurance that bordered on mild sibling rivalry, she said, "If you're her mommy, then you have to be my mommy too, because I'm her sister." Her eyes were hazel, same as mine, and her hair was one shade lighter than her sister's—the same as my birth color before Clairol and I become forever friends.

Awash in wishes wrapped in goosebumps, I said, "Oh! That would be so much fun."

My heart didn't know whether to beat out of my chest or to freeze in those moments when I heard two beautiful sisters call me "Mommy." Long before my (step)children gave me grandchildren, in a span of about 12 years, I had suffered two miscarriages, lost premature identical twin girls at birth (one lived 5 hours, the other 16), and lost a stillborn son.

I never wanted anything more intensely than to have children. To compensate, I adored my nieces and nephews and my students at school, in church and city choirs, and in my private piano studio. And then, when COVID-19 guidelines still stipulated rigorous caution except when outside, two delightful young strangers were acting out a fantasy they felt while my entire being in those few minutes knew for the first time what it was like to be called "Mommy. There was too much joy to relive once again the pain of loss.

The dad paid for their treats and began walking toward a table. He smiled again, and with eyes brimming with a father's pride and playful engagement in their fantasy, said, "Bye, *Mom*."

In unison, both girls said, "Bye, *Mommy*."

I stepped up to the window to order, my skin feeling the prickle of hairs standing on end. The teenage boy with pink braids said, "What'll it be today? One scoop or two?" Since Sunday was butter pecan day, I splurged on two scoops and made yet another promise to myself to stop allowing the indulgence in calorie-laden dessert that I craved during the pandemic shutdown.

The *scooper* called out, "This lady's my favorite customer. Don't you go easy on those butter pecan scoops."

I said, "Looks like I just became an instant mom to those two little girls."

"Yeah. They sure are cute, and they totally trusted you."

I paid for my treat and waved again to the dad and his daughters as I headed toward my car. The girls signaled me to join them. We chatted a minute or two before they both patted the cement bench. In a split-second decision, I declined to join them because the dad, although very friendly, had not echoed their invitation. It just seemed a bit presumptuous to join a family outing when only young children had invited me and when the dad and I had not exchanged vaccination information.

On the way to my car, as soon as I licked the first drips of butter pecan, I regretted not seizing the opportunity for further interaction with all three. When I sat in my car, I whipped out a business card from my purse and returned to their table, uncharacteristically leaving the purse in the locked car. As I handed the card to the dad, I said, "I'm a retired music educator from the local school district and teach piano now. It looks like your older daughter might be about the right age to consider taking lessons. If you ever want to discuss it, give me a call."

She became just as animated as her sister had been when she had first seen me. Bouncing up and down on the bench, she said, "Please, Daddy, please, can I take piano lessons with *Mommy*?" The dad told me that they (he and his wife) had told her they would like her to take piano lessons as soon as she *got into it more*. "But Daddy, I really am into it now. Really. Pretty please! When can I start?"

I interjected that I lived close to a near-by intersection. He said, "We've just bought a new house and will be moving about 15-20 minutes farther west. Do you go out that far?"

"No. I teach in my home. It would not be cost effective for me to travel for lessons. Some of my students live an hour or more away from my house. I have a doctorate in Music Education and teach on a Steinway baby grand."

"Oh. Okay. I understand. I'll talk with my wife—their *other mom*—and see if we can work it out as soon as we get the piano out of storage and tuned."

When the girls again said, "Bye, *Mommy*," I said, "My piano students call me Ms. Sue or Dr. Sue."

The dad's head snapped toward me. "Really? Both of their grandmothers are named *Sue*. One goes by *Suzie*, though."

Meanwhile, my butter pecan was crawling over every finger and dripping from my wrist, taking aim at my elbow. I tossed four soggy napkins into a trash bin. The toddler laughed and pointed to the dripping unfrozen custard. The dad said, "Is she dripping her ice cream?"

The piano prospect said, "Yes. Looks like it's coming out of her skin." She and her sister giggled.

Not caring whether I lost all the delicious creaminess to the sidewalk or not, I ignored the drips and addressed the next remarks to the dad. "I need to let you know that meeting you and your daughters today has been both a delightful and profound experience for me." There was an unspoken understanding that I was speaking only to him. The girls got quiet and focused on eating their cups of frozen custard. "I just had to come back over to talk with you, not so much because of the possibility of your needing a piano teacher, but because this encounter has been meaningful in ways almost impossible to articulate."

I explained in rather clinical terms that my own children had been lost at birth and that I adored children and working with them. "I have (step)grandchildren older than your daughters and miss being around younger children."

He chuckled. "Well, they are obviously thrilled to meet you."

"I've got to get a cup to catch this trickle that is turning into a torrent. I've really enjoyed talking with you."

Again, "Bye, *Mommy*."

I turned around and hurried back to the counter.

At the window, the *scooper* handed me a cup. I placed the cone in it just in time for a gust of wind to topple it onto the damp paper towel I had requested. He quickly wet another swatch of towel as I jerked my hand out of the top mound and snatched more napkins from the dispenser.

The dad and his daughters ate their custard quietly as I rushed to my car, stood at the door, and frantically sucked globs of melted butter pecan custard, trying to get it under control before the saturated cone collapsed. The dregs of a root beer and its melting ice were still in the cup holder. After finally sitting behind the steering wheel, but with the door still open, I used some of the ice to make my hands a little less sticky and finished the soggy cone and melted custard before heading home, wondering if I would ever see *my children* again.

CHAPTER 16

A MAILBOX POST, A FEW SMALL SCREWS AND A MOUNTAIN OF MULCH

When you betray somebody else, you also betray yourself.
Isaac Bashevis Singer
(1902-1991)

Throughout the summer and early fall of 2007, my husband, Chris, and I watched the building process turn an undeveloped lot into complete fulfillment of our dream house less than a year before it became a nightmare for me. Stud by stud and brick by brick, we watched the daily progress as the builders managed work schedules and we managed the selection of every single option for each of the finishing materials. About nine months after moving in, the dream home became a nightmare for me. We lived in those 4,000 + square feet of luxury only a few months before I received the news of his sudden death while I was attending a composer's workshop out of state.

There were too many immediate problems to solve to face the grieving process. After the funeral was over and relatives had gone home, one of the most painful and demanding tasks was to close his law office. Among the papers I found on his desk were my notarized retirement papers, which he should have mailed to Austin that week. It was out of character for him to neglect such a responsibility—one of those unusual things that switches a mistake into an advantage. I knew there was no way I could keep the large house and hoped I could continue teaching in the same district for at least one more year while

I sorted out my plans.

I've heard at least half a dozen different labels used for such a serendipitous happenstance—blessing, God-wink, God-thing, synchronicity, and more. But no one label adequately describes the experience and tends to dilute the sense of awe. I choose to accept my history of synchronous events with gratitude and leave the logic of definition to those who find comfort in concretized explanation.

I gave some thought to the possibility of simply filing the retirement papers and focusing on solving the problem of an oversized mortgage with inadequate income to support it without his income, but felt the need to be with my colleagues and to let both financial and emotional dust settle before I took that final step to end my teaching career.

When I called the school district where I had taught for 15 years, the personnel administrator informed me that I could be rehired at full salary. If the paperwork had been sent to Austin, I would have been rehired at only a beginner teacher's salary. With the help of Chris' closest friend, who also was an attorney, Chris' staff, and many volunteer assistants from my school, we closed the office within a month.

When I called the Director of Fine Arts, I learned that my position had already been filled and that the only elementary music position open required teaching strings as an enrichment program. With strong doubt that I could talk the principal into substituting a choir or other instrumental ensemble for the strings program, and knowing I was not qualified to teach strings, I made an appointment for the interview despite the misgivings.

The principal and I connected professionally and personally. The interview lasted over two hours. She assured me that I could teach the strings program because other music educators she had hired also were not certified in strings and taught the program successfully.

A big advantage for me was that the other music teacher at the school had a brother who played violin with a major professional orchestra. She was a concert pianist and had been at the school for several years. Her brother had taught her the skills to teach beginning strings students and was available if we had questions or concerns. She, in turn, helped me learn to play the assigned piece(s) and to develop basic skills to assure the students would not pick up bad habits from me.

For that entire school year, 2008-2009, I was an emotional zombie—numb with no desire to feel what I knew was churning just under my skin. For the first time since the funeral in late June, I cried on the way home after the last Christmas concert at school when I noticed the wreaths on city lamp posts and felt the emptiness waiting in the big house—no desire, much less a plan, to put up the 9-foot Christmas tree.

But I had four grandchildren who expected to have Christmas with "Gramma Sue." The granddaughters were old enough to remember their Granddaddy well and to have a basic understanding of the finality of death. But the grandsons were not yet four years old and struggled to match their siblings' and cousins' understanding. To maintain their Christmas tradition, I put up their individual three-foot Christmas trees and set out a few decorations to relieve some of the emptiness and unwanted stillness.

The girls came to spend a night with me and to help with the small trees. Emma had turned 6 just weeks before Chris' death. At the breakfast table, she said, "Gramma Sue, your house is too loud."

"What do you mean?"

"It makes noises when I try to go to sleep."

"I know. It's just the new lumber getting used to temperature changes."

Kathryn, barely 8, said, "And when we have on our dress shoes, it makes an echo when we walk on the tile. I miss having Granddaddy with us."

"We all miss him. But we know he would want us to have a good holiday with lots of fun together."

Kathryn continued, "Gramma Sue, do you have a boyfriend?"

"No. But if I ever do, I will call him my man-friend. When you're old enough to have grandchildren, it sounds a little silly to call someone a girlfriend or boyfriend."

Emma stroked my hand and said, "Why do you have to be old?"

"Oh, Emma, I'm not old. I've just had a lot of birthdays." Kathryn looked at me as if to say, *I know you're just saying that, Gramma Sue. I* missed hearing her call me "Gamma Shoe" like she did when she first learned to talk.

When the family gathered for Christmas, Chrisser (Kathryn and Emma's brother) patted my elbow to get my undivided attention and said, "Gramma Sue, did you know we lost Granddaddy? I don't know how, but I guess he got lost somewhere."

I picked him up and held him as tightly as his grandfather had held me. "Do you mean that you think Granddaddy is not with us because we can't find him?"

"Uh-huh, Mommy said we lost him."

"Sometimes grownups use words that mean more than one thing. When people get older, an illness or accident may cause them to kind of go to sleep and never wake up. We'll never get to see Granddaddy again because he had a heart attack and will never wake up. That's what we mean when we say we lost him. We lost him from our life, but he is not really lost. It's a little hard to understand when you are so young, but we'll talk about it any time you want to ask questions."

Chrisser twirled my hair as he said, "Oh. I thought you could help us find him."

His cousin, Jack, who is just three weeks younger than Chrisser, had been listening. I put Chrisser down and started walking toward the sofa where Jack sat in the middle. I sat beside him and motioned for Chrisser to sit on the other side of me. Jack said, "So—Granddaddy is really dead?"

"That's right, but his love will always be with us, and we will always remember him."

Chrisser said, "Gramma Sue, I have your shoulders because I'm strong like you." He could not possibly have had an inkling of what his identification with me meant. To me, it meant, *not sharing DNA does not matter.*

Not to be outdone, Jack said, "I'm going to do music like you, Gramma Sue."

I hugged them close and said, "Let's go over to the piano and sing some Christmas songs."

Chrisser built his shoulders when he joined a gym in high school, and Jack took piano lessons with me for about two years before he went into percussion in middle school.

I completed that academic year, then turned in my resignation and went over to Austin to personally walk the papers through the system. I had reached the point of no longer receiving much of a raise each year because school budgets favored raising entry level salaries over pay increases for long-term employees. I was bone-weary tired, but still had plenty of energy for basic music classroom responsibilities. Accepting long-term sub assignments was the right move for me. For about five additional years, I taught nearly full-time, but did not have the paperwork of lesson plans or responsibilities of planning and producing a concert each semester. That allowed me to finish paying for my piano and to build my piano studio. Once the piano studio schedule could no longer accommodate a full day in the schools, I stopped taking sub assignments and notified the district office to take me off the list. At that point, I also started pursuing courses in Creative Nonfiction and divided my time between coursework, writing, and teaching piano.

Chris' mother died in the spring of 2009. We had leased our smaller house. The real estate bubble had burst while we were going through the process of putting the smaller house on the market and closing on the dream house. She left sufficient funds so that I could consider at least a partial refurb job on the old house. I knew I could not stay in the big house and notified my tenants that I would not renew the lease and needed to have access to the property by June 1st. The news did not matter to them because they had decided to return to the rural county where they used to live.

By then, it was the summer of 2009. Retired from teaching music only a few weeks and finally facing the grieving process, it was time to do as much refurbishing of the old house as possible and pack for the return move. I looked forward to opening a piano studio in the fall.

The couple who had leased the small house had five children, all of whom were homeschooled. They were a lovely family, but five kids are five kids, and normal wear and tear was accelerated. They left the house and yard in a state as ready for occupancy as could be expected, but the house was not ready for me.

A hailstorm had come through that neighborhood the week before I took possession. My realtor suggested that we have the roof checked for possible damage. Most houses on my block had significant damage. The insurance company's inspector was hesitant about approving a claim until the realtor's assistant hobbled on her two metal canes to the foot of the ladder and yelled to him and his assistant up on the roof, "You're not going to tell me that you're going to deny a claim for this widow when she needs to get back in this house with a dependable roof, are you?"

The inspector said, "Well, it's marginal. Other roofs on this block look worse than this one."

"But this one is damaged, right? We can see the upturned shingles from here."

"Yes, Ma'am. But it's not all that bad."

"How many storms do you think it will stand?"

"Oh, I couldn't say."

"Then put on the new roof so that she can be at peace and not have to worry every time we get a storm warning. Treat her like you'd want your mother to be treated."

I hoped he loved his mother.

"Okay, Ma'am. I'm gonna have to put it in as recommended, but not required, though."

"Put it in however you want, but just be sure it gets done ASAP. She's got to move in within two weeks."

I had recoiled at the realtor's assistant's brusque communication tone more than once, but that day, I was thankful that she played every card in the deck to get the 15-year-old roof replaced after obvious hail damage that didn't quite reach the insurance company's definition of "necessary." I wouldn't have been surprised if she had said, "Don't make me have to climb up that ladder with these crutches to make my point."

I put the dream home on the market soon after Chris' death but the burst real estate bubble produced no offers. I attempted to get the bank to agree to a short sale, but they would not agree. I lived month to month not knowing when a foreclosure notice would appear and hearing horror stories about sudden evictions being enforced and furniture being confiscated once a foreclosure was in process. I was managing to make regular payments on the furniture but could not maintain the mortgage payments.

My husband died with neither insurance nor any other financial assets. Every discretionary penny we had was invested in upgrades to the dream home. We were told that the cash we had paid for the upgrades would be reimbursed at the closing with that amount being rolled into the mortgage. But that was before the market collapsed. We learned of the changed financial arrangements at the closing. We felt it was too late to back out of the deal and that there was no good financial decision to be made at the time. If we declined to close, we would lose the money invested in the upgrades and would be back where we started in house-planning, but without any cash reserves.

I moved back to the smaller house on schedule. The foreclosure notice came a few months after I moved. While I did not advertise the fact that the big house ended up in foreclosure, I felt more grief and frustration than shame. I knew it would affect my credit rating, but I also knew I could reestablish an excellent rating.

In hindsight, of course, I would not have agreed to buy the house with Chris if we had had a crystal ball regarding his death or the real estate market collapse, but I refused to take on false guilt on top of the honest grief and frustration. More deeply, I felt gratitude for the help from dozens of people throughout that year along with determination to get beyond the immediate fall-out of Chriss' death.

It was a relief to find out that I would be allowed to keep the furniture and that I would not have to pay income tax on the amount of the foreclosed mortgage. The much smaller mortgage on the smaller house was manageable and would be paid off in a few years. Rebuilding my credit was just a matter of time.

Working within the confines of a tight budget, and with the small inheritance from my mother-in-law, I provided as much of the labor as possible for the refurbishment of the smaller house. The anticipation of removing myself from the nightmare and reclaiming the first house we had bought became the revised dream.

The temperature was in triple digits with high humidity. I had been working for at least eight hours that day ripping up old carpet and vinyl, then cramming the pieces into large black trash bags. On the first day when I piled old carpet, pad, and vinyl at the curb, the trash collector left them there. I called the company to complain and inquire. With more snark than usual, I said, "What do I need to do to get old flooring picked up?"

"Read your service contract, Sweetie. We don't pick up nothin' that's not bagged or bundled. Just stuff it all in those big black bags, and we'll take it for you."

"Okay. Thanks for the information."

That added one more step to the process, but I must admit that the piles of bags looked less tacky than the mountain of ugly used flooring, even if the bags did remind me of body bags. Streaks of sweat and tears of frustrated grief smeared the bare slab. Sprinkles on the bulging black bags blended with humidity while the setting sun lit the sky orange.

On the previous day, I had bought a new mailbox and realized that I needed a new post for it. Thinking it was time for a break from paint fumes and from the painter who was falling short of his reputed standards, I left the house in his inadequate hands and went to Home Depot. After taking my time to find just the right post, I then found an employee to help me get it off the shelf and on to the shopping cart. Pushing the cart at the speed of a student reticent to walk to the principal's office, I managed to guide the post's lumbering bed to the checkout lane without collecting any splinters and without sideswiping merchandise or customers.

Standing in line, I was lost in a review of prioritizing the rest of the evening's work and heard a man behind me say, "Looks like you've got a hot job there." I turned around and saw that he was the best dressed person in the store—a man of average height wearing starched, steam-pressed jeans, a nice plaid shirt, and jaunty suspenders. He appeared to be older than I and spoke with a gentle accent.

"The job's for the handyman, not me," I said.

The man's purchases fit comfortably in his left hand. He opened his palm and explained, "I just had to get a few small screws for repairing an instrument for one of my grandbabies."

"It's nice that you're active in your grandchildren's lives, especially their musical pursuits."

"Yes, I like to go to garage sales and buy discarded instruments, make the repairs, and give them to needy students. But this time, I just needed to fix one of the grandchildren's instruments. They are identical twins, and I'm always looking for something they will enjoy."

Thinking that I might have taught his grandchildren, I inquired as to whether they attended school in the local district. "Oh, no. They don't live here. They live down in the Valley."

When I told him that I had recently retired from teaching music, he looked at me intently and said, "Well, I guess that means you like to dance."

"Yes, I do like to dance, but I haven't done any dancing lately. Since my husband died just a year ago, I've been preoccupied with closing his office, teaching, and moving back to our smaller house."

With no words of condolence, he responded, "Well, since you know all about serious music, I guess you don't like polkas."

"Polkas are okay, especially during Oktoberfest."

His eyes lit up, implying a felt connection. "That's one of my favorite times of the year. I play tuba in a German band in my hometown. Are you familiar with the Melody Ballroom here in Houston?"

"Yes, but I haven't been there for a very long time."

"I thought you would have heard of it. That's where old people go to dance." There was neither a twinkle in his eyes nor a smile on his lips as he made that remark. I thought, *"That's strike one."* I do not use the O-L-D word.

By then, it was time for me to step up to the cashier and pay for my post. As I put my debit card back into my wallet, the man tapped me on the shoulder and said, "Don't leave. We can visit a while longer."

It took just a minute for him to pay for his screws. We walked out of the checkout area and sat down on the mountain of bagged mulch in the front area of the store. I thought sympathetically, *"He must have lost his wife recently and is either really desperate for conversation or is a person who simply does not judge a book by its cover."* My face was as red as an anemic tomato from heat-triggered rosacea; a shower was long overdue; and my gritty hair was pulled back into a stringy ponytail.

After being patient for as long as I could, I said, "I really do need to get back to my house so that the handyman can finish the mailbox job." He agreed that he also needed to get back to his project. As we walked to our cars, he gave me his business card and said, "This is so that you can look me up on the internet and not think I am some kind of a kook." He made no offer to help me put the mailbox post into my Camry. Not that I couldn't do it myself, but a little courtesy wouldn't hurt.

A few days later, I looked up the site listed on his business card and found that he had outstanding professional and academic credentials. He also had asked me to call him if I ever wanted to have coffee together. Intrigued by his credentials, and with some encouragement from my closest female friend, I called him on a Sunday two or three weeks later and suggested that we could have coffee halfway between his apartment and my house. In response to my phone greeting, he said, "Are you the one who used to teach music?" I wondered how many other *ones* he had been talking to but assumed that his question simply reflected the length of time since the initial conversation.

He was not familiar with the area where I suggested that we meet for coffee but assured me that he could find it. As I was turning into the parking lot, my phone rang. He was calling to find out where I was. Being a couple of minutes early was not early enough to suit him. *Is he at strike two already?* I wondered. When we ordered coffee and a light meal, I asked him if he would like for me to split the bill. "Oh, no. This is my treat."

We enjoyed a generic, safe conversation for about twenty minutes. He then glanced at his watch, snapped his fingers, and said, "Oh, no! Hannity's speech has already started." I've never made a habit of watching TV but recognized the name.

Seeing a possible quick and natural ending to the encounter, I said, "If you want to watch the speech, it would be alright if we leave now because I still have so much work to do tonight."

He responded, "Oh, no. This is far more important." Remembering the scheduled speech by Hannity seemed to shift his mental gears into politics. Striking my ears like an accidental crash of symphonic cymbals, I detected a conspiratorial tone in his voice as he said, "Have you tried to buy ammunition lately?"

"No. I have no reason to be looking for ammunition."

As he cranked up into a full-blown political tirade, I interrupted him long enough to say, "You might want to know that you are talking to one of the few Democrats in this area." That just enraged him. He then started ranting about how stupid people were to have voted for Obama.

"You know, we are on the verge of an all-out race war. I have seven pistols at my apartment and four shotguns at my ranch. It's hard to get much ammunition, though."

I was more than ready to separate myself from him when the waiter approached and said, "Excuse me. It's almost time to close. I'm sorry, but we close early on Sunday evenings."

Just outside the door of the restaurant, the Hannity fan turned toward me and said, "I have only one question. Are you over eighteen years old?" Not amused, I automatically nodded. "Good. So am I. We can do *anything* we want." I had already turned down his invitation to go to his apartment to see his night-blooming cacti. I wondered silently, *"What ever happened to etchings?"*

He placed one hand on my shoulder and said, "You know, with most of these old gals around here, they've told you everything they know once they've said 'Hello.'" I think he meant that as a compliment, meaning that he was aware that I had something more to say beyond "Hello." But with his implicit demand that he be the only speaker, he was far too short-sighted to find out what I might have said. I wonder how many of the "old gals" he had tried to corner long enough to spew forth his twisted views had cut him off far sooner than I. He was definitely at strike three and out.

Undaunted by my lack of enthusiasm, he went on with his verbal exploration. "You know, here in Katy, there is a lot of bartering that goes on. For example, I might need to have a button replaced sometime. You might have needs that I could help with too." His tone and delivery carried the air of a wink-wink and a *get it?* innuendo.

I reminded him that I had to get back to work on my house and hurried out of the parking lot so that the aggressive old lecher could not follow me. He was more slime than real threat to me, but I felt that his views were a real threat to the nation.

For quite a while, several of my friends would frequently tease me by saying, "Hey, Sue! Been hanging out at Home Depot lately?" Or, "How 'bout them mulch bags?"

Several years after this unsettling encounter, I saw an announcement from a prominent Texas university that the man I had met at Home Depot had died. The obituary listed his many accomplishments and the honor he had brought to the university right after naming his survivors: wife of over fifty years, children, and twin grandchildren.

CHAPTER 17

SIXTY-EIGHT AND READY TO DATE

*The porcupine, whom one must handle gloved,
may be respected, but never loved.*
Arthur Guiterman
(1871-1943)

It wasn't the first time I had been single, but it was the first time that being single was thrust upon me by circumstance rather than by choice. My husband's sudden death had thrown me into a chasm of emotional solitude from which only I could take life-affirming steps. Family and dear friends were close at hand and solicitous, but they had their own world apart from me and could not possibly fill the gap in my life.

About three weeks before Chris' death, he called me into his home office. He had just received the proofs for a new publicity head shot and wanted my input regarding which to select. I pointed to the one I liked. "That one shows both your serious side and a twinkle in your eyes. People who know you will see your personality, and prospective clients will see you as approachable."

"That's the one I like too."

He then looked up as I stood at his shoulder and, with tears in his eyes, said, "Will you use that one for me?" I knew instantly that he meant that I would use it for his obituary.

"Of course, I will. But that will be at least twenty years from now."

He stood and gave me one of his tight bear hugs and said, "Always remember how much I love you."

Even though I was seven years older than Chris, he always believed that I would outlive him. He released the embrace, placed his hands on my shoulders. and said, "Promise me three more things:

1. Always be a redhead.
2. Don't forget me, but get on with your life.
3. Don't settle."

I said, "I don't know why these things are on your mind right now. Is anything wrong?"

He shook his slowly and said, "No. I'm just so tired."

I went back to my home office and reviewed my flight schedule for the composer's workshop I planned to attend in three weeks. During the remaining weeks until the trip, he did not mention the conversation and did not repeat the sentiment. I did notice his deep fatigue, but believed it was reasonable in light of his workload.

I left for Pennsylvania early on a Saturday, flew into Philadelphia, rented a car, and drove to Lehigh University, about 1 ½ hours from the airport. I learned of Chris' death when I returned a call to the hospital near our house. The prospects of a productive composer's workshop exploded in a frenzy of phone calls, an onslaught of *what-to-dos*, how to get back to Philadelphia without having a wreck, and a million other items on the swelling list that fogged my brain so much that I kept making the same mistake on the Pennsylvania turnpike and literally drove in circles until I finally stopped and asked for directions. The drive doubled to three hours.

To partially distract me from the list of things I could not possibly solve while trying to get back to Philly, I called the person who had sold us the lot for the dream house and had supervised our planning of every detail of the construction. I asked him to simply talk to me about anything he could think of while I made my way back to the Philadelphia airport. He was kind and helpful as he talked, and I kept him informed about my location and progress. Many others assisted me and stood by to ease the way as much as possible.

Two years after Chris' death, at a youthful 68, I began to consider the possibility of dating. Doubting the likelihood of meeting eligible men any other way, and upon the suggestion of a friend, I joined an online dating service. For me, that experience quickly evolved into a serial comedy rather than a viable means to establish social connections.

One of my colleagues had met a man whom she married through an online dating service. I asked, "Cindy, you met your husband through an online dating service, didn't you?"

"Sure did. Got something in mind?"

"I'm considering joining one or two, and you're the only person I know who has used one. What was it like?"

"There are two I would recommend. They both do a pretty good job, but I'll just tell you right now—I had to kiss a lot of frogs before I found my prince."

Based on her comments and my recognition that meeting someone whom I would want to date apart from a dating service was doubtful, I became a member of two online dating services. While they operated in similar ways, their clientele did seem to be somewhat different. I received multiple possible matches from one and only two or three from the other.

Within a week or two, the beads of social non-events began to accumulate on a long rope of heavy-duty jute twine. The first occasion was a lunch date with someone whose picture must have been taken at least 15 years earlier. Conversation was easy as we enjoyed our lunch. After finishing our salads, he leaned back, looked me up and down, and boldly announced, "I'm looking for action." When my response was minimal, he repeated the statement with a louder voice. I didn't give him a chance to clarify whether he wanted to go to a casino or perhaps had something else in mind. So, after a quick goodbye, I archived Mr. Action.

My second venture into a social setting was with a man from another state who had lived in Houston for a long time. It seemed that we were both enjoying getting acquainted at a wine tasting venue when he excused himself, presumably to use the restroom. Instead, he went to the counter and ordered himself a second glass of wine without asking me if I would like a second glass. His email later informed me that there was "no chemistry." So much for Mr. MO.

The next possible contact looked interesting—a former band director who had changed careers and recently retired from his stint in the business world. He sent me his phone number, and I called him. I was surprised to find that he sounded distant on the phone—slow with his part of the conversation, which created awkward pauses. He finally said that he was not able to make a date because he would be out of town for 30 days. At that point, he started crying and said, "I can't believe I'm going to say this, but I am an alcoholic and will be leaving for treatment in two days." I wished Mr. Rehab well, hung up, and blocked him from my site.

Another person I had been in contact with but had not met in person edited his profile. In the edited version, he added five years to his age along with two children. I emailed him regarding my concerns about the changes. He responded by saying that he had made a mistake in judgment by misstating his age and that he was really proud of his grandchildren. He also said that he would never contact me again, which, of course, was fine with me. So long, Mr. Age Adjuster.

Not yet totally discouraged, I made a lunch date with another person for the following week. Two days later, he emailed me and told me that he had met "another gal" and since he had seen her twice over the weekend, he would have to break our date. I didn't want or need to hear anything further from Mr. O. G. Date-Breaker.

My next adventure was with an executive in the financial department of a major company. At his suggestion, we met in the bar of an upscale seafood restaurant. As soon as we were seated, he said, "I don't know why I suggested we meet here because I am temporarily off of alcohol." Over Diet Cokes, he politely asked me to tell him about what I did in my work and for entertainment. I mentioned that I had just attended the dedicatory recital of the organ at the new Roman Catholic Co-Cathedral. With obvious enthusiasm, I was telling him how beautiful both the organ and the building were when he blurted out, "Who on earth would listen to organ music if they didn't have to?" I tried to explain that I thought he might be thinking of bad music played badly on an electronic organ. My possible explanation for his perception was wasted when he countered with his statement that he related organ music to a pop hit of the '60's or '70's and to funeral homes. I could have discussed that mindset at length, but his eyes were glazing over.

Once I saw that discussing the new organ and building was pointless, I regrouped, and asked him about his work. He began to explain the process by which China is attempting to gain a monopoly of the rare elements on the periodic table. He was as passionate about the periodic table as I was about the new organ. Had he been paying attention, he might have noticed that my eyes were about as glazed as his. He was quick to call a spade a spade, and with emphatic gestures said, a la Ann Richards ("That dog won't hunt."), "This train will never track." He was correct in judging that we had nothing more to say to each other, but his handling of the situation lacked tact or finesse. Mr. Periodic Table will have to discuss China's quest to establish control of the rare elements with someone else. And, if I am lucky, maybe at some point I will find someone who will share excitement over a new world-class organ and an architecturally significant building.

As emails continued to come in, I started viewing the entire experience as a voyeuristic glimpse into profiles written by illiterate, insensitive, and, to me, unattractive misfits. At the same time, the companies who were eager to boost their coffers by teasing seekers into either starting or extending memberships showed no concern for the thinly guised inadequate *buyer beware* phrases. At that point, I decided to journal some of the more interesting, funny, and ridiculous statements I received.

One of the profile writers proudly stated that he *"read vociferously."* (Bring your own ear plugs.) Another claimed that a weakness he had was that he sometimes became too *"embossed"* in his work. (Hmmmm—textured tattoos, maybe?) Still another was bold enough to say that he was a *"grate lover."* I was tempted to wish him luck in finding a grate, or even to tell him where to go to find one. For the sake of the high road of civility, though, I ignored it.

Another choice statement was *"I don't need anyone to fore full my life."* One described his ethnicity by saying, *"very traditional, respectful—do take things in, ponder."* (I guess I am not familiar with that ethnicity.) Then there was the one who believed that *"reality will adventurely set in"* (Who said anything about wanting adventures?), and another who said he *"didn't believe in fairy tails."* (How about fairy heads? Fairy tails, fairy heads, what's the difference, and does either have anything to do with anything?)

Perhaps the least inviting claim was, *"I am not a male chauvinist. I have a strong opinion that women should be treated with more respect than they deserve."* (And just how much respect is that?) Perhaps Freud could come up with a calculated answer to that question. A similar line of thought was expressed by a different person when he said that his ideal date would *"respect me for being a male."* (Sorry—my giving of respect requires something more than the luck of the gender draw—or dare I say the luck of the fuck.) The next quote is best if read with an East Texas accent. Among other things the man enjoyed was *"a glass of wine or whatever spirts* (sounds like "spurts") *you enjoy."* (I wonder what type of "spirts" he enjoys.)

Another profile writer listed his marital status as widower and stated that he had *"always been single until I got married."* (Is Yogi Berra still around or just being channeled?) One other said that he liked to *"be in places no one expects."* (Maybe it's time he quit playing hide-n-seek.) A man who claimed to be 25 years old and looking for a woman 21-72 years old said, *"I try to go with the flow of things, but that doesn't usually work out the way you want it most of the time."* (How about how he wants things to turn out?) I've heard of sugar daddies, but this young man seemed to be seeking a sugar mommy. Sorry—my sugar canister is empty and bone-dry.

Every day brings enticements for journaling ear-stinging quotes. It is now just a little over two months since my association with the online dating service began. One of the men whose email arrived recently said he *"would love to travel more with someone that you love."* (What about traveling with someone whom he loves?) I am unable to think of a single soul whom I love who might like to travel with this stranger.) Another warned, *"if you don't have a sense of humor and love to laugh, please don't apply."* (I have yet to see an application form to be completed in order to be considered for a date.)

One friendly person wrote, *"Hi there. My nice guy is here to fine the right woman to fulfill my dreams. If you think you are the one, then come, lets tie the nut."* WHAT!!?? He's going to fine the one whom he thinks is "the right woman?" And exactly how does he think we can tie a nut? Sounds squirrely to me.

The last email of that day stated, *"I like to spin time doing things with horses."* (No specification as to exactly what things he likes to do with horses.). I am aware of spinning ideas, particularly when broadcasting a point of view, but how does one spin time? Maybe he is into time travel. He continued, *"I like being around people, but also like being one on one."* (One people on another people? Very confusing.)

My intent to stop was just ruined by yet another email I can't ignore. Someone informed me that his ethnicity is *Episcopalian*. (I, too, am Episcopalian, but my ethnicity is British Isles.) One was quite proud of his house and described it as *"private and comfortable with a big porch all around and a fireplace built for two.* (What would we do in the fireplace, and what about the bicycle built for two?) One claimed that he was *"not no player."* (He needn't worry—I will not be asking him to play.)

One of the blanks to be filled out on the profile form relates to pets. It even breaks down the category into pets that are liked and pets that are owned. On one of the profiles, the man stated that his *"yellow lab died last summer and would like a golden retriever puppy."* (Is there a doggie heaven where this poor yellow lab can be granted his/her wish for a golden retriever puppy?)

And last, but certainly not least, the person who filled out the last profile I journaled stated that he would *"like to travel to laces I have not seen."* (A lace fetish? Oh, my! The difference an omitted letter can make! That traveler's destination will not be to my laces!)

If my late husband could read this, he would be the first to laugh at the inanity of these writings. I can just hear him say, "Sue, I wanted you to get on with your life, but I hope you can find a better way."

And now, I am past sixty-eight and still ready to date.

CHAPTER 18
CLICK IT OR TICKET

*The test of a person's breeding
is how they behave in a quarrel.*
George Bernard Shaw
(1856-1950)

Texas State Troopers take seat belt regulations very seriously. The reminder, "Click it or Ticket" sits atop signposts along highways of all descriptions, at times breaking the monotony of endless bleak streaks of tumbleweed traffic, and other times being staked within spaghetti bowls of multi-tiered interstates in the state's largest cities, several of which rank among the nation's top ten in population. Drivers in Texas have no excuse for ignoring the signage. Most comply by habit.

It was the first Friday of the month—the night to play bridge with friends at church. But I had received a phone call from my man-friend around noon. "Hi. It's John. I was wondering if we could get together tonight."

"I'd like that, but I've already planned to play bridge with a group at church."

"I have a PBS movie I thought you might like to watch—'Mrs. Wilson's War.'"

"Let me check on how many have signed up to play, and I'll call you back in a few minutes."

I called my friend who was the leader of the bridge group. "Hi, Rick. I signed up to play bridge tonight, but John just called and wants us to get together tonight. Do you have any extras on the list?"

"Yes. I was wondering what we were going to do with an odd number, but we'd miss seeing you and we might be short on deserts if you don't come. You know, everyone calls you either the *hat lady* or the *cake lady*."

"Yeah, I know, and I don't mind. There are much worse names they might consider. You and Keith are the only ones, though, who can call my double glasses the 'grasshopper look.'"

We chuckled, then said in unison, "You crack me up."

Rick said, "Do what you need to do, but you might want to think twice about making yourself available on such short notice when you already have plans. Jus' sayin.'"

"I know, dear friend, but I really do want to see John, and he would never agree to learn bridge. I'll bring the cake to the church office before the secretary leaves."

"Alright. Tell her to leave a note so we'll know where to find it. I don't want to have to declare a scavenger hunt in the church. Being a tour guide on Sundays is one thing, but chasing down a lost cake might not sit well with the sexton. We'll see you for bridge next month."

"Thanks. I promise not to make this a habit."

I called the church office and explained the situation to the secretary. She was planning to leave early, so I would have to get the cake there by 3:00. I said, "No problem. It'll be done by 1:30, so I should be there by 2:45. Rick and Keith will pick it up and take it to the room where we play. Could you leave a note on the counter near your desk, so they'll know where you put it? It won't need to be refrigerated, but it's okay if that would be the best place."

"Sure. I've heard about your cakes."

"I'd better sign off and get busy. I appreciate your help."

I called John and let him know I would be ready around 6:00.

My sour cream pound cake was always a favorite. It was fun to play with the frosting ingredients to vary the appearance and taste. Using a Bundt pan made the frosting job go more quickly than if I used layer cake pans. I had already purchased blueberries and blueberry jam to dress it up.

I made the cake with only a glance or two at the recipe and got it in the oven. While it baked, I made the cream cheese frosting and added just enough of the fancy blueberry jam to enhance the color, texture, and taste—all primed to please the palate and to wear fresh blueberries like adornments on church-lady hats. Knowing I would have to frost the cake before it cooled properly, I made the icing extra thick and put it in the fridge, hoping the chilled mixture would not turn into a runny mess when it met warm cake.

When the cake was done, I cheated and put it in the refrigerator for about 10 minutes to accelerate the cooling time. The cheat seemed to work. The consistency of the frosting and the temperature of the cake worked well together. Once the frosting was swirled, I placed several rows of blueberries on top and placed the last dozen or so in the center well.

I put the frosted cake in the fridge while I grabbed a cardboard box from the garage. Perfect! The domed glass cake plate just fit in the box. I taped the top at the corners to form higher walls for stability in case the usual Friday afternoon traffic forced me to stomp the brake without warning the cake to get a grip.

There was no time for a shower or change of clothes. Every minute was crucial to *get it to the church on time*. Things were going well. Instead of *having my cake and eating it too*, I was going to deliver my cake and have my date too.

No problem with Memorial City mall traffic or with traffic in general, so I let the lead in my foot have its way with the pedal. When I rounded the curve in the far left lane approaching Loop 610, which branches off toward the Galleria, I spotted a sleek black Corvette apparently stalled on the shoulder. Feeling a bit smug to whiz past him in my school-marmy Camry, I heard the siren just a split second before I saw red *pull over* lights flash in my rear-view mirror. I thought, *No way. Unmarked police cars are never Corvettes. Motorcycles or big-ass trucks, but Corvettes?* This was a first for me.

I knew I was speeding, but others were passing me. I just happened to light up his radar screen at the exact moment when he could finagle his fancy car into the lane behind me without getting it sideswiped. *If only I'd stayed in one of the other six lanes.*

"License and insurance card, Ma'am."

"It may take a minute, but I'm sure I have them."

"Take your time. I'm in no hurry."

I rooted in my bulging purse to get my wallet out, pulled out the license and handed it to him. In the attempt to get the insurance card, I forgot whether it was in the wallet or in the glove compartment. I tried the glove compartment first and scrounged through proof of all the oil changes the car had ever had before I returned to the wallet. I soon found the insurance card and held it up for him to take. He walked back to his car to make sure I was the rightful owner and that there were no red flags associated with my driving record. That task must have taken less than five minutes, but it felt like half an hour as I kept vigil on the cake and traffic.

He wore the uniform identifying him as a Houston police officer proudly—no plainclothes to match the unmarked Corvette. About forty years my junior, he was patient and polite. After checking my license and registration, he came back to the window to return the papers and to talk.

"Ma'am, do you know how fast you were going?"

"Not exactly. I thought I was just keeping up with traffic."

"The speed limit here is 60 miles per hour. Do you have a reason for going almost 80?"

I looked him straight in the eye and said, "Officer, I'm on my way to church."

He seemed to notice my grubby, faded t-shirt smudged with icing, my stringy ponytail, and verified the facial proof that middle age had left me long ago. His eyebrows stretched upward.

"Church? What's the occasion?"

"See this cake sitting beside me? I have to get it there before the secretary leaves."

"And why would she be needing the cake?" (I didn't dare lecture him about the possibility that the secretary could be male.)

"It's not for her. It's for the bridge group that will play there tonight."

"You mean that card game?"

"Yes. We play the first Friday of every month."

"So—the bridge game's tonight, but you have to take the cake right now? At almost 80 miles an hour?"

"Yes. I decided not to play tonight because I got a call from my man-friend right before I baked the cake, and now I have an unexpected date tonight. And the church secretary leaves at 3:00."

Realizing that being a senior citizen did not necessarily mean rocking chairs and knitting needles, he gave an "Aha" nod and smiled. "Oh. Now I understand." He leaned down to look again at the cake and said, "I think you'd better fasten the seat belt around that cake. I clocked you at 78 miles an hour. I'm reducing it to 70 so your fine will be less, but you need to slow down to the speed limit between here and the church and keep it like that on your way home."

I had to release my seat belt to pull the cake's belt with one hand while the other steadied the box. The officer said, "That's better. Don't forget, 'Click it or ticket' for your own seat belt."

"Yes, Sir. Thank you, Officer, for understanding."

He handed me the ticket with instructions for the options of either paying the fine, going to court, or taking the driver training course online.

Now the trick was to figure out how to leave the shoulder and whip into traffic while the officer was still behind me. I've never been prone to feel eyes on the back of my neck, but on that day, my neck was ablaze. I wondered, *Does double jeopardy count in traffic law?* It would have helped if he had stepped out and directed traffic for me, but he left it up to me to time the stomp on the accelerator to re-enter I-10 traffic on a Friday afternoon at the frenzied spaghetti-bowled confluence of I-10 East and Loop 610. I darted in between a car and an 18-wheeler. A glance at the dashboard clock told me it was 2:45—the time I told the secretary to expect me.

Feeling both relief and stress, I handed over the cake to the secretary just as she was locking her office door. I said, "Don't ask me about why I didn't get here quite as soon as I thought I would."

She looked at me and said, "Well, you know I have to ask you now."

"I got a ticket for speeding right on the curve beside The First Baptist Church. I still wonder why they capitalize The. I even had to buckle the seat belt around the cake when I told the officer I was speeding because I had to get the cake delivered to the church before the secretary left."

She laughed and said, "Rick ought to take up a collection tonight for your fine."

"Absolutely not! I'll never hear the end of it already."

"Don't worry. I left a note where they can find it. I've already cleared out space in the fridge. I'll stop by the break room and put it there on the way to my car. Be careful on the way home. You won't have a cake delivery excuse now."

With every blueberry still hugging its assigned place, I placed the cake plate in the secretary's hands. "I'll be careful. Thanks."

I rushed home as quickly as I dared, determined not to become as infamous as "The Little Old Lady from Pasadena." Like a poet friend of mine once said, "You can call me *Little*, and you can call me *Lady*, but I'd better never hear you call me *Old*."

PART TWO: RETURN
WEATHER, REAL ESTATE, AND RELEASE

This is the weather the shepherd shuns,
And so do I.
                                Thomas Hardy
                                (1840-1928)

"Time to plant tears," says the almanac.
The grandmother sings to the marvelous stove,
And the child draws another inscrutable house.
                                Elizabeth Bishop
                                (1911-1979)

Courage is the price that life exacts for granting peace.
The soul that knows it not, knows no release
From little things;
Knows not the livid loneliness of fear,
Nor the mountain heights where bitter joy can hear
The sound of wings.
                                Amelia Earhart Putnam
                                (1898-1937)

INTRODUCTION

The lock-step potency of the pull toward adventurous exploration and the push out of emotional toxicity finally brought me back to reclaim the soil of my soul. I had to get away to heal, and I had to come home to reclaim cultural life after age-related macular degeneration curtailed night driving. The deep peace I found right here in DeLand allowed me to write this book of personal journey in much less time than it took to write my first book.

Weather plays a part in lifestyles world-wide. So far as I know, there is no perfect climate. After witnessing more disastrous weather events in the Houston area while I lived there (1980-2022) than any I experienced or knew of in any of the other six states where I lived since 1968, I gave up on trying to identify a place to live based upon the climate. Shunning Houston's weather extremes was only one of the factors that nudged me out of the city I called home for 43 years.

It seemed that I had been *drawing houses* all my life, especially since about two years prior to leaving DeLand. At my urging, my first husband begrudgingly agreed to buy a small house. To me, it signified that we were almost ready to start a family and that once I had children, I would then have a way to give and receive affection. I had picked up my parents' belief that paying rent was a waste of money. He had picked up his parents' belief that any form of debt was taboo, even a mortgage. They agreed in theory, though, that it might prove to be a good investment.

When I filed for divorce not long before leaving DeLand, the first message my attorney received from my husband's attorney was that I should not expect any claim to the small amount of money invested in the house. At that point, I didn't care. But I kept the dream that, in time,

I would own my own home.

That dream of home ownership came to fruition and ruptured twice more in Houston before I sold the house that I had bought in 1999 and moved back to DeLand in 2022.

I don't recall thinking of myself as having courage when I handled each segment of my journey. Yet that is one of the descriptors I often hear now when people comment after reading my first book. My thoughts were more likely to be *I've got to get through this* or *What do I need to do next*.

With hindsight, I agree that my history shows courage. It did take courage to survive the stresses and challenges and to re-start after every set-back. When I most needed it, my high school choral director's reminder, *Young folks, your potential*! echoed in my ears while my eyes recalled the differences between my underclassmen and upperclassman grades. Intermittent successes tempered the incessant doubts and fears that seldom slipped beyond the surface of my mind.

More pertinently, when I think of courage, I must include the little things that demanded compromise from me and that never seemed to yield toward me in return. The *bitter joy* of a recent inadequate relationship was a small matter compared with the familial abuse that had pushed me away from my hometown. When little things pile up for more than ten years, though, the weight and wear are significant, and the relief is huge—so huge that it opens up space for peace and *the sound of wings*.

A network of people, places, and process serendipitously joined forces to guide me home. To document every link in the chain would be impractical, if not impossible. Too numerous and too intertwined to isolate or rank in scope, I recount in Part Two some of the more significant incidents to specify the impact and to honor some of the guides who simply offered parts of themselves with no expectation of reciprocity.

I could not have ended up in this place with this sense of purpose by any other route. Any attempt to speed up the process would have backfired. The encouragers I knew or met along the way strengthened my resolve and powered my confidence as I did the work of weeding out and removing succulent parasites that, by their very nature, survived by gaslighting my energy.

The series of coincidental incidents that led me home sometimes jolted, sometimes calmed. The incidents ranged from meeting people who unknowingly sent out signals and opened opportunities that eased the process of returning home to reconnecting with high school and college friends and meeting up with cousins after not seeing them for decades and to being led to all sorts of professionals and trades people. Each person made the goal seem to be within my reach and by seeming, being.

While at times stunning, these coincidences did not bring stress or pressure. Rather, it seemed as though an inexhaustible battery kept my path lit. Trusting that the light would be there when needed freed me from squandering energy on anxiety, and the forward momentum toned muscles of resolve. Many times, if someone had asked, *How are you going to manage to pull up the roots where you have lived since 1980 and return to your hometown where you have not lived since 1968,* my answer would had to have been, *I don't know, but I have no doubt that I will.*

I became aware of that certainty as I drove back to Houston in March 2022, after attending the Murphy Getaway to Write workshop in New Smyrna Beach, FL, and visiting DeLand before retracing the I-10 route back to Houston. I knew that moving back would not be easy, but ease or difficulty of the move was not relevant. While I had never handled the sale or purchase of a house by myself, I had been through the process enough so that I had a faith-like assurance that I could do it, even if I did have plenty to learn about real estate. So far as I know, in all their moves (about three dozen), my parents never used a realtor. Perhaps that was common for their generation, but for me, it was an example that all I had to do was talk to the right people to make it happen.

CHAPTER 19

GRAMMA SKILTON'S TEACUP AND SAUCER

Men (and women) are not influenced by things, but by their thoughts about them.

Epictetus
(d. 135 A.D.)

When news of the outbreak of the COVID-19 virus blazed the news channels 24/7 and local reports on school closings frequently released updates on options for hundreds of thousands of students in the Houston area, I knew my own study and teaching would be affected. My memoir, *Cries of the Panther on Mockingbird Hill* came off the press that April, 2020. I hosted two pre-launch parties a few weeks before it was obvious that there would be no additional pre-launch get-togethers, much less a bigger celebration to launch my first book into marketing.

Instead of planning book signings, I waited for news about the Get Away to Write course I had registered for that was to be held in late February or early March. After talking with several of my friends regarding my misgivings about heading for Florida, I cancelled my plans to attend. The following day, I received a notice that the course was cancelled. Not much later, I heard that the Getaway to Write course scheduled to be held that summer also was cancelled.

As school districts agonized over the dilemma of fulfilling their mission while also guarding the health of faculty, staff, and students, I also had to face the issue of meeting the needs of my piano students, maintaining my own health, and keeping some momentum in my writing practice. Students helped me learn to use FaceTime and Zoom. Parents adjusted schedules, and I registered for a course offered online by Rice University. Later, I would enroll in two additional online courses taught by Peter Murphy of Stockton University, the sponsor of the Get Away to Write courses.

Writing during the shutdown helped me to maintain some degree of balance between frustration and hope in the eventual return of normalcy. Now, two years later, as I prepare this manuscript, I am grateful that Rice University in Houston and Stockton University in New Jersey both offered online courses that not only kept writers engaged in their craft, but also maintained a sense of community and connectivity when endless hours at home and fearsome times out in public places fed anxiety while medical news gut-wrenched beyond anything imaginable.

This chapter began as an assignment in the course at Rice.

Six months after the Civil War ended, Gramma Skilton celebrated her fourth birthday. Her parents (my great grandparents) gave her a bone china tea set. It was a generous, perhaps extravagant, gift in 1865. I can visualize the little room where her mother taught her to set a small table in anticipation of her dolls' tea parties. The child's table would have been an echo of the one my great grandmother set for afternoon tea when friends came to call in their Connecticut home.

Not long before she died at age 95 ½ in 2001, my mother gave me one of the four cups and saucers from the tea set. The cup holds exactly 1.5 teaspoons of liquid—just enough to quench a doll's thirst, but too little to cause much concern if a child accidentally spilled its contents.

The rim is 1.5 inches across. A gold band circles the interior of the rim and drapes the 7/8-inch handle, which has two holes—one for the finger, and one for design balance. The outside of the cup has a raised pattern divided into eighths, but the interior's surface is flat.

The saucer measures 2.5 inches in diameter. The shallow interior is enhanced by eight raised points that remind me of the shape of a holly leaf. Along the rim there is a coordinating gold border and a total of 16 scallops. It could be used to teach or illustrate basic fractions, but I doubt if my great grandmother, grandmother, or mother thought of it as a math tool.

When I was about the same age as Gramma Skilton had been when she received the tea set, Mother tenderly removed a wooden box from the small trunk that always sat near her bedside in each of the many houses we occupied. The box was so small that she easily balanced it on one of her palms. It was more rustic than elegant, but I soon learned that it held objects of great value.

Like Daddy's tackle box, I knew Mother's trunk was off limits for my inquisitive mind and hands. I felt my status in the family rise to that of a princess when she showed me the tea set nested like bird's eggs in its own wooden box. The lid to the box slid into slots, and the front dropped down, giving access to the miniature dishes. Many years later, I would wonder how anyone could have installed such tiny hinges.

Mother said, "This tea set for dolls is older than I am. My own mother, your Gramma Skilton, died when she was only 60 years old when I was still a teenager. This is one of the few things I have that belonged to her."

Knowing how I longed to explore every inch of the house itself and the contents, she reminded me that I must never pry into Daddy's tackle box or her trunk.

"The hooks on the lures in the tackle box could hurt you, and you might have an accident with the tea set."

She went on to tell me that I could ask to see the tea set at any time, and I also could ask Daddy to see the contents of the tacklebox. Seeing the tears that always came to her eyes when she talked about her mother, I knew not to break those rules.

As I grew in years and understanding, I could never be certain whether Mother's initial intent in sharing the tea set with me was primarily a way for her to reconnect with a tangible connection to her mother, to strengthen the bond between us, or simply to help me appreciate the Skilton heritage. But every time I visited her as an adult, I asked to see the wooden box with the four doll-size teacups and saucers wrapped in translucent tissue, encased by lightweight wood, and buried in the trunk. The complete set probably included at least one additional box filled with a sugar bowl and lid, a creamer, and a teapot. But the history of those pieces is lost to an archive of silence.

It has now been over 75 years since I first saw the china tea set. I assume that my three siblings also received one of the cups and saucers, but I do not know where the wooden box is.

Like my parents, I have moved many times. Despite my careful packing, the cup now has two tiny chips on the rim. The gold running down the arc of the handle and around the rim is faded. It could not have worn off from the friction of a dish cloth because I only cleaned it occasionally when it sat outside a china closet and collected dust. The gold on the saucer is more intact but is inconsistent in width.

Now the treasured cup and saucer sit inside a china cabinet and do not collect dust. Other objects on the same shelf include a full-size cup and saucer in the official Skilton china pattern, a matching salad plate, and one of the ivory napkin rings that graced my grandparents' dining table.

Like me, the tiny cup and saucer from the tea set have lost some of their superficial luster, but their worth has become more precious than the thin gold decoration that made me think the cups and saucers for dolls' tea parties had great monetary value when I first saw them. Also like me, they cannot hide their age, but they set my heart a-sparkle every time I see them or cradle them in my hand, remembering that my great grandparents bought them; my grandmother played with them so carefully that her six daughters also enjoyed them; and my mother, the youngest of her family, preserved the four cups and saucers well enough for each of her children to have one cup and saucer from the tea set that is now 158 years old. I wonder who will curate the pieces of the tea set when my life ends.

CHAPTER 20
SNOWMAGEDDON

Snow—Beautiful show! It can do nothing wrong.
John Whittaker Watson
(1824-1890)

    Texas Governor, Greg Abbott, reassured residents that the state's independent power grid could withstand the unprecedented demands of the powerful Arctic Vortex bearing down on a large portion of the country, threatening to stall over the entire Lone Star State. I finished the last piece of Valentine's Day dark chocolate and watched the latest weather update before going outside to make sure the tape on the improvised Styrofoam coverings on both exterior faucets still gripped the brick.

    Earlier that morning, by the time I had gone to each of the three big box stores near my home, shelves meant to hold faucet insulators were bare. But I am resourceful and felt certain that the two cheap coolers in the garage would suffice. I placed small cardboard boxes around the faucets before adding slabs of Styrofoam snapped from the coolers. Blue painter's tape was strong enough to secure them, and plastic trash bags with drawstring ties added layers of insulation and reinforced the tape. The only uncertainty was whether the tape and brick would bond long-term.

    When I went outside to check the tape, I found it already curling away from the brick like lips tasting quinine, just waiting for a whip of wind to take the entire masterpiece of insulation to parts unknown. I found a roll of packing tape in the garage and was relieved when it seemed to take up where the painter's tape left off. When the two custom-designed faucet protectors resisted my tests of wiggles and pulls, I sent a picture of one of them to my brother, who lives in Missouri and has to prepare for severe weather every year. He texted back, "Looks like you've got the faucets under control. Ole Man Weather doesn't know who he's messing with. You know to leave the faucets running a little and to keep cabinet doors under the sinks open, right?"

"Yes—just like our parents did when hurricanes approached. That's all done. I also filled both bathtubs, but one doesn't hold water very well. I'll keep an eye on it, though, and refill it as needed."

"Do you think you might go to that little hotel you went to when Harvey hit?"

"No. I think I'll be fine at home. Several friends have invited me to go to their place if I need or want to. I'll keep you posted as the storm moves through. It will be far different from Harvey."

"I love you, Sis. We'll be praying for you."

"I love you too, Rich"

I tried not to watch the almost constant weather coverage on TV but could not avoid it. Predictions looked bad, but I felt prepared and knew I could accept one of the invitations if things became worse than expected.

Valerie, a former colleague and mother of one of my piano students, called again. "Sue, are you prepared for the storm? Jason (her husband) can come over and help if you need him."

"I just checked the outside faucets, and they seem to be ready. I have candles and matches in every room and a large flashlight in two areas. The bathtubs are full, faucets are running at a slight trickle, and sink cabinet doors are open. Jason is so thoughtful and skilled. I appreciate his availability, but I think the house and I are about as ready as we can be"

"Okay—just come on over if you lose power. We have a small generator. No need to call; just come ahead, even if you decide you just don't want to be alone. You can use Bronwyn's room upstairs, and she can sleep with us downstairs. That will be a treat for her."

"Thanks. We won't plan on a piano lesson this week. Looks like severe weather will be here all week."

That call came in on Sunday. The power went off in the middle of the night, and my house was all electric. As long as I was bundled up in flannel pajamas, thick socks, and a fleece jacket under 3 blankets, I was fine, but when I got up to use the bathroom, I knew the meteorologists had not been indulging in hyperbolic spin.

Normally, when occasional power outages occurred, they rarely lasted more than a few minutes. But the power was still off several hours later when I braved the walk from the bedroom to the kitchen. I glanced at the thermostat in the front hall—65 degrees.

The growls rumbling in my stomach fueled my determination to stay out of bed long enough to scarf down a slice of bread slathered with peanut butter and to wash it down with room temperature water. I always ask for water without ice in restaurants, but the water on that gray morning might as well have had ice cubes in it. The sound of sleet rapping or scratching on windowpanes, and the sight of snow falling on top of ice while exterior temperatures hovered in single digits made the inside air seem even colder than it was.

Shivers spread from my neck to my fingers and toes. Sixty-five degrees may be almost pleasant for many people, but I am unusually cold-natured, and fear or dread are triggers that worsen temperature-related shivers for me.

I checked the thermostat again on the way back to bed—down to 63 degrees. No way to warm my insides with a hot beverage or food; no wood or safety inspection for the fireplace; and no telling when power would be restored.

Water still trickled from all faucets. I took that as encouragement—at least it was not frozen in the pipes. I told myself to pretend the sound came from a mountain brook, but my attempt to distract with pretense failed. I bristled when I reminded myself that raging rivers begin as a small spring before it is either visible or audible. The memory of the melody of *The Moldau* in Smetana's tone poem, "Ma Vlast" came to mind and briefly replaced the dread of the approaching storm with visual and aural pleasantries.

It was as difficult to breath as on a summer day with triple digit temperatures and air heavy with humidity, but not because of steam room conditions; it was because my lungs had amnesia when it came to long-term cold air. Every cell of my body longed for some of Houston's notorious spring warmth.

As several hours crawled by, there was no relief. Streets and I-10 were silent. Normally, I could hear a constant hum from the interstate and marked neighborhood routines by the sounds of school bus engines revving or idling, children and teenagers passing by, birds singing, and mail carriers stopping at each house on both sides of the block. Even about 35 miles beyond the center of Houston, the rhythm of city sounds soothed in their patterned dependability. But the invasion of the Arctic Vortex immobilized and muted life while it bleached *Esperanza* bushes to anemic shades of thin-soup brown whitewashed with pigeon gray.

Sleep was hopeless. I got up again and wrapped myself in blankets on the love seat in the TV room. With my feet on the oversized ottoman and blankets tucked from neck to heels, I must have looked like a mummy. Occasionally, I jumped at the screech of a dying limb from the *Esperanza* bush when it brushed across the screen over the window behind me. The same bush that festooned the yard with hundreds of yellow blossoms most of the year was being frozen to its roots. I had planted *Esperanza* bushes in the front and back yards because of its blossoms, hardiness for Houston's planting zone, and meaning of its name—Hope—in Spanish. Even though I had no expectation that the power would be restored any time soon, it felt a little less abnormal to be in the TV room than in bed.

I was glad that my niece, Camie, had urged me to buy a portable power bank when we made a trip to Ireland. Even if the phone lost its charge, I could get enough of a re-charge to make it through Monday night with access to news and 911 if necessary. And surely, the power would be on by the next day.

By noon, the thermostat registered 59 degrees, losing at least a degree per hour. I fought the shivers and my fears but felt that I was at risk and began to consider calling Valerie. Thinking I could get the shivers under control was just as accurate as if I thought the power would come on any minute. I added another pair of socks, a second pair of pants, and a heavier sweatshirt. I wondered if I could tug my all-weather coat with the removable liner over all the layers.

I swapped short wooly gloves for the long thin ones and traded the acrylic knit hat for the one made of thick recycled wool. I stretched the cuffs of the sweatshirt over the gap between the gloves and cuffs. Still no decrease in the shivers. The only other time I remembered shaking so badly was when I lay on a stretcher on the way to the operating room where my doctor waited to perform an emergency C-section. I feared I was going into shock and knew it was time to make the call.

No bars on the phone. I frantically grabbed what I thought were essentials. Not knowing how long I would be away, I took the fruit and enough nonperishable pantry items to contribute to whatever meals we would put together. A couple changes of clothes, bedding, medical supplies, and electronics completed the mound to be hauled to the car—and plenty of masks because my friends were very conscious of COVID-19 precautions because of a relative even older than I.

Although I had lived in extreme cold in Iowa for 6-8 years, I had forgotten that locks freeze. The remote for the car lock would not work. Not only was the key worthless, but I knew it was also vulnerable to snapping in two if I gave full vent to my frustration in the twist. I alternated rubbing the key opening with my wooled hands and blowing on it. Bit by bit, it warmed enough finally to let me unlock the door. Since I have two sets of keys, I loaded the take-alongs, then went back inside and let the car warm up before I headed out on what should have been a 10–12-minute drive. I drove 5-10 miles per hour on the snow-covered icy roads and saw only one other car between my house and Valerie and Jason's.

About an hour later, I pulled into their driveway. They were outside on the front porch watching Bronwyn build a snowman. It felt like they had staged a welcoming party for me. Jason came over to the car and started taking things inside. Valerie and Bronwyn hurried inside to put on another layer of clothing and for Valerie to turn on the coffee pot. They came back out and helped me take in the rest of the bags.

Inside, Jason said, "We're so glad you decided to come over. Would you like coffee or tea?"

"I thought you were going to use the generator only for heat and the refrigerator."

"We haven't lost power yet. We're trying to conserve, though, because we don't want to stress the grid. So many are already without power. The water's hot for whatever you prefer."

"It's going to take a little while for me to thaw out, and coffee will be the best way to help. Black, please, to keep it hot longer."

I continued, "How about your cell service? I tried to call, but I had no service." I checked my phone and saw the bars were lit again.

Valerie said, "We haven't really felt any effects from the storm, but we think it will be with us for a while. We're so glad that you are here."

We settled into the den. Bronwyn, a gifted fourth-grader, sat close to me. I pulled off my gloves and let the cupped warmth of coffee and care from my friends thaw my veins. She said, "Here, Ms. Sue. Now you can use this beautiful blanket (afghan) you made for us for Christmas. I use it all the time."

"I'm so happy you like it. And now I'm glad that I made it a little larger than the pattern suggested. It's big enough for both of us to stay warm."

"I like the color. Will we have my lesson here now?"

"We could, but since it's not scheduled until Wednesday, let's wait and see how things work out."

She patted my hand and looked up at me. "Did you know you are going to stay in my room?"

Valerie added, "It will be a treat for her to sleep with us downstairs, and you can have her room upstairs for as long as you need it." She was already beginning to gather up my stuff to take upstairs. I followed and helped her change the sheets.

The next morning, we enjoyed a hot breakfast, still marveling at the power staying on. Jason said, "Once it gets up above freezing, we can go over to your house and see if everything's okay. Would you prefer to lead or follow me? I think we should take both cars in case there's a problem."

What I didn't know was that he was already thinking about what tools and equipment he would take and that he would rather pack those in his car. Around noon, he came to the breakfast nook where Bronwyn was teaching me a new card game. "We're at 32 degrees now—the projected high for the day. Want to take a look at your house?"

"Sure. I'll be ready in just a minute."

"Toss me your keys, and I'll start your car so it can be warming up. I've already started mine. We'll give them a few minutes to warm up. That's better for the engine and for us."

I went upstairs and dropped the keys from the landing. He headed out the front door. When he came back, he said, "The streets are still covered by ice with snow on top of it. You've driven on snow and ice, haven't you?"

"Yes. I lived in Iowa for quite a while. That was the coldest climate I've ever lived in. But I also had to drive on snow or ice in South Carolina and Maryland and when I visited my family after they moved to Missouri. It's been a long time, though, since I moved back here from Maryland."

"You'll be fine. There's hardly anyone on the roads. Just go slow. I'll lead because I know a back way out of this subdivision. Flash your lights if you need to stop."

The drive took about 45 minutes instead of an hour but was still treacherous. When we arrived, I parked on the left side of the driveway, as usual. I hadn't seen Jason pack his car, so didn't realize how much equipment he brought. I almost ran to unlock the door while he took out a toolbox *just in case*.

As soon as I turned the doorknob and cracked the door open, I heard the rush of water as though we were at Niagara Falls. I yelled, "I hear water!"

"Where's the main cut-off?"

I pointed. "Right there, near the curb."

He ran to the city's access box, heaved the heavy lid aside, and tried to turn off the valve. It wouldn't budge. He ran back to his car. "I need a wrench. Go on in and start taking pictures. I'll be in as soon as I get it turned off."

I could tell the sound was coming from the kitchen. I thought, *What happened? I know I did everything I was supposed to do to get ready for the storm.* The stream was gushing from a hole in the ceiling right in front of the refrigerator. Water also streamed down the corner of the upper cabinets beside the sink. Jason was inside in just a minute or two.

I had frantically grabbed bath towels to try to keep the water from getting to the piano and dining room furniture.

He immediately unplugged all the appliances and reminded me to take numerous pictures at every step of his intervention. I grabbed a yard stick to document the three inches of water in the kitchen. The water was breeching the threshold into the living room, forming a tributary to the dining area.

I moved the dining chairs to bedrooms while Jason moved the full curio cabinet beyond the water's threat. He moved one of the sofas away from the large window and flung one end of the Oriental carpet over the back of it. Once he had moved everything that had to be placed away from the water, he started ripping up the engineered hardwood floor in the living and dining areas. The water had stopped about three inches away from the piano and large china cabinet. I toweled as much as I could into the sinks.

Jason went up into the attic to assess the damage. When he came back, he said, "I can see one ruptured pipe, and there might be one more. You'll have to replace quite a bit of insulation, and I'm not sure whether the water got between the walls or not. Do you have a plumber?"

"I've used the one you recommended a time or two, but he's really expensive."

"It's going to be hard to get one at any price."

I called the one he knew and found that he was already booked three weeks ahead even before the storm hit.

I then called my neighbor who had given me referrals to a couple of workers. "Patty, could you recommend a plumber? I've just discovered a ruptured pipe. A friend is here and has found the problem in the attic, but he's not a plumber. Is your house okay?"

"Oh, Sue, I am so sorry you've had to come home to this. I had a busted pipe too and just found a plumber down the street. It wasn't too bad, and he fixed it while he waited for his helper to go get some parts from their warehouse. You know that house on the corner with the orange tree near the curb? Well, that lady's son is a plumber, and he's there fixing her broke pipe right now. I'll give you his number. I hope he can work you in soon. They're all going to be so busy. You better call him right now before he gets away."

I thanked her and called him. He said, "I'm 'bout ready to go home. Without no electricity, I can't hardly see to work in the attic."

"My friend has a hat with a light on it—the kind that miners wear. Would that help?"

"Yes, Ma'am. I'll be over in a few minutes and see what I can do."

The plumber arrived in less than 15 minutes. I had already asked Jason to go up into the attic with him because I knew Jason's integrity and trusted his assessment of the plumber's skills. They were up there for just a few minutes.

When they came back down and stood in the kitchen, Jason stood behind the plumber so that he could signal to me without alerting the plumber to the communications if he needed to signal silently. The plumber said, "Ma'am, there's just one slit that has to be repaired right away. I've got a length of pipe on my truck and can get it done right now since your friend said I could use his light."

"I don't have cash for this. Can you take a check?"

"Sure." He grinned. "I know it'll be good 'cause I know where you live at."

"What will the charge be?"

"$200-$225, depending on how long a piece of pipe I have to use."

I looked at Jason with a question mark on my face. He gave a small shrug and a thumbs up sign. I said, "Okay. Let's get it done."

The assistant who had come with the plumber went out to the truck to get tools and materials while Jason and the plumber went back up into the attic. Jason had already taken pictures of the damage and continued to take shots of the repair.

It must have taken about thirty minutes for the plumber to fix the pipe. They turned on the water valve and tested for leaks. It looked like a successful repair. They agreed that the water valve should be left off that night because the prediction was for continued single digit temperatures for the rest of the week.

I gave the plumber the check and got his card. He gave me the 12-inch length of copper pipe with the one-inch slit in it. He said he believed that there was only one rupture and that the other place Jason was concerned about just needed a little tightening. They also checked the section over the master bedroom where Jason had found the source of a slow leak coming down between the bed and armoire when I had called him after his bedtime on a school night not long before the Arctic Vortex appeared. The plumber said that area could use some more insulation, but the repair looked good.

The next day, Jason and I went back to my house. He brought a hazmat suit and a roll of insulation he had in his garage. He hauled down all the soggy insulation and replaced it with what he had on hand. I had a supply of extra-large black trash bags, which he used to contain the insulation before he placed it at the curb.

Just like twelve years earlier when I had done the partial refurb on the house, the black bags looked like they were in a holding area at a morgue. Within days, they were dwarfed by other bags full of warped flooring, stacked furniture, and ruined appliances and accessories such as ceiling fans dotting the curbs up and down the block. It was reminiscent of the mountains of drenched belongings we had seen when Harvey stalled over Houston in 2017—not a good memory to be triggered by a winter storm equal to Harvey's strength, but different in affect simply because one came in the early fall and the other just beat spring's pollen and blooms.

I later learned that the damage to my house was similar to what almost every homeowner on my block suffered. Some had a little less damage, and others had more. But neighbors shared what heat, water, and groceries we had as each of us reconciled insurance claims and competed with the entire city for competent, available craftsmen to restore our property and sooth our souls.

CHAPTER 21
TWO GALLON LIMIT

*The violation of some laws is a normal
part of the behavior of every citizen.*
　　　　　　　　　　　　Stuart Chase
　　　　　　　　　　　　(1888-1985)

Now that the United States has surpassed 170,000 deaths from COVID-19, the numbers of positive tests, hospitalizations, and deaths reported in Texas hint at stabilization. Nothing is normal, just a little less bad. But as soon as we took slight comfort in the latest numbers reported, we heard that not one, but two, tropical storms were entering the Gulf of Mexico, either or both of which could hit Houston as Gulf-intensified hurricanes. And in case that was not enough to spike the anxiety scale, we heard that a meteor was hurtling toward Earth. The universe was spinning the ball on the roulette wheel called Earth.

Many, if not most, seasoned Houstonians still flinched at the word, "hurricane." It had been only three years since Harvey's unwelcome visit, and most who suffered total loss of property and belongings still reeled from the nightmare's impact and the memories. My back door still showed the mark where raging water had threatened to breach the weather stripping.

I was lucky, though, with almost no property damage. Yet my usually calm and steady nerves quivered when I thought of the nights I spent in a newly opened motel near my house so that I could be in a second story room on those nights when rain fell in feet rather than inches. The extreme rainfall that Harvey dumped on concrete and saturated ground was attributed to its stubborn refusal to move on. It either loved or hated Houston too obsessively to find other dumping grounds as quickly as most tropical storms or hurricanes do.

In 2021, with Harvey's memories fresh, a pandemic shutdown, two potential hurricanes, and a meteor trying to add a skyward exclamation point, I scrolled through Facebook postings of the supposed approaching end of the world. It reminded me of the hysteria that preceded the turn of the millennia when Y-2K was about to slingshot Earth into terminal chaos. I considered the mindset and beliefs that are the source of such predictions and moved on to more palatable subjects such as the utter necessity for voters to mandate changes in the next election.

Twenty-eight years earlier, I vowed to never again be my own hair colorist. But that was when the natural red was still simply fading and the copper needed only a light polishing. Now, in week four since the last trip to the salon, the roots show not as faded auburn, but as silver worthy of someone much older than I feel.

Eager to use precaution, but without manufactured masks readily available, I fashioned a mask out of an old sock. It was the third try at protective gear. The red bandana seemed flimsy and too western for my east-coast soul. A polyester scarf folded multiple times offered better protection with its tight weave, but it slipped easily. Finally, I resorted to online instructions for the sock mask. Almost instant, two cuts—one at the toe and one at the heel—plus two small clips to create ear loops got the job done. I didn't hesitate to use the obviously misplaced garment and anticipated using plastic produce bags for gloves

While at the grocery store with a mission of stocking up in preparation for two potential hurricanes forming in the Gulf, I indulged in some time in the aisle that held bottled miracles for hair color. I dreaded attempting to color my hair after having had it done in a salon for many years, but I dreaded more intensely the possibility of seeing a faded shade of auburn take over. Satisfied that I had made a good choice of the product to use, I aimed the cart to the aisle with bottled water.

In addition to bottled water, I needed ice and canned goods. Getting one bag of ice was not a problem. Shelves for bottled water were not bare, but there was a sign about every two feet stating a limit of two gallons per customer. That had been routine since news of COVID-19 first hit months prior to the double storm prediction. Even toilet paper was almost always available once the initial hording was curtailed by limits.

My house was just old enough to have a few age-related quirks. One was the cold water line in the kitchen. Occasionally, tiny shiny black particles came out of the cold water faucet there, but never from any of the four other sinks in the house.

Because of the less than pristine cold water in the kitchen, I used bottled water for all kitchen needs. Although I had initially stocked up, I had let the supply of water become low since grocery stores were not having any difficulty keeping it stocked, thanks to the long-standing limit.

I knew of the two gallon limit but thought I could talk my way into being able to at least double that amount, even if it meant playing the age card. Because of my age and absence of the vaccine at that time, I tried to avoid going to the store more than about once every ten days. After discovering I had left my "wallet" of credit cards in the car after filling the tank, I asked a supervisor at the self-check lanes to watch my cart while I retrieved the plastic case holding the credit cards. He took one look at the cart, puffed himself up to his full 6' 2" height, and said, "You'll have to remove two of those waters. There's a two gallon limit."

"I know, Sir, but I'm 78 years old and don't need to be out in stores. Could you make an exception this time?"

"No, ma'am. My boss told me to tell everyone that we're not allowed to make exceptions."

"I understand the need for limits. Does this mean I'll have to make other trips in order to prepare for the storms headed this way?"

Either waffling or being tired of me, he said, "I'll call the manager."

I watched as an officious man came from about six or eight check-out lanes away. The one I had been talking to started walking toward the man who I assumed was his boss. I didn't want him to deliver a self-fulfilling message such as, "I can't let her buy more than two gallons, can I," so followed and politely made my case. When I got the same pat answer, I tried to smile and said, "Okay. I guess I'll have to spend additional time going from store to store to get enough water. Hope I manage to dodge the virus."

Finally, a definite waffle. The manager said, "Well—as long as they're separate transactions, I guess it'll be okay."

"So—I can buy more than two gallons if I pay for them separately?"

"Don't say I said so."

Feeling relieved, I went to the checkout lane. I should have used the self-check lane where the man who first talked to me had returned. But as they say on Facebook, I am not an employee of that or any other store.

I was proactive as I greeted the cashier. She was young and earnest—a rule-follower and proud of it. When I thought beyond my own concerns of the moment, I felt sorry for her and realized that she was doing the best she could to have a job and to keep it. I explained that the water on the bottom of the cart was to be rung up separately. She said, "No, ma'am. We can't do that. There's a two gallon limit."

Remembering that the manager did not want to be quoted, I said, "I understand that a separate transaction is permissible."

"No, Ma'am. I ain't gonna get fired for nobody."

I didn't engage. (She who blinks first loses.)

"I'm gonna call my manager."

"Okay."

She dinged her bell, turned around toward the next aisle's plexiglass, and flailed her arms. A woman came over and listened to the clerk explain that I wanted to buy two additional gallons of water.

The supervisor said to me, "You just talked to the head manager, right?"

"Yes, after I talked to the self-check supervisor. He watched my cart for me while I went to the car to get my wallet (easier than explaining that it was a plastic case with my credit cards in it). He called the manager over, and I talked with him. I'm 78 years old and don't need to be making extra trips in and out of stores when so many people still refuse to wear a mask."

Again, "I ain't gonna get fired for nobody." (And I thought I was obstinate.)

The supervisor responded, "It's okay. I saw her talk with the manager. Just ring it up as a separate transaction."

The bagger had left the scene of the inquisition and returned just as the supervisor was moving on to the next crisis. The cashier explained to the bagger, "She got two extra gallons on the bottom of the cart. I done tole the supervisor I ain't gonna get fired for nobody, so don't you go tellin' nobody I let this lady do this."

I thanked them for helping me and put the cart into over-drive to make it to the trunk of my car before I had to get special dispensation from anyone else. Even the thought of running out of bottled water can stretch behavior beyond what was the old norm back when making any number of trips to a store was no cause for concern.

Then, as the storms approached and the meteor sought a landing spot, it was time to think about when to fill the bathtubs with water to be used for bathing or flushing the toilet if one or both hurricanes hit Houston. And then there was this thing about trying to sleep.

CHAPTER 22
MEAD IN THE ELUSIVE GRAPE

*One can return to the place of her birth,
but cannot go back to her youth.*
John Burroughs
(1837-1921)

If I had never known the space where The Elusive Grape wine bar is housed as any other business, I would have only noticed the feel of the welcoming air as I inhaled the aromas from the kitchen and bar. From both curiosity and a friend's recommendation, I had just ordered my first glass of Mead, which was brewed in DeLand. For a while, I alternated between burying my head in editing a chapter and taking in the charm of the bar with the Hatters light fixture and the various seating areas that looked more like private conversation pits than seats for a business. In the midst of the reverie, it felt more like a type of dislocation—a gentle jolt to take in the current configuration of the space I had idealized decades ago.

For me, Fountain's Store for Men was the epitome of a high-class shop for men. In high school, I went there to buy small gifts for my first boyfriend, Jack, and nice handkerchiefs for Daddy on Father's Day. The first time I gave Daddy a box of handkerchiefs from Fountain's, he gently reminded me, "You know, you pay less per handkerchief at Sears or Penny's." I think he intended to teach me frugality, which was ingrained in himself.

"I know, but it's more fun to shop at Fountain's, and these last longer." I was trying to practice my newly honed shopping skills I had learned in my Home Economics class and felt justified in my choice of stores because I used my own money, which I earned by checking groceries at Winn-Dixie and babysitting.

The thing that stuck out in my memory as I sat in the plush chair at the Elusive Grape was Daddy's story of buying his blue serge wedding suit there in 1926. Even though that splurge went against his grain monetarily, his pride in ownership of that suit never waned. Mother gave me the wooden hanger from the store after his death, and I eventually passed it on to my brother. There I was, though, waiting for my mead, and trying to reconstruct my memory of what the store looked like before it was repurposed.

I wondered, *Did the less expensive suits hang where the red or the white wines rest in anticipation of a sommelier or large group selecting them? Did my father peruse the entire selection or limit his shopping by his notion of which suits were affordable?* I feel certain that he never would have even considered the possibility of paying more for a suit than he knew he could afford. Not one to covet or wish for more than he had, he would have asked a sales attendant to direct him to the less expensive suits. Had he been a drinker, he would have asked for the house wine, never a particular bottle, even if he were hosting a sizable group.

The bottles line the racks like middle school girls wondering which boy will find the courage to request a dance—categorized by color, vintner, and degree of sugar content. They are further divided by texture—the amount of effervescence determining whether they are siblings or cousins to each other, as though a personality trait defines their worth.

I turned my attention away from the wine inventory and focused on the menu. The granite-topped table between me the sofa held my writing journal and pencil. I quickly decided on the fancy ham and cheese sandwich and returned to scanning each area for items of distinction and comparing what I saw with what I remembered.

The sofa nearest me was a warm shade of coral, almost the same tone as the accent color in the granite in the kitchen and bathrooms of my newly purchased home in DeLand. The other sofa, the one facing the coral one, was separated by an oversized dark wood coffee table—a table that should be called a wine table since its space is in The Elusive Grape. Long before bottles of wine lined the walls and smells of panini stuffed with ham and cheese filled the air, suits made of the finest fabrics and worn for the most joyful and solemn occasions filled about ¾ of the floor area.

The other ¼ of the square footage was filled with dress shirts, ties, and a variety of leather belts meant to complement Florsheim dress shoes. The small section where I could find gifts I could afford was near the center where the cash register rang up the sales and heightened my pride when I received the tissue-wrapped treasures for Jack or Daddy.

For my father, the purchase of his blue serge wedding suit in 1926—one of the few, if not the only, suit he ever bought—it was a life-long memory. I feel certain that the durability of the double twilled weave of the serge piqued his sense of practicality and accounts for the long life of the wedding suit. Decades after their marriage, he still wore it when I was a teenager on those few occasions when he needed to dress up. More often, though, he wore dress slacks and a white shirt with a conservative tie on Sunday. A friend or one of his brothers occasionally passed on a sport coat, which he would add on cooler days.

For his daily attire, Daddy wore a khaki or dark green uniform. He usually purchased the pants and shirts from either Sears Roebuck or Montgomery Ward catalogs, but also sometimes purchased the sturdy work clothes from JC Penney, located in the Dreka building on Woodland Boulevard. Men looking for work clothes knew not to go to Fountain's.

The Dreka Building still stands proudly on the corner of the block where my father worked at the Standard Oil Service Station owned by Lou Skillman. Now, there is an empty lot where the station stood. The lot next to it is also empty except for parking designations—the lot that once supported the red brick building that housed the heavy printing presses of the DeLand Sun News. That same building became the site for the Ford automobile dealership after the DeLand Sun News moved to a different location—more signs of dynamic change that can be viewed as progress or with regret.

My mind wanders as I wonder if that concrete holds molecules of Daddy's sweat. And does the adjacent lot hold memories of the hum of the printing presses and the aroma of ink mixed with the sounds of

Ford engines and the smell of exhaust fumes. Do the fronds of palm trees recall the shade of red in the cooler that held small bottles of Coca Cola? And did that red match the red in the Lance glass jar that held nickel bags of peanuts destined to drown in the Coca Cola liquid as we tossed them in, salt and all, swigging the nutted Cokes quickly before the peanuts lost their crunch? Much of the partially chewed peanuts lodged in large tooth cavities, serving as partial protection from the pain that stabbed when sugar in the cold Coke found a direct path to a sensitive nerve.

My mind shifts back to the present and notices the cork-lined pillars that define the space for the bar. I assume they are weight-bearing and have always been there, but I do not recall seeing them long ago. Perhaps the decades have clouded some of the memories, but that was so long ago, and I did not go into Fountain's very often.

I notice the Stetson Hatters chandelier right over the center of the bar and smile. When I attended Stetson, students were not allowed to drink on campus, and a sign of any sort with *Stetson Hatters* on it would never have been seen anywhere near a bar. Now, it is so much simpler and more honest—a forthright recognition that whether or not a person drinks alcoholic beverages is up to the individual, not the institution, and the chandelier in The Elusive Grape is only a sign of welcome to students, alums, and both residents and visitors of the town because it is impossible to separate the town from the university. Once inside the Elusive Grape, there seems to be an unspoken agreement that for those moments while we are united with the Hatters chandelier crowning the warmth, we all are Hatters and DeLandites.

Beyond the bar and front half of the floor space, there is a glass wall with etched art on it. I wonder if that is where the fitting rooms were. Perhaps it is merely a means of separating the front from the back sections of the room. But since I can't be sure of that, I guess I will just have to go back to the Elusive Grape soon and investigate. Perhaps I can also learn the story behind the presence of Christmas lights strung along the wall near ceiling level. And maybe I will talk again with the same people I have met there. Or perhaps there will be new friends the next time who I will need to meet for the first time.

CHAPTER 23
COINCIDENTAL INCIDENCES THAT LED ME HOME

(S)He thought (s)he saw an Albatross
That fluttered round the lamp:
(S)He looked again, and found it was
A penny postage stamp,
"You'd best be getting home," (s)he said,
"The nights are very damp."

Lewis Carroll
(1832-1898)

It felt like nudges from the universe surrounded me—not in a knotted circle to contain me, but in a chain-linked path to guide me home. Hurricane Harvey and the Arctic Vortex not only made climate change real in thought, but in personal consequences.

Harvey's stall over Houston brought the two-block-away-creek to my back door and sent me to a hotel for safety on the second floor. My property and I fared much better than millions of others. Even while I met the challenges of the flooding all around me and watched news coverage of utter disaster, the impact did not fully wrench my gut until I got out to help deliver food to workers tasked with mucking out houses in all socio-economic neighborhoods. They raced the build-up of toxic black mold with minimal self-protection.

When the entire contents of a home are piled by the curb, the replacement cost of those possessions and the income level of the occupants are irrelevant. Heartbreak knows no neighborhoods. I thought that was the worst natural disaster I would ever experience.

Four years after Harvey's visit, the vortex reminded me of the foolishness of my previous assumption about natural disasters. I got through Harvey without having to call on anyone to help, but the vortex reminded me of the limits of personal independence and stubbornness. The aftermath of near total house refurbishing after ice sliced one pipe gave me both pride in the finished product and confidence in solving problems of home maintenance. But the deepest feeling was of gratitude for the friends who sheltered me as the snow, ice, and wind swirled in single-digit temperatures. I asserted to myself that I never wanted to repeat such a project.

While recognizing the folly of my wish, I wondered if I could at least find a place I loved where I would not be at the mercy of a climate out of control. I had to admit to myself that long-term residency in the United Kingdom was not realistic at my age. I *what-ifed* every state I thought I might enjoy but could not identify one with the right combination of climate, beauty, and affordability.

On the heels of Harvey and the Vortex, COVID-19's forced isolation impacted everything and everybody. I witnessed two verbal assaults on store managers when virus denier customers refused to comply with the manager's request that they wear a mask. Cops were called, and I fled in my car. The first time I ventured to a grocery store after the shutdown began and before the vaccine came out, I used plastic bags as gloves in the produce department and donned a mask made from an old sock. I trained myself to stand at least six feet from fellow shoppers and realized how much I missed talking to strangers.

My friend, Valerie, taught me to use FaceTime and Zoom for teaching piano. High school students volunteered to host the Zoom meetings. A few high schoolers dropped out because the challenge of preparing for piano lessons while trying to maintain academic progress and music ensemble preparation was simply too heavy a load to bear. I cancelled lessons with that year's youngest beginners because online instruction was impossible for that age group. Students, parents, and I all missed the recitals, which we normally held at the end of each semester. But for those who did continue lessons, and for me, the reward of maintaining contact and continuing musical progress outweighed the deficits of online lessons.

I tried to market my book that had just come out by sending custom-designed post card announcements to independent bookstores nationwide. Admitting that it was a complete waste of money made a bite of bitterness dull the excitement of publication. But it kept me busy and maintained hope that I would eventually be able to market in person. I reminded myself that I was an author still learning not only the craft of writing creative nonfiction, but also the business of publication.

Idle hours alone at home encouraged deep reflection. I recalled how happy and free I felt on vacation, particularly when travel included writing retreats and workshops. I asked myself why I didn't feel that way in Houston. I had told visitors many times, "Houston is impressive, but it is not beautiful." And I joined others who said, "I will never be a Texan, but I am a Houstonian." I was there by marriage. It was my city-in-law, but not my home.

Houston treated me well. The city and most of the school districts supported fine arts in the schools. I earned my doctorate at the University of Houston. I met and married my last husband, grieved his death, and adored my grandchildren his children had given me. Yet, I still missed DeLand. As I thought about the low-level, but constant, feeling of discontent, slowly, the reasons came into focus with such strong clarity that I not only could, but felt compelled to act upon them. I pondered why I rarely felt so alive as when I travelled.

I took several online writing courses during the pandemic shutdown and began shaping my writing toward what became this book. Then, once the dreaded daily numbers reporting infections, hospitalizations, and deaths from COVID-19 dropped to a point of reasonable safety, Peter Murphy announced that the course sponsored by Stockton University would resume at the Atlantic Center for the Arts in New Smyrna Beach (less than 20 miles from DeLand) in March, 2022. I registered for the course as soon as I saw the announcement and counted weeks and days until I would leave and make the familiar drive from Houston to DeLand.

On the Sunday before I left for New Smyrna Beach, my friend, Rick, came up to me in the Great Hall at church and gave me a big hug.

"Hey, Sue. I am so happy to let you know we will resume the bridge night this Friday. Will you be able to come?"

"Oh, Rick, that is wonderful news. Will it still be 6:00-9:00?"

"Yes. That seems to be the best time for most folks."

"I can't attend this week because I'm going to Florida for a writer's workshop. What concerns me, though, is that I don't think I can participate any more because it is getting so difficult to drive at night. The injections in my right eye are maintaining peripheral vision and depth perception, but there is a blind spot that cannot be treated because of scar tissue. I'm afraid my night driving time is over, especially on busy interstates. The other eye is still doing well."

"So many of my friends have the same issue, but I don't think we can change the time for bridge. The Dean wants us to expand it to include board games so that families can come and socialize. I hope you have a great time in Florida. We'll try to get together for a small bridge party when you get back."

As I drove home from church that day, I thought about what it would be like to drive at night in DeLand. Driving times would be measured in under 10 minutes. I felt certain that even night driving would be comfortable for the short distances within the town. I knew I could attend cultural events at Stetson almost daily and never think twice about driving issues.

With that mindset, I packed for the trip to the workshop and planned to spend an additional week in DeLand split between several days prior to the workshop and additional time after its conclusion.

One of the town quirks in DeLand is that many of the downtown businesses, particularly restaurants, close on Monday. Trying to avoid chain restaurants on the outskirts of town, I strolled the boulevard, hoping to find a place for breakfast. On a whim, I went into *Lace and Accessories* for suggestions. I waited while another customer paid for her purchase. I eyed the *church-lady* hats in the back of the shop while I waited, noting that I would come back before I left town to buy an Easter hat.

Assuming I was a tourist, the customer turned to me and said, "Hi. My name's Amy. What brings you to DeLand?"

"I'm a DeLandite but haven't lived here since 1968. Any suggestions for a breakfast place?"

"I guess you know Hunter's is closing. This is their last week in business after three or four generations. They're closed on Mondays, though."

"I'm sorry to hear they're closing. Didn't they just reopen after the old restaurant burned?"

"Yes. The new location is just off the boulevard on East Rich Avenue."

"I remember Nancy from high school. She was a year or two ahead of me. I always eat there at least once when I'm in town. Guess it'll be a chain restaurant today, but I'll go to Hunter's tomorrow."

"You know that Nancy passed away recently, don't you?"

"Yes. I saw it on Facebook. It won't seem the same without her there."

Amy put away the receipt the cashier handed her and continued, "Are you visiting family?"

"No. Most of my family live in Missouri now. I've often thought about moving back and buying the house my maternal grandparents built and renting out the extra bedrooms to Stetson students. I even googled the address recently and found it had just been taken off the market. I learned it has four bedrooms, but only one bathroom, so my dream wouldn't work without a lot of expensive renovation. I'm here primarily for a writer's workshop in New Smyrna Beach. But I can't be that close and not spend some time here."

"So you're an author?"

"Yes—as of April, 2020."

"What do you write?"

"The book is a memoir that tells the story of my history of sexual abuse by a family member and my recovery from it. The thing that makes my story different from millions of others is that a cousin published a book of so-called genealogy in 1999. In it, he claimed that I accused my father of the abuse. That false claim mandated that I set the record straight."

Amy reached into her purse, pulled out a business card, and handed it to me. She said, "If you ever get serious about making the move back, just let me know."

Thinking she was simply being friendly, I didn't look at the card until after I returned to the hotel room hours later. Amy lowered her voice almost to a whisper and continued. "You are so brave to tell your story. I've got to talk with you. I work part-time with girls and young women who are victims of sex trafficking. Do you have any of your books with you?"

"Yes. They're in my car. Would you like me to get one for you?"

"No. I want you to get me six copies. I want everyone I work with to have a copy, and I want one for the library in the safe house. Do you use Zelle?"

"Sure. My car is less than two blocks away. I'll be happy to get them for you now."

I walked to the parking lot and loaded my arms with the six books, excited to have connected with a friendly stranger who valued my work.

When I placed the six books on the countertop, Amy handed one to the store owner. She said, "I already know you're going to love this book. I counted you in the number of books I bought."

The owner looked at the cover, thumbed through to see the pictures, and said, "Yep. I can tell that's you even in your junior high school pictures."

Amy then said, "In case you decide to move back, do you have a realtor in Houston?"

"No. I used a friend years ago, but she and her assistant have both retired."

"I have a dear friend who is a realtor and used to work in Houston." Her thumbs were already clicking away with a text. He responded immediately. She then said, "Are you familiar with an area called *Katy*?"

"Am I familiar with Katy!? I'm retired from the Katy Independent School District. My mailing address is Houston, but the boundary for Katy is half a block away from my house."

"I can't believe it. I've never heard of it, but it's where the realtor my friend recommends is located. I will text you her contact data. Do you know this address?"

She showed me her phone screen. I glanced at it, then said, "I know exactly where that is—about five minutes from my front door."

"I don't know this particular realtor, but my friend highly recommends her. She is the daughter of the broker who my friend used to work with. Anyone he recommends will do a good job for you."

Later that evening after spending the day driving up one street and down the next looking for *for sale* signs (there were none), I looked at Amy's card and was surprised to see that she was a real estate agent. I had expected her card to relate to her work with sex trafficking victims, but with reflection, it all made sense. I called her.

"Amy, I didn't realize you are a real estate agent."

"I work part-time in the office and do my other work from home. And now, I'm your agent here in DeLand. I work with my brother, who is the broker."

"This may be tender turf for me because I have a cousin who is a real estate agent in New Smyrna Beach. I need to talk with her before I agree to work with you. I would not want to stir up a family controversy before I even get home."

"I understand. I'm guessing, though, that if she works the coastal area, she does not work this side of the county. See what she says. Either way, I'm here to help in any way I can."

"Thank you so much for the referral to Erica in Katy. I will let you know how plans are developing. I'll be back in DeLand after the course is over."

"Okay. Enjoy the workshop."

With that cushion of comfort and encouragement, I called the cousin and made plans to get together the day the workshop ended. I did not say anything about the possible plans, though, because we had not seen each other in thirty years. When we met for a seafood lunch a little over a week later, I still did not mention the possibility of moving because her husband and brother were there, and the place was too noisy for serious conversation. We needed every minute to catch up and reconnect.

The next day, I went back over for another lunch with her. After we finished lunch, her brother went to his home. She and I returned to her home, and her husband went out to do errands. Finally, the atmosphere was right to talk seriously about my dream and developing plans. Her first response was, "You know I'm a real estate agent, right?"

"Yes. I had seen that on Facebook, but I didn't know if you were still working or had retired."

"I just renewed my license for another 2 years. The market is too good to hang it up yet."

"Do you work in the Deland area?"

"Not really. I stay pretty much on the coast. I could help you through multiple listings, though."

"I would love to work with you, but I need to think about it before I decide."

"I completely understand. I think we could make it work, but you might want someone who specializes in that part of the county."

We spent another hour or so reminiscing about the times we spent together as children when our dads—mine the oldest and hers the youngest of their siblings—fished together and gave us the happiest times they could.

With so many of the restaurants closed on Mondays, I had to wait until the next night to have dinner with the friends who had read the first complete draft of the memoir. Georgia is a high school friend and wrote one of the testimonial blurbs for the book. ClaireBeth is the daughter of Paul Langston, who was Dean of the School of Music at Stetson University when I was a student there. She was one of the first to write a review on Amazon. Her mother, Esther, taught elementary school music and influenced my career choice when she asked me to substitute for her.

We talked non-stop about the old times, the tight connections, and our current lives as retired women. Georgia, the high school friend, had become an Administrative Assistant in the elementary school I attended in DeLeon Springs. ClaireBeth was the Assistant Principal there after the former principal (also my fourth-grade teacher) retired. It was uncanny that they even knew other because of the difference in their ages, much less that they had worked together.

Over dessert, I said, "I have what may be a hairbrained idea and need to run it past you two. I'm seriously considering moving back to DeLand, but I think it might be a good idea to try staying here for one-three months before making such a major decision. Living here could be vastly different from visiting."

Georgia spoke up, "Sue, I have an extra room completely separate from my house. My late husband built it for a workshop. It has everything you'll need except a shower. You can use the guest bathroom's shower, though. There's a window unit AC and a ceiling fan, wifi, a desk, and outlets for your electronics. You can come and stay as long as you want or need."

"That sounds ideal. What would the rent be?"

"Not a penny. Just come when you want; stay as long as you need; and come back if you need to when you are looking for a house."

"That would be a godsend. I talked to Bobbie at the tea room about my idea, and she told me about a person who winters here and might want to rent out their house for the summer. I called and found that the rent would be $1600 per month plus utilities."

"Don't even think about money. The room's yours as long as you want."

ClaireBeth interjected, "I can't believe all these connections. Have you two been in touch all these years?"

I said, "No. I contacted Georgia to get her feedback on the memoir because I knew she had lived here almost the entire time since we knew each other in high school. I especially needed her feedback regarding the description of this area. I needed your input as it related to references to your father and others connected with Stetson."

Georgia added, "Sue and I knew each other in high school. She was a year behind me, but we sang together in the Glee Club and Madrigal Choir and in a mixed quartette. I was the robe custodian, and Sue did some of the accompanying. Did you know that our Madrigal Choir was the first one in a high school in Florida?"

ClaireBeth said, "No, but I'm not surprised. My father was fond of Mr. Auman and respected his work."

I reminded ClaireBeth, "Your father was one of my major professors and an outstanding role model for me. Your mom's timely laryngitis launched me on my career in Music Education, and now, you are part of that extended circle they both cast. I am so happy to know you and appreciate your reading one of the early rough drafts of the book.

"My pleasure."

Georgia said, "Now when will we get to read the next one?"

"It will be a while yet, but I'm working on what I hope will become the story of my homecoming to DeLand."

I gave each of them a gift bag with Texas wine. They headed to their homes, and I headed to the hotel, my mind ping-ponging with what-ifs and to-do lists. My heart felt cradled in the most comfortable and fertile soil of my soul.

I left DeLand with short-termed sadness and inevitable comparison between the road I was close to embarking on and the almost endless search I had been on since 1968. I thought about how long it would take to complete refurbishing the Houston house. That had to be done, no matter what I decided about moving. But if my plans became definite, the work had to shift into overdrive. I speculated that if I made a firm decision to move to DeLand, I could make it happen in 6-12 months. I was aware that the market was very good, but I did not know it was crazy in both Houston and DeLand.

Mulling over all the what-ifs was exciting until I turned off of I-75 onto I-10 going into the panhandle of Florida. A torrential rainstorm hit and was almost as stubborn as Harvey had been. I turned off the CD and turned on the radio to local stations as I drove much slower than the speed limit. I also set the phone to the weather app and held it in my left hand for frequent checks, but the sky was so dark that I couldn't read the screen. I pulled off for coffee when there was a bit of reprise in the rain. By the time I parked, the sky was even darker. A truck driver was unloading at the convenience store. I parked beside his off-ramp, lowered the window enough to make him hear me, and asked, "Is the weather better or worse west of here?"

"It's fixin' to get real bad here. Go west as fast as you can. I just heard a tornado warning for this county."

"Thanks! Be safe."

I eased back onto the freeway without coffee or a comfort stop and adjusted the radio. The driver was right. "The National Weather Service has issued a severe thunderstorm warning with tornado watch for this area. Take precaution and stay tuned."

I've driven through many storms in many different areas of the country. Each was a little different, but the concerns are always the same. *Do I stop and risk the worst of the storm hitting here? Or do I go on and risk going into even worse conditions?"* I tried to relax my shoulders, not daring to indulge in the distraction of music. I hoped that the few others on the interstate had their lights on. I fumbled around on the steering wheel trying to find the hazard lights button, but gave up on it. I hoped I would not have bruises on my thumbs like I did when I drove through a bad storm between Houston and Missouri. On that trip, I saw more than a few 18-wheelers flipped onto their sides on the median, and I gripped the steering wheel for all it was worth as the winds threatened to add my little Hyundai to the heap.

The radio host was an extreme right-winger spouting conspiracies mixed with weather alerts. Every time I crossed a county line, I had to find another radio station. But they might as well have been the same one.

The general consensus seemed to be, *The weather's bad, but it's gonna'get worse.* I fought the tenseness by trying to focus on the possibility that my next trip on this stretch of I-10 would be when I returned to Houston to supervise loading the moving van.

Ifs became *whens*—first in my thinking, and then in my plans. Whatever residual fog remained in my mind about wanting to make the move finally distilled into three conclusions:

1. Houston is too big for night driving.
2. John's commitment is too small.
3. DeLand is just right.

I knew that I did not need to spend any time in DeLand to make sure I would want to move permanently. It was clear, and my mind was settled.

After what seemed like 12 hours, but wasn't, I was close to the Alabama state line. Rain and sky both lightened. By then, it was mid-afternoon—not my usual time to stop for the night, but I felt it was time to find a hotel. When I approached the front desk, the clerk said, "You been drivin' in this storm long?"

"Too long. I left DeLand this morning and have been in severe weather since hitting I-10. I think it's time to get off the road and plan to get an early start in the morning."

"Where ya headin' to?"

"Houston. I usually stop in Biloxi, but this weather has about got the best of me."

"Lemme jus' check the weather app for ya.'"

"Okay. That would be very kind of you. Mind if I use the restroom while you do that?"

"Sure, Hon—right over there."

When I stepped back up to the desk, the friendly desk clerk said, "You might as well go on if you want to. You've made it through the worst of the storm. The rain will stop after you cross into Alabama."

"That is encouraging, and I really do want to make time if the weather will ease up." I made an estimate of time on the road and thought I could get to Biloxi by a reasonable time. I thanked her again and left.

She was right about the weather, but the abundance of drivers who apparently had weathered the storm somewhere off the highway and the number of spring breakers who had headed home from West Florida beaches had the interstate jammed bumper-to-bumper. And there were miles of stretches where one lane was closed due to long-term construction. I had traded the nightmare of weather for the frustration of traffic.

With minimal exception, though, there was no impatience or imprudence among the drivers. I saw no wrecks until weather had greatly improved and lanes had opened up. Traffic was still slow. At one of the entrance ramps where the on-ramp descended a hill, an 18-wheeler had jack-knifed off of the ramp and was in a twisted pile between the ramp and the highway. At least half a dozen emergency vehicles were scattered around from the ramp to the ground. Several responders were at the cab, probably trying to get the driver out.

I recalled the multiple flipped 18-wheelers I had seen on that trip to Missouri and remarked to myself that even though it was horrifying to see so many heavy trucks turned on their sides, it was nothing compared to that one truck that looked like a giant chicken with its neck broken and turned backwards, upside down.

I made one more stop and called to see if the Beau Rivage had a room. It was full. I drove on, assuming I could find a room somewhere else. I arrived at around 9:00 PM and found a room where I had stayed once before.

I texted Georgia to let her know that I had made up my mind and would not need to stay with her for an extended period of time while deciding about the move. She responded, "Well, you know the room is here whenever you need it. Keep me posted on your exciting news."

Biloxi is only about seven hours from Houston—a relatively short drive. But traffic remained highly congested. I wondered if Biden's funds were already at work. It seemed that every bridge was being repaired or replaced and many stretches of highway were in the same condition. At least we were moving faster than the previous day, though, and the weather was good.

Erica, the realtor Amy's friend recommended, called the next day and made an appointment for a couple days later. When she arrived at my house, she presented a portfolio of real estate comps. Her outgoing personality and professional demeanor left no doubt that Amy's friend had guided me to the right realtor. I trusted her with the negotiation of one of the biggest financial decisions of my life.

Erica said, "Let's look at the calendar. Things are crazy-busy now. This house won't stay on the market more than three days, and I wouldn't be surprised if we get an over-asking offer in less than 24 hours after the open house. The kitchen alone will sell it."

"I want to finish the refurb and list it for top dollar, and I don't know how long it will take to finish the bathrooms. The contractors I've been using for the kitchen and painting were highly recommended by one of my piano families. They were outstanding, but a little slow in their work. The ones they suggested for the tile work are difficult to work with due to limited English. They are really good, though. I've seen their work."

Erica assured me that her firm had a group of contractors on call who could finish the work on the house and do odd jobs to help me prepare for the move. She estimated that they could finish the refurbishing in less than two weeks, then take the photos and produce the brochures and have the open house the weekend after the brochures were printed. She planned for two open houses—one exclusively for realtors, and one for the public. As things turned out, a generous offer came in from one of the realtors, making only the first open house necessary.

My mind spun with the speed and efficiency of her projections, but I felt so sure that I was making the right decision that all I wanted to do was match her work ethic and get the job done. We took care of the initial paperwork, and I went to several big box stores to stock up on packing supplies. My attention turned to the issue of informing my students and their families about their need to find a new piano teacher. One of the biggest dilemmas, though, was how and when to tell John about my decision to move to DeLand.

Erica and I talked almost daily. When I reached the point of near panic trying to get rid of household items and untold bags of clothing, she came over in gym attire and took two loads of donations in her Suburban to a charity donation center. I followed her with my Camry just as loaded as her van. She was certainly an *in the trenches* realtor.

She and I had a slight difference of opinion about setting the asking price for the house. I held firm on setting the price higher than the highest comp in the neighborhood. My house was the largest in the subdivision. Even though there was *a whole lotta' flippin' goin' on*, I knew that my choices of materials, particularly the countertops, were much more expensive than most—porcelain instead of granite. She agreed to use my price suggestion. The open house was set for a Sunday afternoon. She called as soon as she locked the lock box to let me know I

COINCIDENTAL INCIDENCES THAT LED ME HOME 229

could return to the house. I expected a cursory report on traffic and interest expressed, but the glee in her voice let me know that she had good news. She said, "Congratulations! You are now under contract at $30,000 above your listing price."

I blurted out, "I told you so! I knew someone would fall in love with the kitchen."

"Actually, they fell in love with the size. They are first-time homebuyers with two children. The dad works from home, so he fell in love with the separate office, and the three bedrooms appealed to the mom. She really liked the kitchen, but I think the practical issues were at the top of their list."

"I can hardly believe it! This will make the purchase in DeLand so much easier. What next?"

"Inspection and appraisal, but that should be routine. I'll be in close touch. Call if you need anything or have questions."

"I am so grateful for all the help you and the contractors have already given. We'll have lunch before I head east.

Managing the calendar became tricky. I could not buy a house without the proceeds from the sale. The market in Florida was at least as hot as the Houston market. Since my lender promised a 21-day closing or $5,000 in my account if it took longer, they were highly motivated to get the papers processed. I had to time an offer in DeLand after the Houston closing, but as soon as possible.

I tried placing online offers through Amy's company several times, but each time, the house sold to a higher offer. It became clear that I must be in DeLand to stand a chance to have an offer accepted. I called Georgia to let her know when I would be coming down to look for a house. She again assured me that the room was available for however long I might need it. On the way to DeLand, I spent a couple of days at the Beau Rivage in celebration of all that was happening. Once I got to DeLand, I met with Amy and her associate, Brenda. Amy explained that she had asked Brenda to handle my purchase because Amy's mother was ill and needed her help. Brenda was just as competent and as easy to work with as Erica. She helped me put in several offers, but everyone hit the same bidding war as online. In hindsight, I am so happy that it worked out as it did.

The last house on my short list was listed *For Sale By Owner* and would not be available for realtor showings until after the owners held their open house. I had been in DeLand almost two weeks when Brenda found out that the open house had been set and we could see the house the following day. I was almost ready to make an offer when I stepped into the foyer. I already loved the curb appeal, but the colors in the tile and countertops and the size of the dining room and master bedroom sold the house to me. I am very picky about color and texture and needed rooms large enough to accommodate my furniture.

Brenda asked the owners, "How was the open house?"

"We had a little traffic, but no offers."

She explained, "I'm not surprised because in a market like what we have right now, most people want an agent working for them. Things move so fast, and there is so much paperwork to be done that people just feel more comfortable with someone taking care of things for them."

While I measured room dimensions and looked at every nook and cranny, Brenda negotiated with them so that they would pay at least part of the commission because she knew how much work she would have to do for them. She later also asked me to pay 1% of the commission, which I was okay with because Erica had given me a 2% discount because of the connection with Amy's friend. As we left, Brenda said, "I'll be in touch after Sue and I have a chance to talk."

Back at the coffee house, I agreed to make a formal offer slightly above asking price because I did not want to lose the house to a higher bidder; it was a fair price in light of the market conditions, and I really liked it. I clocked it at six minutes from Stetson's campus, eight after parking. The house was a little smaller than the Houston house, but the lot was double the size and beautifully landscaped. I felt it was the right house in the right place for me.

They accepted the offer. In a day or two, I received notice that the electronic closing on the Houston sale was set at a title company in downtown DeLand. That would give me the money in time to ease cash management. I was sitting in the title company's conference room doing the electronic closing by myself when I heard a knock on the door. I turned around and saw Amy in the doorway, smiling and as bubbly as ever.

"Mind if I sit with you a while?"

"Perfect timing. I got to the part where I have to upload my license and hit a snarl."

"This system is a little different than the one I usually use. There's a title company right next door to our office in Orange City. We usually do our closings there." She stepped out and went to the front desk. When she returned, a title agent was with her.

"You don't mind if we have a little help from Elaine, do you? Once we get the license uploaded, it will be easy to go through the forms and sign everything."

"Technology is not my forte. I would appreciate the help."

Elaine said, "This is just a slightly different process than the other title company uses. Having a remote notary also makes the system seem a little more complicated. It's easy if you do it every day but can be daunting when you're not familiar with it. It won't take but a minute to make sure everything is ready to roll."

She stood beside my chair and prompted me each step of the way. Once she saw that I was following the prompts on my own, she said, "Okay. You're doing fine now. I've seen your name and the order for the closing on your new house. It will be right here. I'll see you then."

Amy stayed long enough to make sure I made the connection with the remote notary before she slipped out to continue her day. I waved as she left, then kept signing until I finally reached the last page. The receptionist brought in a folder with the printout a few minutes later. She said, "See you soon for the closing on your new house. Welcome home!"

Back out in DeLeon Springs, I picked Georgia's brain for everything and everybody I might need—everything from health care to yard maintenance. Her knowledge of people and places in West Volusia Country is encyclopedic, and her memory is perfect. By bedtime I had a long list of people to call and their contact data.

I repacked my suitcases and let Erica know my move-out plans. She had included a 30-day free lease-back clause in the contract, but

I hoped to move out in 2-3 weeks. Most of the household goods were already packed and stacked in the garage, but I still had to clear out the attic and finalize arrangements with the moving company and piano technician.

CHAPTER 24
DISCOVERY OF CHILDHOOD HOME

*No great artist ever sees things as they really are.
If he did, he would cease to be an artist.*

Oscar Wilde
(1854-1900)

Identifying places where my family lived almost always included the street address and sometimes a name. Perhaps that habit developed because we moved so often, mostly within the same town. When street numbers became irrelevant, the street name sufficed. The earliest two homes of my parents simply became *Anita Street* or *Grace Avenue* even after Grace Avenue became Grace Street on the signage.

When my parents bought a larger home toward the end of World War II, it was set in my memory as 142 North Adelle Avenue in DeLand. The location was ideal. My older sisters could walk two blocks to school, and the service station where Daddy worked was just a few blocks away on the corner of West New York Avenue and Stone Street. I mentioned the house located at 142 N. Adelle in my earlier book, *Cries of the Panther on Mockingbird Hill*, not knowing that it would impact my life again after I moved back to DeLand less than a year ago.

Through the decades since I left DeLand, when I visited, I always drove by all our former addresses. Driving by 142 N. Adelle triggered memories of my brother's birth, our trip to Washington state, and Mother's description of it as the nicest house they ever owned. But like most of our homes, it was not a long-term residency.

When we returned to Florida after just a few months in Washington, we rented the house across the intersection of Adelle and Rich Avenues.

As a four-year-old, I did not understand why someone else lived in our house. But I adjusted and enjoyed renewing my friendship with *Mother Holmes* who lived on the opposite corner from the rental house and diagonal to the house we had owned. Because I wrote extensively of the family history previously, this chapter focuses on the house I knew as *142 N. Adelle*.

I drove by that house in 2015 and almost cried. It looked as though it was abandoned, had withstood too many storms, and had fed too many termites. I feared that by the time I returned, it would be a pile of rubble.

Seven years later, in 2022, I gripped the steering wheel tightly when I turned from West New York Avenue onto North Adelle Avenue. At the end of the first block, there was a vacant lot where my childhood home had sat except for a detached garage, which I think was added after we moved out, and a small bulldozer sitting near the sidewalk. It felt as though I were visiting a cemetery, but I had no flowers to lay or hymns to sing. I stopped long enough to lower the car window and take a picture to share with my brother. Although he does not remember living there because he was an infant, he recalls hearing Mother and Daddy reminiscing about our time spent there.

I speculated that someone had purchased the lot and was preparing to build a new home and hoped the new owners would honor the architectural and historic context of the house my parents had owned when I was a child and etched my first memories. Feeling both downcast and hopeful, I turned onto West Rich Avenue to drive to the house I had placed an offer on. While driving slowly to take in the house we had rented when we returned from Washington, I scrutinized each house I passed. Several houses beyond the corner, I noticed a house on the left and wondered if the owner had restored it or had built a new home in a historic style. House, yard, and detached garage all were impeccable in style and upkeep. I wished there were a *for sale* sign in the yard and that I could afford to buy the property. The attraction to the house was so strong that I turned around and drove as slow as possible to get a better look—two stories with center dormer triple window; generous front porch; large trees in the back yard, but none in the front; detached three-car garage—probably much more house than I needed and certainly out of my budget even if it were for sale. I noticed the street address—524 West Rich Avenue—the same street number as the house where we lived when I was in high school—524 North High Street. There seemed to be a connection, but one that I could not yet identify.

For several months after closing on my house in DeLand, I occasionally drove down Rich Avenue just to enjoy seeing that house and to watch for construction at the 142 North Adelle lot. I also tried to get a glimpse of the house we had rented, but it is so canopied with trees that very little of the house is visible from the street. It appears that it is still the same house as the one we rented. The house that *Mother Holmes* owned looks much like the image filed away in my memory bank, but the yard does not measure up to her landscaping that filled the air with fragrance.

In the early fall, I went to the West Volusia Historical Society (WVHS) office to register for a guided tour of historic homes in DeLand and Lake Helen. After signing up for the tour, I talked with several employees and shopped for books.

When I saw the cover for *A Field Guide to DeLand's Buildings*, I gasped. There was a picture of the house at 524 West Rich Avenue. It felt more familiar than ever when I saw it on the front cover of the book that lists historic buildings. I realized it was not a new construction in historic style but was a refurbished house. I wondered if it could be an example of a Sears Kit House like my maternal grandparents had used for the house they built at 408 East Rich Avenue.

I opened the cover and read the paragraph, "About The Cover." It stated that the image was selected because it represented "a meticulous restoration of an historic building." It was originally built in the 1880s for Silas Wright, son of DeLand's first mayor, Cyrenius Wright, and was originally located on the lot at 142 North Adelle Avenue. The house was described as "dilapidated and scheduled for demolition" before "restoration carpenter Mark Keane" rescued it. His process included taking it apart board by board and reassembling it at 524 West Rich Avenue. WVHS featured it on the 2018 Tour of Historic DeLand Buildings, and Mr. and Mrs. Keane received the Society's 2018 *Preservationist of the Year Award*.

My insides quivered as I sputtered, "I knew it! I knew I knew that house, but I couldn't quite identify it. My parents owned it in 1944 before we left for Washington state—when it sat on the corner at 142 North Adelle Avenue. I don't know exactly how long we lived there, but it must have been at least a year. My brother was less than a year old when we moved to WA."

Words kept tumbling out as I told the patient docents how I loved to play on the embankment on the Rich Avenue side of the yard. Mother was terribly afraid that I might fall off what I thought was a hill and land in the street where a car could run over me. The kind listeners shared my excitement and assured me that Mark and his wife would be cordial if I contacted them. I bought two copies of the book—one for myself and one for my brother.

I recalled the work my family did when we tore down our dilapidated farmhouse out on Mockingbird Hill in DeLeon Springs and built a new house with the salvaged lumber. I know how difficult the process is and can imagine the added concern of refurbishing with architectural integrity rather than building a new and different structure.

On one of my drive-bys at 524 West Rich Avenue, I stopped and knocked on the door. When no one answered, I left a copy of my first book with a note in which I introduced myself and asked the owner to call me. The next day, when I received a call from an unknown number, I uncharacteristically answered it. A warm voice said, "This is Mark Keane. You left a book on my front porch and asked me to call." It felt like I was talking to a friend I had not seen for a long time. He assured me that he and his wife would love to visit with me. We agreed to set a time for a visit as soon as our respective calendars aligned.

Rather than serving as an incident that helped guide me home, this uncanny encounter verified for me that I am where I need to be. It was one more example of being at home and welcome even though Mark and I had never previously met.

Not long before completing this manuscript, I received a call from Mark. He told me that he and Linda were home from a vacation and then invited me to visit them and see the house. We set the date for a few days later.

When I drove over for the visit, it was like going to Las Vegas for the first time—a sense of unreality coupled with exhilaration at the thought of being exactly where I wanted to be in that moment. My diaphragm didn't know whether to work overtime and cause me to hyperventilate or to sit idle while I held my breath.

I heard Mark's voice as I walked up the sidewalk, "Come on in." He introduced me to Linda, and they took turns pointing out features of the house and décor. I felt most at home in the front area of the house. They explained that when my family had owned the house, the attic was not finished and that they had removed one or two walls downstairs to open up the space.

For me, the most beautiful part of the house is the restored wood throughout the downstairs and appropriately complementing wood upstairs where they built out the attic space into several bedrooms. I especially appreciated their adherence to authenticity without *fussiness*. Because of their hospitality, I felt at home and had a sense of *déjà vu* even if the house sat on a lot around the corner from where it was when I had lived in it.

Before I left, we were sitting in the living room talking and drinking water. Linda pulled an object out of the corner and indicated that it was for my bottle of water. It looked like a smaller version of a fern stand, but had a small crocheted doily in the shallow bowl on top. It seemed familiar, but I did not realize what it was until I thought about it on the way home and looked it up on the internet. The original function for the piece was as a pipe smoker's ashtray. Daddy had one very similar. I saw pictures of elaborate ones with spaces added to hold a collection of pipes, but the simple one like Linda placed in front of me was what Daddy used. He never had more than one pipe at a time, so would not have needed anything fancier.

It was almost time for me to leave when their granddaughter arrived. Mark went to the back door to greet her. She was the same age as I was when my family left that house. I relished the obvious affection between her and her grandparents, but especially between her and Linda. It reminded me that Grandmother had lived with us in that house in the mid-1940s and was my primary caretaker while Mother taught school. It felt as if I were seeing my own attachment to Grandmother as we left for Washington, not knowing if or when I would ever see her again. I had no doubt that I had identified our departure from DeLand and Grandmother as my first emotional trauma.

CHAPTER 25
INSTRUCTIONS IF I WERE A HOUSE

My secrets cry aloud.
I have no need for tongue.
My heart keeps open house.
My doors are widely flung.
Theodore Roethke
(1908-1963)

Encased in a wrapping as thin as phyllo dough, nothing about my personal exterior matches my self-image. My thoughts turn to *what ifs* as I recall the recent refurbishing of my house after the Arctic Vortex hit Houston in February, 2021.

If I were a house, I would be longing for a remodeling contractor to restore my youth, modernize my functions, and extend my life expectancy. People who don't know I am nearing the point of being decorated with a "Historical Site" bronze plaque that could put me on the historic home list might not guess my age. Or they could say something like, "Not bad for an old one," but I prefer to hear a simpler statement—something like "Not bad!" I need no *fors* embedded in compliments, just an occasional "Wow" would suffice and ring in my rafters long beyond the sound wave's demise.

I know my paint is peeling and follows the perpetual pull of gravity. Microscopic flakes dot my floors and coalesce into what humans call *dust bunnies*. Sometimes I see my image in large rain puddles and wonder if paint is imitating the scales on fish that one of my owners guts and filets on my back porch. Fish scales are uniform, but my flakes have shades of ghostly white, brown, or red—all on a bed of itchy multi-troughed crepe paper—but no purple contusions yet. You'd think the paint gods would have a better sense of color coordination and texture. But they seem to think turning tiny old freckles into large sepia-toned spots that beg for ineffective lemon juice and hydrogen peroxide is their job. Or maybe their easel has an affinity for giraffe markings.

My skeleton stands on a thick concrete slab. Make sure there is no crack before you spruce up the rest of me. I know that all my interior systems will soon pass inspection, but there is no required inspection of exterior matters that bug my interior control center. It's odd—external issues churn my innards, and prolonged interior issues show on the outside if allowed to linger too long.

Realtors like to brag about the *good bones* of their listings. A machine determined that my bones "look good," but nobody sees them. How can on-lookers know that I have good bones when only high-tech machines can see beyond my walls and between my studs? Perhaps a strong breeze will let me give myself a pat on my roof with a shingle for having a good grade on my bones' report card.

Frequent heavy rains sagged my shutters while swirling whirlpools set them askew on loosened hinges. The losing battle to keep the shutters dry rubbed the edges raw and threatened to rot my frame before rains subsided and sunshine returned. I hope someone will straighten and trim them to let in more light. Enough sun rays get through so that I know who visits me, but I long to see long-range vistas and visitors as they approach from afar.

Even in streetlight after the sun sinks into the river, I know I am sturdy, flexible, and sound by the nocturnal sounds of my bones expanding or contracting as they recalibrate when temperatures and humidity fluctuate. Dynamic movement is life, and these organic diaphragmatic pulsations are the irregular rhythm of inhalation and exhalation. When my bones are stagnant, I hibernate, content to wait for sounds of life to reset my sensors. If you can find one, install a pacemaker so that I can experience the constancy of regulated breaths.

Joists creak, and joints groan. Rusted hinges screech and need to be saturated with lubrication. No need for steel wool, though—the rust is too long-lived for that—and scratchy wool makes my pipes leak and may send my chimney into a sneezing fit. Slather the rusted spots with a thick paste made of either vinegar or baking soda. Let it set before you rinse off the paste; then pat me dry with a fluffy towel and buff my metal with a soft cotton cloth. If that doesn't quiet the friction, spray me with Rust-O-Leum or WD-40 Specialist Rust Remover. Having screechy hinges is embarrassing. In the world of residential real estate, it might be considered a housing fart—an unintended release of gaseous pressure, and I have no way to say, "Excuse me."

Numerous hurricanes tested my strength, and torrential rain pooled in the neighboring houses, but the roots ignored erosion's threat and held tight. With enough sway in the wind to withstand the stress, my thick weather stripping barred rising water that lapped my doors. And still, ever with flaws and imperfections and no longer in the midst of a storm, I stand without collapsing.

When invasive insects tried to satisfy their insatiable appetite for savory wood or sweet sap from green lumber, those who care about my longevity found a way to chase away the unseen offenders. But the creatures that gnawed and chewed left cavities in some of my beams and pitted my ribs. Tear out and replace all pithy wood to solidify my strength. The surface of my top-most bed has scratches from claws and nails of nocturnal animals that entered my eaves and tried to homestead under my roof. Maybe a refurbish expert will polish those surfaces to make my broad expanses shine and will plug the holes of invasion.

Perhaps the contractor will paint me green. Any shade from light sage to deep forest foliage will suit me well. I've heard humans say that green stands for renewed growth and that it reminds them of lush fields in a place they call Ireland. (*That's a funny word—how can a land have ire?*). When cars need to cross an intersection, a green light controls their timing, allowing them to proceed only with permission. On even the darkest night when foggy mist halos streetlamps and 18-wheelers hog lanes and block sightlines, the regulation of green lights protects the traveler before a switch triggers it to silently shout "Go."

I'm smart enough to know that houses do not grow like animals and humans, but some people fail to think about the interior of houses growing or shrinking except through physical addons or teardowns. Our rafters swell with the warmth of love, and our wooden bones shrink when the crack of a broken heart chills hinges and tightens ligaments into stubborn contractions. Like a thermostat, our interior control center depends on the circumstances of occupants and whims of weather for direction.

Nerves that carry power and veins that pump our blood of water also are sensitive to forces we can neither control nor define. Perhaps when I am remodeled, there will be a promise that these intestines of realty will carry a *can't fail* guarantee. The A-Fibs of electrical or plumbing systems may not be fatal, but they can be debilitating to those we shelter.

Reroof me with a roof so strong that the gutter splash pans no longer clog with coarse shingle sheddings. Don't be chintzy with my nails. I want to keep every single shingle, so hammer the nails deep where their integrity survives even the highest wind speeds or the sharpest bombardment of snare-drumming hail. You might even consider using green shingles like I see on some of the younger roofs.

Rip up the matted, crushed carpet whose tufts of shag required a rake when it was new. Shred the disintegrating speckled pad into oversized plastic bags to contain the particles filled with allergens. Air out every room so that the musty odor of multiple spills and cat pee dissipates. Even if it were new today, shag carpet would mark me as outdated and uninformed. If my flooring's surface is marred or dull, gently sand me and restore my luster with a thin coat of clear varnish. Expose my grain, but feel free to place a few small area rugs to enhance the color and texture of my space. I hope when someone looks at me and an appraiser estimates my value, they will find my restored floors a bonus. Place the old carpet and bags of pad beside the curb for the trash collector to haul away. If any creaks remain, especially on the stairs, ignore them. They are part of my daily percussive rhythm and remind those who listen that even oak or maple require a certain amount of bend when pressure is constant or acute. Some might describe the sounds as part of my charm or character—so much livelier than the silent steel and concrete angles of industrialized construction.

Those who wish to live in artificially sterile perfection will need to find a different neighborhood. My appearance will appeal to those who also have a history to share and who look forward with optimistic hope neither fearing longevity of dwellership nor wallowing in regrets for having lived elsewhere. My refurbishment will place me at the top of someone's list, and that appreciation will encourage my serious consideration of an offer. The market is still hot even with rising interest rates and high homeowner association fees.

While you're working on my insides, tear down some walls. I want to be open so that my dwellers more easily come and go, and temperature-controlled air more easily flows from one area to the next. With fewer walls, concentric sound waves from the piano will spread harmonic vibrations farther while the aroma of treats baking in the oven waft as they wander and pleasure neighbors' nostrils when not constrained by walls.

Don't neglect my front porch. It is like open outstretched arms to anyone who approaches in friendship. Fill some clay pots with bright flowers that will make bees and butterflies light and visitors inhale and smile. Be sure a watering can is handy. Add a swag of swing for decoration and quiet relaxation. If the porch rail has a gate, be sure the lock is in plain sight and opens easily. Install a screen door in the front and back so that I can invite breezes in to freshen my air. Add plenty of bookshelves, but don't worry about excessive storage space for mountains of accumulated stuff. I intend to discourage the storage of items no longer relevant to me or my occupants.

I want those who live in my space to be at peace with no worries about repairs or constant maintenance. Assure them that my bones are still good, all my systems are repaired or replaced, and that I feel comfortable garbed in either earthy or elegant attire. I'm ready for my next iteration with more efficient power than ever, here where others see only my exterior while I exist with granules, splinters, and cells that define my interior and defy assumptions.

As you take care of all these suggestions and requests, remember that if you are doing a favor or giving a present, it is usually wrapped in lovely paper, tied with a beautiful bow, and might even be adorned with a miniature package decoration. Wrap me loosely in the smoothness of silk or cashmere, but weave enough texture for my paint to hang on to its pigment and for each touch of the elements to cling long enough to nurture me before they follow their own natural course.

Once someone selects me, plan a big housewarming with gourmet food and a well-stocked bar. Put out table games and decks of cards inside and croquet and corn hole outside. After desert and coffee, invite guests to play the piano. My rafters long for the sound of music and the vibrations of music-makers who love their craft.

Be sure the painter blends the paint to uniformity. Have fun with my roof color. Open my shades; take down some walls; and finish me off with my key under a flowerpot near the front porch swing. Leave the windows open. I will blow on the *close* button if the air becomes too wet, too cold, or too hot. Make me shine with care and sparkle with joy—not to outdo my neighbors, but to state, "I am restored, and I am loved" because I intend to wear that bronze plaque and to host a welcome mat for a very long time. I want to shine!

CHAPTER 26
CAR REGISTRATION AND FLORIDA TAG: APPLICATION

Good Morning—Midnight—
I'm coming Home—
Day—got tired of Me—
How could I—of Him?

Emily Dickenson
(1830-1886)

My to-do list might have sent a certified list accountant into cardiac arrest. I anticipated that the to-do list for moving home to DeLand would be long and tedious, but I did not expect it to be hooked on rapid growth hormones. Every time I checked off an item, I took a deep breath of satisfaction and scanned the remainder to estimate when I could transition from the *must-dos* to *want-to-dos*. Too many times, additions outnumbered checkoffs.

Once the utilities and electronics were all working, the kitchen was functional, and enough boxes were unpacked to carve a room-to-room path, the next thing I wanted to do was get my Florida license tag. Since the day I left DeLand in May, 1968, my heart had revved a bit whenever I saw a Florida tag. I lived in seven different states between my departure from and return to DeLand. Invariably, when I saw a tag from my home state, I would look at the first digit to see if I recalled the county it identified. I remembered that the system I grew up with was based on the population of the county in which the car was registered. For many years, I recognized Dade County (Miami) as number 1; Duval (Jacksonville) as 2; Hillsborough (Tampa) as 3; Pinellas (St. Petersburg) as 4; Orange (Orlando) as 7; Volusia (DeLand) as 8; and

Seminole (Sanford) as number 17. Mother used to quiz my brother and me on the tag numbers we saw around DeLand, so it was a well-practiced habit.

What I had to learn online was that the first state-wide automobile registration was enacted in 1905, the year my mother was born. The fee was $2.00. The addition of county codes began in 1938 and was the standard until 1975, seven years after my long-term departure from DeLand.

As Florida's population shifted and grew, the registration system expanded and adjusted beyond the county designation. At some point, I noticed that the design of the Florida license plates no longer included the county number, but I still scrutinized Florida tags to check for an auto dealership or other reference that might indicate what part of the state the car came from.

The slogan, *Sunshine State,* first appeared on the license plates in 1947, the year I started first grade. But there were two exceptions when that slogan had to wait for reinstatement. *Keep Florida Green* replaced *Sunshine State* in 1951. I recall hearing Mrs. McInnis, my fourth-grade teacher and the school's principal, tell us about the importance of doing our part to keep the state beautiful so that everyone could enjoy it far into the future. With her encouragement and some help from Mother, I wrote my first song, which was based on the *Keep Florida Green* slogan. I still remember the melody and words for that first song, but the most long-lasting effects were the sense of geographic pride and the urge to express myself in creative ways.

Again, in 1965, the slogan was changed to commemorate the 400th anniversary of the founding of St. Augustine. Even though I was preparing my senior recital at Stetson University when the quadricentennial was celebrated, I took a day off to visit St. Augustine to be a part of the momentous celebration. That visit was a precursor to my celebrating Charleston's tricentennial five years later when I was working on the Master of Music degree at Winthrop University (then Winthrop College).

Sunshine State returned to its place on the Florida tags and, so far as I know, has remained there ever since. It is not on every single

Florida license plate due to the variety of design selection, but it is on the bottom of the basic entry level tag with *myFlorida.com* on the top.

The background of the plate depicts an outline of the state with two ripe oranges and three orange blossoms superimposed on the outline. I wondered why the designer included both ripe fruit and blossoms and had to satisfy my curiosity online. Because Florida's climate allowed more than one season of citrus crops per year, it is correct to show both ripe fruit and blossoms on the same branch. I had not noticed that on the trees in my family's yard but do recall hearing Mother remind my brother and me that if we kept using small green oranges for games or fights, we would not have very many oranges in the next crop.

Several weeks after moving into my new home in DeLand in June, 2022, the to-do list had shrunk enough to let me feel it was time to locate the tag office and get the longed-for Florida license plate. I looked forward to seeing the floral reminders of my native home on my car and hoped there would be an option to include *Stetson University* on it.

A high school friend and I had talked about singing what we knew as the Florida Song every day in DeLeon Springs Elementary School—not the official state song, *Suwanee River,* by Stephen Foster—but the one that began with "I want to wake up in the morning where the orange blossoms grow." Stephen and Mary Lynn Ulrey wrote the lyrics.

Most of the groves whose fruit and blossoms earned their place on the Florida license plates by largely building the economy in much of the state were lost to freeze and suburban crawl long before I returned to DeLand. Similar in appearance to the luminous edelweiss blossoms immortalized in the movie, *Sound of Music*, many Floridians feel a sense of personal identity with the small white blossoms that almost glow against lustrous green leaves, making the contrast of tiny golden dots of pollen dance into focus. Their number compensated for the small size and filled yards and groves with the aroma of home.

Now I wake up not where orange blossoms grow, but where a family of sand hill cranes nest and serenade me with their gobble-esque sound. I catch a whiff of candles on the nightstand and watch squirrels hop from one buried morsel to the next when I pull back the drapes. Occasionally, I hear the train whistle just a few blocks away.

I sometimes recall the failed attempt by a perfume company to capture the smell of Florida in a bottle and sell it in dime stores and drug stores when I was in high school. But orange blossom honey did make its way onto grocery shelves and into boutique shops such as *The Anointed Olive*, one of the DeLand shops that caters equally to residents, winter *Snowbirds*, and summer beach babes and bros who stroll historic DeLand streets when too much or too little sun nudges them westward. Besides sweetening teas, orange blossom honey has a keen affinity to blend with medicinal whiskey for minor sore throats—a welcome relief from pesky allergies. Even though the fragrance could not be captured, it is eternal, and needs no bottle or atomizer to trigger the olfactory nerve.

When I went to purchase the tag, I had to test my rusty parallel parking skills around the corner from the County Clerk's office. I think I still would have earned an A on that part of the Driver's Education exam and may have even earned some brownie points if the Florida Highway Patrolman who administered my driver's exam in 1957 had been in the passenger seat with his clipboard ready to note any shortcoming or exceptional success.

Not only did I maneuver the parking requirements; I also managed not to hit or disturb the family of ducks that had claimed the rain puddle my car had to straddle. It just took a little patience for the ducks to decide that the slow-moving car might have a bigger claim on the puddle than they had. When I got out of the car, I took a couple of pictures as they waddled off toward the next puddle. I recalled Mother's frequent admonition, "Walk like you have some place to go," when we walked along Woodland Boulevard in the evening waiting for Daddy to close the Standard Oil service station located just south of the Dreka department store building before the wrecking ball made space for a parking lot. I certainly had a place to go and was eager to get there.

I had checked the street address for the County Clerk's office and knew I had arrived. Immediately inside the entrance of the building I entered, I found an Information desk where a friendly gentleman held the last bite of a sandwich in his hand while he chewed.

Hoping he would swallow before trying to answer me, I said,

CAR REGISTRATION AND FLORIDA TAG: APPLICATION   249

"Could you please direct me to the office for license plates?"

He swallowed with a gulp. "'Scuse me, Ma'am. Just finishin' up ma' lunch." He tilted his head back and washed down his food with the last of his coffee. "Exit this buildin' right there at the Exit sign; follow the brick sidewalk 'round to the left, and go right on in the next buildin'."

"I thought this is the address for the County Clerk's office."

"This here entire complex got the same address. Each buildin's got their own office numbers. You'll see some real nice benches where you can sit and wait after you check in with the lady at the main desk. Looks like she's in a cage, but she's real nice." I smiled, hooked on the charm of one so eager to help a home-comer in need of assistance.

Relieved that I was only one building off, I thanked him and left.

I had walked only a short distance in the hall before I discovered that I had left my credit card case in the car. On the way to town, I had filled the gas tank and was so focused on the purpose of the errand that I left the case on the console. Not wanting to pass by the man who had given me directions and risk having him intervene with redirection, I walked around that part of the complex outside and went to the car. No ducks on the sidewalk; no roadkill in the street. I wondered where they might be.

With card case in hand, I retraced my way back to the correct entrance and saw the benches beside the door. The courtyard was lively with workers outside on lunch break and customers who I presumed were there on county government business. Inside, I checked in and received a number that would be called when a clerk was available. Since the system used text messaging to alert people when their number was close to being called, I opted to go back outside and sat on one of the *real nice* benches. A friendly stranger and I chatted about the changes I had observed in the town, especially in the courthouse complex.

When I received the text alert, I went in and sat in the only available chair, the one against the back wall. The few minutes before my number was called gave me enough time to notice the pictures of license plate options hanging on the wall to my right. There must have been at least twenty. I visualized what one would look like with the oranges, orange blossoms, and *Stetson University* on it when I saw that other colleges and universities were on some of the examples.

The announcer called my number. After taking all the pertinent information and documentation, the clerk said, "You don't seem to be in our system. Did you own a car before you left the state?" I felt an internal wince and fought the urge to explain that I had not abandoned Florida but garnered the strength of equilibrium to stay on task.

I responded. "Yes, but I don't know if my name was on the title. I left in 1968. The car was probably in my husband's name, but it was given to me as part of the divorce settlement. Can you check by my social security number?"

"I've already tried that. I'm sorry to say this, but since you never paid an initial registration fee, your total bill this time will be over $400.00. That will carry you 'til the renewal date in 2023."

"What about renewals? How much will they be?"

"If you go ahead and pay for 2023, renewals starting in October of 2023 will be less than $70."

"Alright. Do I get the license plate today? I've waited 54 years to tag my car with the state of my birth."

"I still need to go out and verify the VIN number after we finish up a little more paperwork. Do you have the title with you?"

"No. I think it's with Toyota Financial Services until the final payment is made in January of 2023."

"Then I won't be able to finalize the registration today. We'll have to have them fax it to us. You'll need to send them the fax number to make sure we get it. Most finance companies seem to respond quicker to customers than to government offices."

"I'll call them right now so that you know the call has been made."

I placed the call, and after getting through the automated system to a person, asked to talk to someone who handled title issues. Once transferred, I asked the title specialist if he would talk with the County Clerk's representative. He was eager to help and assured the clerk that he would fax a copy of the title to me and the original to the Volusia County Clerk's office.

Trying to sound more eager than impatient, I said, "Now is it possible to get the tag today?"

"No. I'm sorry, but we can't do anything until we receive the title. I still have to verify the VIN number while you're here. Could you please pull the car around to the lot on Rich Avenue, just around the corner? I'll meet you there and follow you to wherever you can find a parking place. It won't take but a few more minutes."

"When do you think I will be able to get the tag?"

"It usually takes at least four weeks for the title to reach us. Toyota will probably send your copy the same time they send the original to us. As soon as you hear from them, come right in, and we'll be able to get the tag released."

"Okay. I'll be at the Rich Avenue lot in a couple minutes."

Disappointed, but satisfied that I had done all I could do to make the system work for me, I headed to the car and for the rendezvous with the clerk. The ducks had also gone to Rich Avenue.

When I turned off of Florida Avenue onto Rich Avenue, I saw that traffic was stopped all the way to the Boulevard and for almost a block in the opposite direction while the ducks took their time crossing the street, apparently confused as to which way to go to the next puddle. I wondered if they were trying to get to the large pond across the Boulevard and how they would manage the traffic there. A young woman had stepped out of her car and was *mother-henning* them by trying to direct traffic. No duck or duckling was to be harmed on her watch. This was a new thing for me. With dozens of lakes in West Volusia County, it was never uncommon to see many types of animals near the lakes or out by the St. John's River, but seeing them on a major street down town was a novelty.

Once I could move along, I saw the clerk standing at the parking lot entrance, shielding her eyes from the sun, looking in my direction. I pulled into a parking spot almost directly across from her, thinking my mission qualified me to use one of the clearly marked *reserved* spots for people who were sworn in and wore badges. Less concerned with the sun's brightness than with my breach of parking protocol, she frantically waved both arms in a way that screamed, "No!" and then motioned me to the parking lot entrance. If the ducks saw her, they would have wondered which traffic control human to obey—the self-appointed Chief of Duck Patrol or the Director of Sue.

As I pulled out of my first-choice parking space, the clerk's representative continued to wave me into the lot. While I drove down one side of the lot, she walked down the other. When a car pulled out, she stepped into the area, and with one hip thrust out to support one hand, she slapped her other hand like a mime would do if defining a box, and silently shouted, "Don't even think about taking this spot" until I could make the turn to come up her side of the lot and claim the space. I wonder if I will ever have someone physically hold a parking place for me again.

Feeling both foolish and defensive for trying to park in a reserved spot, as soon as I parked correctly, I rolled down the window and started explaining myself. "I thought that they might allow parking in reserved slots when a car is being registered. It was the closest one to you."

"No way," she said. "You'd get a ticket quicker there than anywhere else. You're lucky none of the officers saw you there."

"I'll remember that."

It took the clerk's representative just a few minutes to check the VIN, look the car over, and assure me that all was in order. She handed me a stack of papers, and I thought of the onerous task of filing them and finding them once I had my copy of the car title. I offered to drive her back to her building, but she declined. "It's so nice outside. I'll just walk back. See you in a month or so."

I left the courthouse complex a little disappointed to still be sporting Texas license plates, but grateful for such helpful personnel both on site and from Toyota Financial Services. After waiting 54 years, I could wait one more month.

CHAPTER 27

FLORIDA TAG: RECEIPT AND INSTALLATION

*Perhaps love is the process of leading
you gently back to yourself.*
                              Antoine de Saint-Exupery
                              (1900-1944)

My home office held the last 12-15 boxes of files, along with several plastic crates full of the inevitable *miscellaneous* odds and ends waiting for organization. The urge to avoid the bane of my office and the need to shop for small furniture pieces for additional storage space made the weeks between my first and second trips to the Volusia County Clerk's office pass quickly.

I received a copy of the car title and a text from the clerk's office on the same day. The following morning, I lingered in my driveway long enough to photograph the family of four sand hill cranes foraging under one of the oak trees in the front yard. They let me take a few steps toward them, but sauntered off toward the neighbor's yard when I dug my phone out of the depths of my purse and took a few pictures. I hope they allow me to get a frontal head shot some other time.

A few minutes later, I parked near the historic courthouse in the lot not quite as close to the tag office as the one I had used on my previous tag mission. There were fewer people waiting, and my number, 162, was less than 10 away from the first one called after I sat down inside.

"Number 153." The announcer's voice brimmed with cordial, but firm authority.

The man sitting in the chair beside mine looked toward one of the plexiglassed stations and called out, "She left."

That put just eight ahead of mine, and there were eight windows, most of which had a clerk working behind them. Every time a person left, we heard again, "Number 153." Each announcement of that number was a notch louder, but not yet strident.

By then, the clerk assigned to number 153 relied on the man beside me to keep her informed. He called out again, "She's still gone; she'll be back, though." I speculated that Number 153 must have designated this man as her agent before she left.

My phone dinged with the text alert. "Please be ready. Your number will be called soon." The *be-backer* rushed in with a handful of disheveled paper poised to set sail for the floor.

The number assigner stepped out of the cage and up to number 153's assigned clerk. She stage-whispered, "Our *be-back* is here, Hon."

Turning back toward the *be-backer*, she waved her arm like an usher and said, "Step on up, Honey." I did not hear an eye roll in her voice, just a statement with a *heads up* infused.

"Calling number 153." Tension in the tone teetered on the cliff of agitation.

Someone who had heard that number called one too many times huffed vociferously and said, "Really??!!" His tone sounded like an impatient toddler on the verge of a meltdown. It appeared that the Volusia County Clerk's office believed in 2nd, 3rd, and 4th chances.

A woman farther away from me looked toward the "Really??!!" guy and said with equal exasperation, "Seriously??!!" The scornful look on her face let me know that her outrage was at the impatience, not at Number 153 or the announcer. Her voice sounded like a mom talking to an adolescent.

The clerk greeted number 153 with a smile, looked through the plexiglass, and scanned the seated other numbers. She said, "Sorry, folks. You won't hear that number again."

I looked at the man beside me, smiled, and said, "Oh, the charm of a small town."

"Yeah. We try to keep it friendly, but that guy must *realllly* be in a hurry." We chuckled.

A minute or so later, the announcer called, "Number 161." The man beside me, number 153's agent, stepped up to a window, which was identified by a letter.

Half a minute later, I heard, "Number 162, Window H."

The clerk at Window H was friendly and, like everyone else, said, "Welcome home!" when I told her I was a DeLand native but had not lived here since 1968.

"Did you own a car before you moved away?"

"When I was here about a month ago, they could not find a record to document my having a car."

"Yeah—I've tried every way I know to search, and I'm not finding any record of previous ownership. Everything else is in order, though."

"Does that mean I'll be able to get the tag today?"

"Yep."

I asked, "What about those special tags shown on the Wall? Do you have a printout of the options?" Since they had ones with public colleges and universities noted, my hopes for one with *Stetson University* grew stronger. I said, "I had no idea there would be so many choices."

The clerk handed me a set of eight laminated pages of examples attached to a key ring. All but a couple of the pages had 27 choices. The others had at least nine examples, making an estimated total of 180 images to choose from. Still looking at the first page, I was about to ask if they had one for Stetson when the clerk said, "There are several different prices, but a portion of the cost goes to whatever organization or institution is featured on the tag." She then placed her fancy-nailed index finger on an image and said, "For example, you might like this one right here. You'll see the price listed above each image."

I saw the price, $57.00, and didn't think twice. My pulse accelerated when I saw the picture under her finger. My decision took less than an instant. The base of the picture showed green blades of grass bending as if the Atlantic breeze caressed them. A head shot of a tawny Florida panther sat in the middle of the grass, basking in the warm shade of palm fronds as the background color reflected a light amber sunset rather than bright sunshine.

The statement at the top of the tag was, *Protect the Panther*, not *myFlorida.com*, and the lettering on the bottom was simply FLORIDA without the *Sunshine State* slogan. The realization that this example did not include the well-known slogan or *Stetson University* did not matter. It was clear that *Protect the Panther* was enough. After all my obsessing over wanting a Florida tag with the state's historic icons of oranges and orange blossoms, along with perhaps the addition of *Stetson University*, I knew that the clerk had guided me to the perfect choice.

When I studied the picture of the panther more closely, I saw that the eyes looked calm. Its ears were alert, but not tense. No tears dropped from the eyes, and no drool dribbled from the open mouth. Two long teeth showed, but there was no forward momentum that would hint at an attack. Its pink tongue lolled behind the teeth, not ready to taste a juicy bite of prey. The picture of the state land animal of Florida could almost pass for a large, domesticated pet. A sense of peace engulfed my entire being. I felt as protected as I hoped the remaining wild panthers would be.

With goosebumps prickling the hairs on my neck and arms, I raised my head to make eye contact with the clerk and said, "I've got to tell you why I will choose this option. My book, *Cries of the Panther on Mockingbird Hill*, was published in April, 2020. In the beginning of the book, the panther represents my fear and dread and my wish that I could cry like the panthers that roamed our property out in DeLeon Springs when I was growing up."

"Oh, I love the pancake house at the Old Sugar Mill Restaurant. Did they have that when you were a little girl?"

"The mill was there, and the mill wheel turned, but there was no restaurant. We did have a high dive board and a slide, though. For a while, there was an underwater observation deck and even an elephant in a ski show in the lake where the overflow from the springs runs. It tried to compete with the ski show that made Winter Garden famous. The student teacher in my high school PE class was in the show. Once it became a state park, though, all of those unnatural attachments were dismantled."

"Wow! It's fun to hear about the old days. I've heard they're gonna' close the restaurant. I hope the rumors aren't true."

"I've heard that, too, and checked it online. The restaurant is changing managers, but it will be closed only a few weeks while they make some repairs and get ready to reopen."

"Good. So what's your book about?"

"It tells the story of my history of sexual abuse by a family member. By the end of the book, I have become the panther who can cry and has taken on the strength and maternal nurturance symbolized by the panther. Some might say it's my spirit animal."

The clerk rubbed her forearms and said, "I've got goosebumps. I have to learn more and would love to read your book."

I reached into my purse and gave her a business card and bookmark. "You can find it on Amazon. Feel free to call me if you have questions or want to talk about it."

"I will. Now for the bad news. Since you're not in our system, the charge today is well over $400 plus $57 for the special design. You still want your tag today?"

"Absolutely!"

"Okay. I'll have my supervisor look over the papers to make sure everything is completed; then I'll get your tag." I wondered if she were a new hire but felt confident that she was well-trained.

She walked to the middle of the area. I watched as the supervisor flipped through the pages, pointed to various spots, and nodded her head. After she flipped the last page, the woman helping me took the file and went over to a cabinet that ran along most of the back wall. It reminded me of an oversized pre-computer card catalog. She opened the drawer marked *Protect the Panther*, pulled out one tag, and returned to her desk. "MCM 525," I read. "Not quite my house number, 505, but close." My mind wandered and noted that MCM looked like Roman numerals. I wondered what the value equivalent would be.

The clerk looked at me and said, "That would have been more than I could stand if your tag number had matched your house address."

"I wonder how many panthers are still surviving. When I researched it for my book, there were only about 50 left, and they were living down near the Everglades."

"Yeah—they're still endangered. I don't know the number, but I hope there are more now."

After I paid for the tag and registration, she stuck the renewal date—10-23—onto my tag since I had opted to pre-pay for next year rather than go through the renewal process the following month. "I don't believe it! 10-23 is my birthdate."

The clerk rubbed her arms again. "I can't wait to read your book. I hope you're happy here in your hometown."

"Happier and more at home than ever. Now my car will be properly attired for its home too."

As soon as I pulled into my driveway, I went inside long enough to grab a Phillips head screwdriver, went right back outside, and put on the tag. I took a picture and sent it to a few friends in Texas. When I removed the license plate frame that I had used for over 20 years, I noticed that the words, *DeLand, Florida* on the top and *Stetson University* on the bottom were no longer discernable unless you already knew what had been there. The faint lettering reminded me of ghost signs on industrial brick buildings. I then discovered that the holes on the frame did not align with the Florida tag and realized I would have to put the old frame in the recycle bin. It had served its purpose and was no longer needed to nudge my thoughts of home, for I am home.

A new image replaced the shadows of connections and represents my journey and the Florida panthers' current struggle. Off with the *Lone Star* tag and on with the *Sunshine State's Panther*; no need for a stenciled slogan on a license plate to remind me of a sunny clime because I breathe in sun-painted air, even if clouds or rain appear.

After installing the tag, I refreshed my memory of Roman numeral values and found MCM to equal 1900, the year Aunt Marian was born—the aunt who bought my first piano for me. By then, the association hardly surprised me and was more like a final verification that all the other coincidental associations on the way back home were valid links in a chain of permanence.

Later, when I went back to town to do a few other errands, I noticed that I still had a Texas tag on the front of the car. I could hardly wait to get back to the house and take off that last external mark of having lived somewhere other than DeLand for so many years.

I looked up the current status of Florida panthers. The number has grown to 120-130. I wondered why the designer of the tag chose to use the singular, *panther* rather than the plural, *panthers*. Perhaps it is a mindset of saving the species one panther at a time. For me, it is a personal reminder of all those who helped to nurture and restore me. I hope it is a forecast of the ultimate return of a sustainable number of panthers in their native habitat so that they can continue to be at peace in a rich environment that allows them to reach their full strength with no threat of extinction. I will gladly pay the extra cost for the license plate that reminds all who see it that the plight of the panther deserves attention and remedy. The happenstance of the suggestion that the clerk made reminds me of the long journey that kept me far away from DeLand for 54 years and the string of coincidental incidents that helped guide me home.

WELCOME HOME ME

CHAPTER 28
RELEASE TO PEACE

From harmony, from Heavenly harmony,
This universal frame began.
When Nature underneath a heap
Of jarring atoms lay,
And could not have her head,
The tuneful voice was heard from high,
Arise ye more than dead.
Then cold, and hot, and moist, and dry,
In order to their stations leap,
And Muse's power obey.
Through all the compass of the notes it ran,
The diapason closing full in man.

A Song for Saint Cecilia's Day (From Stanza 1, 1687)
John Dryden
(1631-1700)

Every *to* requires or implies a *from*. But not every *from* requires a gut-wrenching pull, and not every pull offers a parachute or safety net. For me, it was impossible to go to DeLand without going from Houston. Leaving Houston reconnected me with the place where I am most grounded, the place where peace oozes from bodies of water bathed in breeze, where internal peace cradles thoughts and ambitions, where peace of place maintains a lifelong lease.

Living in DeLand renewed my ability to participate in community and cultural activities without worrying about driving at night. The timing of the move let me maximize profit on the sale of the Houston house, which allowed me to buy a house in DeLand.

Throughout the process of moving back to my hometown, the underlying pushes and pulls combined to provide space in which I could release old issues and settle into the peace I sought for 54 years. Initially, I released the hold of long-term dread of ever having to see my abuser again. That dread extended to his large family, but it no longer pollutes my joy. If any of his family members ever do show up and are willing to have a civil conversation, I am prepared.

I released my concern for driving at night by purchasing a home within an easy drive to Stetson University so that I can continue attending cultural events without thinking twice about driving home after dark. Now, comfortably established in DeLand, I am in the process of realizing the release of my performance phobia so that I can reclaim the skills needed to play the glorious pipe organ(s) on campus. And, with a little bit of luck and careful planning, I may realize my dream of having a practice organ in my home.

Leaving Houston required that I say *goodbye* to long-term friends, my (step)children and (step)grandchildren, and my piano students. I knew that I could never replace any of them or their place in my life, and I knew I would not be able to equal the community or the live music I loved at Christ Church Cathedral. Yet I also knew that staying in Houston would have negative consequences for me.

The process of release from students required my counseling them and their parents regarding their search for a new teacher. I also needed to assure them of my care for them and of my confidence in their ability to be successful in their continued musical studies. I saw them more than I saw my own family, and I socialized with them as though they were extended family members. Most had studied with me several years; some for as much as eight years.

None of the releases mentioned above made me feel that I needed to be released from my relationship. I was not seeking a way to run away from anything or anybody. Rather, I felt the need to release students to their own sense of autonomy without me. They needed to understand that it was possible to find another piano teacher and that it was not only possible, but desirable, that they like and respect a new teacher. As I met with friends and said my *goodbyes,* I knew and felt their unconditional support and sense of celebration as I prepared to leave.

There was only one person from whom I needed to release myself, and that was John, my long-term man-friend. I never had expected that my relationship with him would ever be more than it was. Yet there was a thread of hope or wish that once we got through whatever required his focus on something other than us, he would at least commit to more time together. There was no question that he enjoyed our time together just as much as I did, whether on trips or just spending time together mostly at my house. But the frequency of visits, the day of the week, and the amount of time he spent at my house before he went back to his house were consistently set according to his terms.

For over ten years, I had been tethered to my relationship with John, but had not allowed myself to slip into a state of dependence on it. That relationship was secondary to the work I was doing in therapy to heal from the trauma of abuse.

I first consulted the therapist for short-term support when John pulled out of the relationship for about 10 weeks at the two-year point after we returned from our first trip. After telling me that he was "moving on romantically," he called unexpectedly and said, "Well, I think it's time for us to plan our next trip." I told him I would have to see a lot more of him before I would join him on another trip.

The first therapy appointment set in motion the sessions that continue today, now at a much less frequent rate and via Zoom. After addressing the issue of the immediate situation with John, I brought up the history of the sexual abuse and maintained the visits with the therapist primarily to process the long-term history.

Through the years from 2010 to 2022, John and I took six trips together. Two were vacations, and the rest were to his professional conferences. At the end of each of the trips, he pulled back in what seemed to be an urgency to give me a message, *Don't count on being together this much except on trips*. It seemed that his reticence said, *If I spend more time with you, you might get a notion that I care about you more than I do*. He talked about relationships he knew of where common law marriage was a concern, but he never would talk openly about our own relationship.

After the re-start following the 10-week break, I felt certain that he would do so again. And he did—not to the point of verbally putting a stop to seeing each other—but always offering some excuse as to why he would not be able to see me more frequently than every other week when we returned from a trip. It was just enough to keep me tethered, but with enough distance to make me keep the tether loose, not tied. I could write a long chapter's worth of speculation and my understanding of his mindset, but that would be pointless and could contain unintentional inaccuracies. I will limit what I say here to what I observed and what I accepted as obvious conclusions.

If it suited him, he would see me once a week for a while, but most of the time limited it to once every two weeks. In case readers wonder, he was not married and had been divorced for decades. There was no objective reason for his stinginess with time other than his preference. While I had always known intellectually that he would not make a firm commitment, I would not accept it until I admitted to myself that coming out of the pandemic shutdown would not affect his willingness to spend more time together and that he would never run out of excuses for limiting his availability. Once the COVID-19 restrictions were lifted, I admitted to myself that his lack of commitment would not change, and the tether slipped its loop and disintegrated.

John came out for a visit soon after I returned from the workshop and the visit to DeLand in 2022. It turned out to be the last time I saw him. That evening, he commented on how happy the visit to DeLand seemed to have made me. I deliberately did not discuss the possibility of the move then because I wanted to give myself enough time to make sure the plans were firm. I needed confirmation from the realtor that selling the house would not be a problem, and I needed to get a feel for the market in DeLand. I also simply wanted to have a pleasant evening with him, thinking there was plenty of time to talk with him and see him before the move could possibly take place.

Two weeks later, when he normally would have planned to come out for a visit (he lived close to an hour away from where I lived), I informed him that I had found contractors to complete the refurbishing of the house. He chose to postpone plans for a week so that the tile and countertop work would be completed. Extreme dust was a real health concern for him.

When he checked about getting together the following week, the text came in while I was away from the house doing errands and could not respond to the text immediately. But I knew that I couldn't let him come out without talking to him about the lock box on the door and waited until I was home to contact him. Right after I pulled into the driveway, Erica stopped by to check on the contractor's progress and to let me know the photographer would be there in two days and that she would hold the open house that coming weekend. She was on her way to the office to pick up the *for-sale* sign and expected to bring it back later that day.

Knowing John was at work, I decided to email him the news and let him know that I still wanted to see him that night. He responded and said that the news was a big surprise, but that he would be out at the usual time. He contacted me about an hour later and said he might not be able to come out because he had not slept well the previous night. He said he would see how he felt later in the day and would confirm whether or not he felt up to a visit. He waited until mid-afternoon, then let me know that he felt too tired to come out.

To me, it was just one more excuse for him to avoid open communication regarding the state of our relationship. It was all the confirmation I needed to know I had made the right decision to move to my hometown. He may or may not have been seeing others, but his staunch commitment was to his work, his staff, and his dog. He never even called to say *goodbye*.

Rather than feeling like my life was coming unglued or unraveled, every step in the decision-making and planning processes seemed to sparkle in the light that guided me. I felt stronger than ever as I sold the Houston house, purchased a house in DeLand, and supervised the movers. My earliest estimate for when I would make the move had been 6-12 months. It turned out to be three months.

I fought the temptation to fuss at myself for allowing John to hang on to a situation that met his needs and preferences more than my own and for the foolishness of not acting upon the obvious shortfall of what

I needed and preferred years earlier. But I soon forgave myself and chose to relish the good decisions I had made, let the good times with him settle into their slot in my memory bank, and focus on the future.

Not only was it time for a new house in the town of my birth, but it was time for me to follow the opportunities and offers of loving support that guided me home. Perhaps most of all, it was time for me to reclaim my undergraduate training on the Beckerath organ at Stetson University, a dream long brewing in the back of my mind.

Reclaiming the training I received from Paul Jenkins, beloved Professor of Organ at Stetson (Students often affectionately called him *PJ*), had niggled my mind off and on since I first left DeLand. I did continue to study organ in my master's program and practiced when I taught at Frostburg State University in Maryland (1991-1993) but have not been on the bench seriously since then (1993). I had experienced a dismal memory lapse on a student recital at Stetson and struggled with a performance phobia ever since. I believe that I have released the hold of that phobia and that I am ready to practice and resume organ lessons with Boyd Jones, current Professor of Organ at Stetson, who also studied with Paul Jenkins.

Back then, probably in the spring of 1964, I walked onto the stage of Elizabeth Hall, ready to play a piece of organ music from memory on the weekly student recital. The mighty Beckerath organ beckoned anyone who was either ready to play or to learn to play. The frontal pipes seemed to extend arms of welcome while standing in balanced design within the case. By then, the organ was about three years old since being assembled in Elizabeth Hall in 1961 following its creation in Hamburg.

I had worked hard enough to stay out of the *C* grade zone, but had not been able to pull up higher than a *B*. After hearing a rumor of speculation that the only way to earn an *A* was to play from memory, I had memorized my piece and was almost confident that my grade would advance from *B* to *A* that semester. And just in case I felt the panic of last-minute adrenalin and was tempted to chicken out, I left the score in another building as a deterrent.

PJ had listened to me play the piece the day before and encouraged me to go ahead with my plan to play from memory. He said, "You're ready. The registration works well. Your pedal technique is smooth, and the counterpoint between the manuals is nicely articulated." Those words rang in my ears as I mounted the organ bench the next day.

Performances during the second semester of the sophomore year were especially important because if things did not go well, that was the point at which professors felt compelled to advise the student to consider a different major. Professors typically knew their students well and were aware if there was something to account for *sophomore approval* flaws. And a dreaded *C* in a student's performance area in any semester called for a *We need to talk* statement from the major professor. I knew I needed to do well, not just to boost my grade, but to cross that checkpoint at which the entire faculty had some degree of authority.

At my request, I was the first on the program, not wanting to wait backstage and not wanting to follow another organist, all of whom I believed learned more quickly and played with finer technique and more nuanced musicianship than I did.

I took a sip of water, three deep breaths, and strode on stage, ready to share my progress, proud that PJ thought I was ready. No problem as I read the first two pages from my mental score. It felt like the *King of Instruments* and I were in total sync and that I had full control of the music I had memorized. But as the pedal solo ended, the mental image of the next page went blank as though my brain had short-circuited. As the seconds stretched in agonizing length, I tried to remember at least the melody. A repeat of the first two pages could not begin if I could not even remember the *cantus firmus*. No re-start to serve as a running start for the section where I had stalled. No musical battery to jump-start my memory.

Usually, Charlie, my classmate who was the stage manager, stood beside the bench, ready to turn pages or pull stops. But since I was trying to play from memory, I was alone with the spotlight of inadequacy blazing a hole straight through all that I wanted to be and to do. I sank to the bottom of a pit from which I might never have emerged.

It felt as though the 16-foot pedal pipe was tying itself around my neck, suffocating the breath needed to sustain the musical phrases and me. The pedal board thrust my right foot onto the *swell* pedal and my left foot onto the crossbeam of the bench. None of the three manuals invited my hands to search for the right notes. I was frozen in dry ice, hands gripping the edge of the bench and feet tucked away hiding the organ shoes that longed to play while my reddened face thought the sting of shame would burst into flame. But I dared not cry.

It seemed that the steam from the dry ice pointed a finger at me and said, *Here she is—right here—a worthless pretentious fake, just like her brother-in-law told her so many times.*

On that day, in the hall described in the *Alma Mater* as "classic . . . temple," after my short-lived pride turned to humiliation, I heard loud claps—first from only one pair of hands and then a polite smattering from some of the audience of students and faculty. Then I realized that the first claps came from where Paul Jenkins always sat. I knew that he was signaling for me to get off the bench and off the stage. It was not a stern admonishment or a musical *gotcha*. Rather it was the gentlest way he could find to help me and, in effect, say *You deserve a hand for trying. We'll continue working at your next lesson.* But all I could feel was how far short my attempt to play from memory had fallen and the fear of being "sophomored out."

When I walked in for my next lesson, dreading that I would hear that I needed to find a different major, Mr. Jenkins motioned for me to follow him to the stage entry. I stretched my legs to keep up with his lanky gait.

He led me to the exterior backstage door and stopped. He said, "Now start your stage entry here. Do not wait until Charlie opens the stage door. Your walk starts here, and your momentum builds until you take the bench. Remember what you say to yourself when you acknowledge the initial applause: *You're a cabbage head. And you're a cabbage head. And so are you.* And then you sit down, and you play. At any rate, whether you have a score or not, you play the music; you breathe with the phrases, and you extinguish extraneous thoughts. I know you know the music. Now let's restart from right here. Go out there and play."

I pulled out the score and retraced the walk, sat down, and played to his and my satisfaction. He sat down in his chair and said, "Now what's really going on?" And that question turned on the embarrassing tears I fought so often to control. My list of ways in which I was miserable was long—each item related to then-current issues, all of which could account for the disastrous meltdown on the recital—but nothing of the decade-long history that most directly caused the memory freeze. He lightened the moment when, in response to the report of serious marital problems, he said, "Have you tried an iron skillet on top of his head yet?" It seemed that everyone knew that the marriage was falling apart before I admitted it to PJ. But nobody knew of the longer history because I dared not break the code of silence.

With the wisdom of a therapist and the care of a master teacher, he assured me that he had already talked with several faculty members and had told them that he had full confidence in my ability to continue and to succeed in more advanced repertoire and that I would more than make up for the memory problem on the next recital. While I never tried to play from memory again, I did continue to make remarkable progress and graduated, still making a strong *B* in organ performance, but working as hard for that grade as others worked for their *A*. Once I calmed down, he directed my attention back to the lesson. " Now let's take a look at the new piece you are learning."

Decades later, at a Homecoming event, I found out that at least six of my classmates had felt the same misgivings. Our common thread of negative self-talk was that each of us had believed we deserved a parchment that read *Least Likely to Succeed*. As we took turns expressing the same misgivings from the time of undergraduate struggle, it was clear that our internal schematic had been so alike that we could have shouted in unison, *How could you possibly deserve such a title when you played so much better than I did?* Our individual reasons for such a damaging message to ourselves were as varied as our personalities and histories, but equally strong.

It is remarkable that Paul Jenkins was willing to take on the challenges we gave him. Between his pedagogical expertise and care and our tenacious ambition, each of those I recall who shared their undergraduate mindset with me when we talked at the Homecoming gathering earned advanced degrees and became leaders in our fields. Most were either professional organists in churches and/or universities. Some of us found our way into Music Education or private studio careers. But without exception, those of us who entered as floundering freshmen returned to Homecoming to express gratitude for the nurturance we were given while we managed to find a way to meet requirements and to continuously raise the bar of low expectations we had laid in our own respective paths. Our transformations emerged once we began to achieve even beyond Paul Jenkins' and other professors' expectations.

For 30 years, in the classrooms where I taught Music, I would not even play "Happy Birthday" without the score in front of me. But now, well into retirement, I have memorized several piano pieces and feel comfortable playing them for guests in my home.

More significantly, Boyd Jones offered me the security code for the organ practice rooms. My hope is to get back on the bench, not to play from memory, but to reclaim the skills, enjoy the repertoire, and to feel the full-body experience of my feet dancing on the pedal board while pipes sing as my fingers control the valves to the pipes. And perhaps Paul Jenkins' organ shoes, which are enshrined in the organ case, will send the music up to him, and he will clap not to get me off the bench, but to congratulate my homecoming to DeLand and to the magnificent Beckerath organ whose bench still invites me to *Hop on.*

With this final release from the phobia that constricted my musical expression and pleasure since that day when my memory short-circuited, I am preparing to get back on the bench by practicing a few organ pieces on the piano while I wait for my new organ shoes to arrive. Once they arrive, I will be ready to accept the kind offer to use the practice facilities at Stetson and to reclaim at least some of the skills I lost. Of all the *Welcome homes* I have heard, perhaps the most meaningful will be the sound of the pipes and the feel of the trackers releasing the valves to the pipes when I sit on the Beckerath's bench with full focus on remastering my command of the *King of Instruments* just as I learned to reclaim my sense of self and followed the long path home.

Now, within days of submitting this manuscript to the publisher, I can report that I have purchased an organ for my home—not the *real* pipe organ I have dreamed of since the 1960s—but a previously-owned Johannus digital two-manual that gives me joy every time I look at the picture I took in the showroom and when I look at May 1st in my calendar and read *Organ delivery*. To those who have only a superficial knowledge of organ building and design, it appears to be a *real* pipe organ, but the pipes are only decorative. It will meet my needs and be more than adequate for my purpose as it fulfills my dream.

I will still accept the offer to practice on campus to get the full benefit of mechanical response from the instrument. But I also will love having access to my own instrument at any hour of the day or night and to having my home reflect my love of the instrument and the repertoire—in effect, expressing who and what I am.

Reclaiming the organ at this age and stage of my life reminds me of what Paul Jenkins' wife, Janice, told me. She taught my freshman class Music Theory and was the Music Librarian at Stetson. When I returned to Stetson after being out for about two years, she told me, "Don't worry about that time away. You will get back to your previous skill level much more quickly than it took initially to develop those skills. She was right.

THANKS BE TO ALL!

ACKNOWLEDGMENTS

I am grateful for the leadership of Stockton University in New Jersey and Rice University in Houston during the long months of isolation while COVID-19 restrictions halted in-person classes. Without the online courses offered by both universities during that time, I could not have completed a book in the time since my first book was published in April, 2020.

Through Stockton, Peter Murphy offered instruction, inspiration, and supportive community to new students and *re-Peters*. Rice offered courses in creative nonfiction that complemented Peter's courses.

While it was of vital importance that both universities encouraged students to maintain the writing practice, it was even more urgent that they provided a way for participants to feel connected and to share a sense of accountability both as writers and as mutual encouragers.

Once the first draft was complete, Roberta Clipper gave editorial guidance for strengthening this manuscript. Her expertise in the craft of writing and keen sense of creative expression combined to help me tighten the verbiage and clarify chronology.

Every attempt has been made to be accurate and to let the reader know when I was offering an opinion apart from objective verification. Where needed, I left out or changed names of people mentioned to guard their privacy.

Any remaining flaws in this manuscript are solely my responsibility.

EARLY READERS

Nancy R. Billingsley	Diana Norton-Jackson
Chris L. Allred	Claire Poole
Elizabeth W. Hedges	Catherine Jenkins Reeves

www.ingramcontent.com/pod-product-compliance
Lightning Source LLC
Chambersburg PA
CBHW020746160426
43192CB00006B/260